CW01502070

Prologue

NOT MAKING IT TO THE LONDON PARALYMPICS IN 2012 should have marked the end of my sporting career.

Instead, the day the games opened in London, I was in New Delhi, at Rashtrapati Bhavan. At a glittering investiture ceremony, I received the Arjuna Award from the President of India, in recognition of my sporting achievements.

This award, a dream for so many athletes, filled me with both pride and humility. Yet my heart yearned to be in London.

I could have just accepted the award and returned to my home in Ahmednagar, content in having proved to the naysayers that all my sacrifices—leaving my home, my daughters, my restaurant—were worth this moment. I could have retired at my peak.

But that's not who I am.

I didn't 'retire' from living when I first became bedridden with a spinal tumour at the age of five.

I didn't 'retire' from life when I was dealt with paralysis from the chest down at twenty-nine years old.

I wasn't going to let missing the London Paralympics force me to retire, even if 'retirement' came with the golden handshake of an Arjuna Award.

To everyone who tried to stop me, who counselled me, who told me to quit at the pinnacle of my career, my answer was to accept the challenge, double down and work even harder to achieve my goal—competing at the Paralympics.

To everyone who doubted me, I said: Bring it on!

Throughout my life, I've battled on so many fronts—as a child, a woman, a mother, a sportswoman.

The challenges have been multiple, but my response has been the same: Bring it on!

Many see only my medals and awards. They call me *lucky*. I'm tired of being called lucky.

Setting a new milestone in the Limca Book of Records by swimming in the Yamuna during a torrential downpour had nothing to do with being lucky. It was the result of hours of training, months of staying away from my family and years of challenging societal norms.

Many see me as a 'biker babe', lucky that I got to ride with John Abraham and appear on *MTV Roadies*. They don't know that I had to spend ten hours in a motor workshop, sitting in a soaked diaper, just to persuade someone to customize a bike for me.

My life has been a continuous test of proving myself, over and over, at every stage. My challenges are as much to do with being a person with disabilities as with being a woman. And starting a sports career at thirty-nine, when most athletes think of retiring, I faced ageism. But I silenced all my doubters when I won a silver medal at the Rio Paralympics in 2016, at the age of forty-six.

The hand of fate may have sketched the outlines of my life, but I've painted in the colours myself. I reply to every challenge with three words: Bring it on!

BRING IT ON

DEEPA MALIK

with SONI SANGWAN

BRING IT ON

THE ᴧ STORY OF MY LIFE
Incredible

HarperCollins *Publishers* India

First published in India by HarperCollins *Publishers* 2025
4th Floor, Tower A, Building No. 10, DLF Cyber City,
DLF Phase II, Gurugram, Haryana – 122002
www.harpercollins.co.in

2 4 6 8 10 9 7 5 3 1

Copyright © Deepa Malik 2025

P-ISBN: 978-93-6569-093-4
E-ISBN: 978-93-6569-174-0

The views and opinions expressed in this book are the author's own
and the facts are as reported by her, and the publishers are not in
any way liable for the same.

Deepa Malik asserts the moral right to be
identified as the author of this work.

All rights reserved. No part of this publication may be reproduced,
stored in a retrieval system, or transmitted, in any form or by any means,
electronic, mechanical, photocopying, recording or otherwise,
without the prior permission of the publishers.

Typeset in 11.5/15.2 Adobe Garamond Pro at
HarperCollins *Publishers* India

Printed and bound at
Thomson Press (India) Ltd

MIX
Paper | Supporting
responsible forestry
FSC® C010615

This book is produced from independently certified FSC® paper
to ensure responsible forest management.

To my parents and my daughters—the generation before me and the generation after me. Both have motivated me to tread the path of ability beyond disability.

Contents

PART I

1

Knock, Knock. Who's There? Cancer.

I HAD COME TO DELHI FROM JAIPUR FOR A CHECK-UP with the neurosurgeon. I came alone, leaving my daughters—Devika, eight, and Ambika, three—and my two dogs, Snoopy and Angel, with my mother. My medical records had been sent to the doctor in advance, and I sat in the waiting room, anticipating my name being called. My outward calm did not betray the turmoil going on inside.

As I waited, the faint whirring sound of helicopter blades reached my ears. They were bringing in casualties from the Kargil battlefront. My trepidation at what the doctor might say was drowned by the wave of compassion I felt for the brave injured soldiers being airlifted from the battlefield to the hospital and my fear for the safety of my husband, Bikram, stationed in the same warzone.

When my token number flashed on the display screen, I picked up my bag and walked into the doctor's room.

He looked up from the papers in his hand and peered at me over his reading glasses.

'Please bring the patient,' he said, taking in my jeans and T-shirt, my long, voluminous hair—it had often been compared to Dimple Kapadia's—my tall, slim figure. I looked anything but sick!

I continued to walk towards his desk.

He repeated his request, this time in Hindi. '*Madam, aap patient ko le kar aaiye.*'

'*I* am the patient. Deepa Malik,' I said.

He sprang up from his seat, beads of perspiration on his forehead, the colour draining from his face. He glanced repeatedly from the papers in front of him to me, muttering, 'Oh my god, oh my god.'

He sank back into his chair and motioned for me to sit. He re-examined the papers as if to confirm he had the right reports. Composing himself, he said, 'Deepa, you're a mess. You should have taken to your bed at least three months ago. Why have you been nurturing this tumour for so long?'

All this happened too fast for me to react.

Before I could formulate my answer, he stood up abruptly. 'I need a coffee,' he said.

We went to the hospital canteen, where, over a cup of coffee, he gave me the diagnosis.

The tumour was huge. It had been growing for some time now, causing me back pain and my foot to drag. It was pressing against my spine, crushing the nerves going down my left leg.

At some level I had anticipated this diagnosis ever since the MRI in Jaipur. But the prognosis was something I neither expected nor accepted.

'Deepa, the tumour is so big and deeply entrenched that removing it will involve cutting into your spinal cord. We don't know how deep we'll have to go. It's a very risky surgery, so there are no guarantees. I don't know how to tell you this ...' He paused, before continuing, 'After the surgery, the chances of you being able to use your legs are slim. You'll probably never walk again. And that is if you survive the surgery.'

I only heard what I wanted to hear. The rest didn't register. There was no way I wouldn't survive. As for not walking again—we'd see about that. When I was five, I had overcome a similar spinal tumour, and through sheer determination and diligent physiotherapy, I had not only walked again but also played state-level cricket.

I realized that my doctor was still talking. 'We'll have to schedule the surgery at the earliest. The tumour could burst at any moment. Let's get you admitted now.'

That last part caught my attention. 'I can't be admitted now. I have two young children to look after. My husband is in Kargil.'

'I can't just let you go. Never in my career have I seen anyone with such a large tumour walking around like you are. It's a ticking time bomb.'

I explained that I had had an MRI about two years ago, which showed nothing of alarm. He clarified that the MRI had been of the lumbar region, while the tumour was in the dorsal region.

I told him that I had been active—I did surya namaskars every day during yoga. Expecting approval, I was shocked when he was aghast. Because the tumour was pressing on the spinal cord, the twisting and stretching of the spine could have caused it to snap. Exercise was actually worsening my condition.

The conversation went on in this vein until, finally, he agreed to give me time to get my affairs in order. 'I can give you one week to prepare for surgery. Seven days to celebrate walking,' he said.

My train was in the evening—the Delhi-Jaipur Shatabdi. As I sat on a bench in the front garden of the Army Research and Referral Hospital, waiting for the clock hands to move to 5 p.m., I wept.

On the train ride back to Jaipur, I composed myself. The practical side of me decided to begin planning everything I had to do—

arranging care for my daughters, installing a ramp to make my house wheelchair accessible, finding where to rent a hospital bed and a gel mattress for my prolonged recovery. Meanwhile, the eternal optimist in me dismissed the doctor's prognosis. There was no way I would never walk again. I had recovered before; I could do it again.

Dying was not even an option.

When I reached home, I couldn't bring myself to tell my mother everything. Instead, I told her more tests were required and that I'd be going to Delhi again the next week.

We had been living in Jaipur for a little less than a year, just a few houses down from my parents'. After completing his course at the Defence Services Staff College in Wellington, Bikram was posted to Gurez, in the high Himalayas, while I managed the home with two little girls and two big dogs. This had been especially challenging due to the persistent backache I had had since my second pregnancy. The pain made me subconsciously drag my left leg. Initially, it was barely noticeable, and I was able to hide it with smart boots. But when the pain refused to go away, I decided to seek professional help from a physiotherapist. Devika, who was recovering from hemiplegia caused by a childhood accident, also needed physiotherapy. So we hired a physiotherapist to come home, and we settled into an easy rhythm.

However, I had to pause my routine when Ambika and I went to celebrate my birthday in Gurez with Bikram in September 1998. Devika stayed back with my parents to continue her physiotherapy. It was on this trip that I realized my problem was serious. To get to Gurez, we had to fly to Srinagar and then travel several hours by road as part of an army convoy. I rode in an army Jonga, a sturdy vehicle with two seats in the front and two benches facing each other along the sides in the back. Not the most luxurious, but suitable for tough terrains. For me, the ride was unbearable. Unable to sit because of the pain, I lay down on a sleeping bag on the floor of the Jonga. I reached Gurez with a splitting headache, which was attributed to the high altitude.

We spent about three months there, my symptoms worsening every day, but I was also enjoying the social life, so I wrote off the aches and pains as being caused by the cold weather and the altitude. My baking skills, honed in Wellington, were put to good use. In Gurez, a small army camp with hardly any amenities, my home-baked pizzas, puff pastries, Black Forest cakes, stuffed buns and bread loaves were a big hit.

But while Bikram and I continued to be the merry couple, happily disregarding my foot drag, his commander was more observant. He noticed my limp and urged us to get it checked out.

I returned to Jaipur when the cold in Gurez became too harsh. Throughout the winter in Jaipur, I continued with my physiotherapy.

When the summer came, I took up swimming. At the pool, I met a young army doctor who was interning with Dr P.K. Sethi, the renowned innovator of the Jaipur Foot. Dr Sethi, a Magsaysay Award winner, had been in the news for providing a prosthetic limb to the famous dancer Sudha Chandran, who was able to resume dancing even after losing her foot.

This young intern would watch me walking from the changing room to the pool and back. Initially I was a little offended by his ogling, but then one day, he came up and introduced himself. I soon realized his interest was purely professional.

'Ma'am, what are you doing about your foot drag?' he asked.

'I've been doing physiotherapy,' I replied.

'If I may suggest, you should consult with Dr Sethi. He's designed many products that could help you walk properly,' he said.

Before I could ask how to meet this famous doctor, he offered to fix an appointment.

The hospital happened to be close to my cousin's house and a shop that sold party decorations and gifts. With Ambika's birthday approaching, I needed to visit the party store anyway. That was why I agreed to see Dr Sethi, just because it was convenient, not realizing at the time that this decision would end up saving my life.

The appointment was fixed for 5 May, Ambika's birthday. I'd planned a big party for her, inviting my parents, cousins and friends, along with Ambika's and Devika's friends. A local garden restaurant had been booked and an appointment for me at the beauty salon had been fixed.

On the day of the appointment, I squeezed in the hospital visit between all the errands I was running for the party in the evening.

Dr Sethi was a frail, yet radiant, elderly gentleman. As I walked through the door, before I even reached his desk, he stopped me. 'Your issue isn't orthopaedic—it's neurological. I suspect nerve compression. You need an MRI.'

He turned to his assistant. 'We need a dorsal MRI, not lumbar. The compression is on the dorsal spine.'

With that, I was rushed for an MRI—out of turn. This did not sit well with the staff, who muttered to each other about the long list of patients already waiting and how *some* people thought they could just waltz in and jump the queue. Their irritation must also have been because I didn't look ill in any way, except for my foot drag. I was casually dressed in jeans and a T-shirt, working clothes for all the errands I was running, and totally out of sync with how a married woman my age was expected to dress. There were no jangling bangles or bindi. I was also in a bit of a rush, having expected a quick consultation rather than an MRI.

The attendant handed me a gown and told me to hurry, as many people were waiting their turn.

As I lay on the metal table, my nearly naked back feeling the cold, my ankles uncomfortably contorted, my thoughts drifted back to my childhood. I remembered the months of uncomfortable, almost torturous medical investigations I had endured. One test had me strapped to a bed, injected with a dye and then rotated to look for any blockage. Though the MRI was intimidating, I thanked god that I wasn't being spun around this time.

With my eyes closed, I gritted my teeth against the cold and listened to the clicks and whirrs of the machine.

A few minutes into the test, the attendant returned, her manner completely changed. 'Madam, are you okay? Do you want a blanket?'

'Yes, please. Could you also get me a pillow? My neck is hurting,' I replied.

She immediately brought both, placing the pillow beside my head since it couldn't go under my neck.

The doctor who was reviewing the images on the screen asked if I needed a break. I wondered if they had all suddenly realized that I was Dr Sethi's patient and needed special care. In reality, they had recognized how ill I was.

The test was soon over. They asked me to return with a companion in about fifteen minutes for the report. 'Why do I need someone else?' I asked. 'My husband is in Kargil and my father is working in South Africa. I have too much to do today to find someone to come back with. I'll collect the report myself.'

I went about getting things for Ambika's birthday: balloons, party hats, party poppers, bunting and knick-knacks as return gifts.

When I returned to the hospital, they hesitantly handed me the report and told me to go back to Dr Sethi. He took barely a minute to review the report, and then asked about my childhood illness. 'This is urgent,' he said, scribbling down the details of a neuro physician in the same hospital. 'You've already ignored this for too long. Don't delay.'

The neuro physician didn't use the word 'tumour'. Instead, he told me that there was compression on my spinal cord, causing a bulge, and that it was a serious matter. He suggested I go to a skilled surgeon for the likely complicated surgery. He also hinted at a severe post-surgery outcome and advised picking a hospital with good post-operative care. He was preparing me for a prolonged hospital stay.

I understood that the 'compression on the cord' meant my childhood problem had returned, but I was too focused on Ambika's party. It was already 3 p.m. and the party was at 5.30. I left to get my hair done, to change into my chiffon saree. We cut the cake. We popped the party poppers. We played games.

I was still in denial the next day. I had beaten the tumour when I was a child and would do it again. I would get better. I went to the army hospital in Jaipur, and, after reviewing my reports, they referred me to the Army Research and Referral Hospital in Delhi.

Not wanting to worry my mother, I told her that I had to go to Delhi for further tests as the hospital in Jaipur didn't have the necessary equipment.

And that's where I got my diagnosis.

I returned to Jaipur determined to face the challenge head-on. I still refused to believe that these were going to be my last seven days on my feet. I was confident that within two years, with intense physiotherapy, both Devika and I would be fine. By the time Bikram was due for a peace posting, we would all be in good health. With that timeframe in mind, I began packing up my home and making it wheelchair-friendly.

The first thing I did was put my jewellery in the bank locker and withdraw some money. I bought a microwave oven, thinking it would make cooking easier—even the kids would be able to use it. I packed my sarees, lehngas and salwar suits into trunks, mothballed to keep them intact for two years in storage. I bought a remote call bell. I told my daughters' teachers about the surgery and that my mother would be looking after the girls for some time. I hired my domestic worker's son to take care of my dogs. I asked a carpenter to instal ramps at the entrance of my home. I spoke to a relative who owned a nursing home about renting a hospital bed and a water gel mattress.

I still hadn't told my mother the full story. All she knew was that I was getting investigative tests done. She kept insisting that I speak to the neurosurgeon who had operated on me in my childhood. He was in Pune, and I had consulted him two years ago, when we had been on our way to Wellington. He had recommended a lumbar MRI, which showed nothing. I spoke to him and told him what the dorsal MRI had revealed. I asked him why he had not suggested we get a dorsal MRI. He replied that when the lumbar MRI had shown no abnormalities, he did not want me to get another expensive test done. He was extremely sad at the recurrence of the tumour and urged me not to delay the surgery even by a day.

I didn't tell anyone about the diagnosis.

I don't like talking about my problems. Maybe it's because I've faced so many. Two years of my childhood were spent dealing with paralysis, surgery for the tumour and physiotherapy. Then, at twenty, Devika was born premature, and as a toddler, she was hit by a motorbike, leaving her left side paralysed. I had surgery for gallstones. During my second pregnancy, I gained a lot of weight from stress eating. I developed a foot drag. And now my spinal tumour was back.

For over two years, I had dealt with my back ache and foot drag on my own. All because I didn't want to be seen as the invalid, the patient, the 'defective piece'. I was always striving to be the perfect daughter-in-law, the perfect wife, the perfect mother. My need for validation and perfection outweighed everything else, including my health.

I also harboured a false sense of bravado—a belief that I could do everything on my own. I was an army officer's wife. I couldn't burden him with my illness while he was fighting for the nation. I didn't need to—I was brave and strong.

And so I kept my silence, not telling Bikram or my in-laws, determined to face this battle alone.

On the second day of my final week of walking, I had to make a heart-wrenching decision. Angel, my Dobermann, had also been suffering from a serious medical condition. Fluid would keep accumulating in her abdomen, requiring regular trips to the vet to get it drained. There really was no cure.

At home, she was my constant companion, following me from room to room. In the kitchen, she would sit by my side while I cooked. I couldn't bend down, and she couldn't stand for too long, so I would place my leg next to her. That small connection was enough for her. We were both suffering parallelly.

Then came the day the vet sat me down for a difficult conversation. The conclusion was clear—it was time to set Angel free. She was ready for mukti.

I held her paw as the vet sedated her, whispering her name and stroking her head as her soul departed.

Even now I believe Angel took on a fate that might have been meant for me. Maybe I'm alive today because she sacrificed herself for me.

I took the Shatabdi from Jaipur to Delhi. and went straight to the hospital, where I was admitted for surgery. My mother still had no idea about all this—she thought I was going for more tests.

At the hospital, I ran into my husband's uncle and his wife, Amar and Anjali. They had lost their young son in an accident, and their daughter had suffered a head injury and facial paralysis. They were at the hospital for her therapy. They became the only relatives who knew about my upcoming surgery.

In the days leading up to the surgery, scheduled for 3 June, I watched Kargil casualties arrive at the hospital. Seeing those brave young men, many of whom later became amputees, smiling through their pain filled me with courage. Their conviction in their patriotism inspired me. I found strength in my motherhood—I had to get better for my girls.

When it came to deciding who would sign the consent form for my surgery, I laughed and said I would sign it myself. I didn't want to call Bikram. I knew from the news how hot things were in Gurez.

The doctors realized I was being cavalier when it came to the matter of consent and spoke to Amar Chacha. He had no choice but to inform my father-in-law and my mother, who immediately came to Delhi with my girls. He even spoke to my father in Johannesburg, who had been there for only six weeks. This job was his big chance to make some serious money and leave a monetary legacy for his children and grandchildren. But the moment he got the news, he took the next flight back and was by my side in the hospital. My guilt was bested only by my gratitude.

The night before the surgery, I finally got to speak to Bikram. In those days, there was no cell phone connectivity, and even landlines were hard to access where Bikram was. The only way to connect was through the old-fashioned radios used in military communication.

'They're saying I'll never be able to walk again,' I told him.

'*Koi na, koi na*. I'll carry you in my arms all my life. Don't worry about your legs,' came Bikram's voice, faint and crackling over the radio. Despite the static and the distance, this brief exchange brought me warmth and strength. He was my knight in shining armour, ready to carry me through any challenge.

I felt ready to face whatever came next.

I was prepped for surgery, sanitized and gowned, my hair tucked into a surgical cap. Before the orderlies wheeled my gurney out of the ward and towards the operation theatre, the doctor asked if I wanted anything.

'I want to walk to the surgery,' I said.

The nurses objected, saying they would have to sanitize me all over again. But the doctor said, 'Let her walk.'

I slipped on the pair of black rubber slippers they handed me. When the nurse tried to usher me towards the lift, I said, 'No, I want to take the stairs.' What I didn't realize was that my left foot had no grip. As I lifted my foot, the slipper fell off. Irritated, I simply picked it up and walked with one slipper and one bare foot. The slipper may be slipping, but I was not going to let my life slip away.

'This is going to be the most challenging surgery of my career,' the doctor had said to me in the OT. 'I wish you had come to me earlier. This is going to be a redo surgery at the same site where you had surgery as a child. The tumour is huge and deeply entrenched. I'll do as minimal damage as possible. But please forgive me for any harm done when you wake up. Stay with me.'

The operating table was shaped like an inverted V, and I lay on it face down. The last thing I saw before the anaesthesia took hold was a sea of masked faces illuminated by a bright light. The countdown began, and before they reached zero, I was out.

2

Papa ki Pari

MY FATHER HAD A SCOOTER. IT WAS A LAMBRETTA. In a family of four in 1970s India, this meant my father was in the driver's seat, my mother on the pillion, my older brother squeezed in between them and I, the youngest, was standing in front of my father, the driver, holding on to the handlebars.

My childhood memories come not just in technicolour but also with smells and sensations, and my happiest ones are of the wind blowing on my face and through my hair. When I stood in front of Papa, holding the handlebars, I felt like I was the one driving. The proximity to my dad created a special bond between us—I was the pilot and he was the captain. I was the scout and he was the sharpshooter. My overactive imagination turned our mundane scooter rides into grand adventures.

The seeds of my love for bikes and all things with wheels germinated here. The roots of my free spirit grew from these experiences.

Apart from the sheer joy of those scooter rides, it was here that my belief in the power of my father developed. With him driving and me standing within the protective circle of his outstretched arms, I felt invincible. I never wanted to leave that shielding embrace. But when I began growing taller, my head reached his chin and my hair, flowing freely, would tickle his nose.

'Maybe it's time Deepa started sitting in the back. Her hair keeps getting in my face as I drive,' I overheard him say to my mother one day. 'She could sit on top of the stepney. Our drives are usually short, anyway.'

That day I begged my mom to get me a haircut. I preferred short hair over losing my position in front of Papa on the scooter.

I was a typical daddy's girl—clearly his favourite, more so than my brother. Bhaiyya was quieter and more introverted, while I was the brat, thriving on the attention the younger child typically gets. Long before the term *papa ki pari* became popular, I embodied it.

And while he was my hero, I was equally his favourite. As a child, I had a habit of climbing onto tables, chairs, windowsills—anything to reach higher ground—and then flinging myself into my dad's arms, shouting, 'Papa, catch!' These jumps were often unannounced, which meant my father had to be constantly vigilant. They were literal leaps of faith on my part. I was confident that Papa would never let me fall, never let me hurt myself, always be there for me.

One day, when I was three years old, I flung myself at him the moment he walked through the door. Forgetting the lit cigarette in his hand, he threw his arms up to catch me, and I ended up with a small burn on my inner wrist. That was the last day he smoked a cigarette.

We were a typical middle-class fauji family of four. Money was there for necessities, never for luxuries. But even in those financially tight times, we never wanted for anything. Our table was always set with the healthiest and most delicious food, our house was always the best in the neighbourhood and we always made the most of whatever we had.

In the army, family accommodations are assigned from a pool of available army-built houses based on seniority and whether you're coming from a non-family station or not. Rather than wait for the best available house, my father would opt for the bungalows that no one else wanted—the ones that needed repairs, that had bigger grounds that required more maintenance, that made up for their disrepair with character and history.

He and Mom would transform those dilapidated bungalows into dream homes through hard work and creativity. Once, we got a house where the ceiling was literally peeling off and practically caving in. My father got us some beautiful block-printed tent fabric and used it to create a false ceiling. We must have been the first family in India to go glamping!

For milk, we kept a cow. For vegetables, we had a kitchen garden. Of course, this meant that my parents had to work hard every day. I don't remember either one of them ever sitting idle. They were always doing something. Caring for the cow, getting its fodder, milking it, tending to the garden—these outdoor chores were done by Papa. Mom's job was to ensure that we always had the most nutritious meals. Along with our breakfast, we were given five almonds, soaked the night before, every day. And to feed our minds, my father bought us an expensive encyclopaedia set on monthly instalments.

They were an eye-catching couple. Dad, tall and handsome. Mom, beautiful and talented. She had three party sarees and hardly any jewellery, yet she outshone all the other ladies. She could sing, dance, conduct social and official events. Her talent shone so brightly that her oft-repeated sarees were the last thing anyone noticed.

My brother was only a year and a half older than me, but our personalities were poles apart. Against my boisterousness, he was reserved. To my outgoing nature, he was introverted. To my adventurousness, he was cautious. Even when we were children, he seemed like a grown-up. I don't recall the exact circumstances, but

I do remember a bigger boy bullying him at school. We were in Nasirabad then, attending a missionary school. This boy wouldn't let my brother take his turn on the swings. Far from feeling intimidated, I was enraged at the boy's audacity—how dare he bully *my* bhaiyya. I marched over and shoved the bully with all my might, securing the swing for my brother. This became a celebrated story: 'Deepa pushed a boy because he wouldn't let Vikram swing in the playground.' The same Vikram went on to join the Indian Army and rose to the rank of brigadier.

Childhood mornings for me were defined by the scent of agarbatti and the sound of the mandir bell tinkling as my mother began each day with prayers in our small home temple. As I said earlier, my memories include smell and feel. This agarbatti smell is something that has remained with me even today.

Everyone at home had a job—Papa's was to provide for and protect all of us, Mom's was to hold the fort by managing the house, and Bhaiyya and I had to be regular with our schoolwork and be well-behaved. But I made it my job to play—for as long as I could. Running, jumping, cycling—anything that involved physical activity. I loved playing with dolls and pretty things too, but it was while I was outdoors with the neighbourhood kids that I was most in my element. People often joked, *'Bhagwan ke paas mitti kam par gayee, nahin to Deepa ko ladka hi banate.'*

There was one cycle between Bhaiyya and me, which became a bone of contention. Our boisterous games would continue until sundown, when everyone would head home—except for me. I'd hide under the stairs even as the neighbourhood echoed with calls of 'Deepa, *ghar aa jao*', while I tried to sneak in one more round on the cycle.

Looking back on it, through the sepia tint of memory, it was a picture-perfect childhood. Yet it was during this seemingly perfect time that things began to unravel.

At first, the changes were subtle, barely noticeable. I lost my enthusiasm to jump on my dad when he entered the house. I felt a strange heaviness that I could not articulate. My desire to play outdoors clashed with a strange lethargy that gripped me, an inexplicable malaise. These feelings were easily overlooked in a busy household.

But one morning at the bus stop my father noticed something that even I had not. We went to school in army trucks, and that day, as he watched us board, he saw that I struggled to lift my leg to climb in.

Everyone thought it likely to be a muscle pull, so my mother began massaging my leg with oil every day. When this didn't work, my father took me to the doctor. This marked the beginning of the seemingly endless hospital visits. Despite all the poking and prodding, a barrage of blood tests and several X-rays, the diagnosis was: nothing.

The doctors were unable to figure out why a once outgoing, physically active child was becoming slow, lethargic and morose. My father began to wonder if the problem was psychological. Papa was way ahead of his time, remarkably enlightened. Even today, mental health issues are often left unaddressed, yet he felt it was time to consult a psychiatrist. Unconcerned about what people would say, he was determined to understand what was troubling his darling daughter.

But the visit to the psychiatrist yielded no concrete results. 'She's stopped playing outside and being active. It's possible that the constant remarks about her being more like a boy and the expectation for her to behave like a girl have affected her,' the psychiatrist said to my parents after the consultation. 'Maybe there's some unsaid pressure on her not to act like a boy.'

He asked them whether there had been any differential treatment between Bhaiyya and me at home, specifically asking whether my mother was pampering my brother, her raja beta, more than she did me.

His questions and reasoning were well-founded, considering the context of the 1970s, when gender discrimination was the norm.

Women's emancipation and campaigns like 'Beti Bachao, Beti Padhao'—for which I am now the brand ambassador—were still pipe dreams. In 1970, the year I was born, Kamaljit Sandhu became the first Indian woman to bag a gold medal in the 400 metres at the Asian Games. Her record remained unbroken for a decade. Kiran Bedi, tennis champion, broke into the boys' club of the Indian Police Service in 1972. But between 1972 and 1978, there were only four women in the IPS cadre. So while the 1970s saw Indira Gandhi as prime minister, the birth of a girl child was rarely celebrated.

But in our small world of four, there was no discrimination. Bhaiyya and I were given the same food, the same education, even the same clothes! I grew up in a family that valued the maxim 'waste not, want not'. Bhaiyya's hand-me-downs came to me, so I grew up wearing his pants, shorts and shirts. If Bhaiyya was given five soaked almonds every day, so was I. If he got milk with Bournvita and I did not, it was a matter of taste, not favouritism. If anything, the scales might have tipped more in my favour than his.

When the doctors had no answers for my failing health, my father did not shy away from seeking divine intervention.

In those pre-television times, the radio was our source of information and entertainment. Ours was a prized possession, and we had a mechanic on call for repairs and regular maintenance. One day, while fixing the radio, he learnt of my health issues.

'Saab, aap log maano ya na maano, magar kabhi-kabhi bacchon ko jinn ki hawa lag jaati hai,' he told my parents. He was convinced that some evil spirit had cast a spell on me. 'There's a revered peer baba nearby. If you take her to him, I'm sure she'll recover,' he suggested.

So every Thursday, Papa and I would go to the mazar. Those visits grew precious: we were going to find a cure for me, I got to spend time with my father and the prayer at the mazar offered me a deep sense of calm.

The mazar was always bustling on Thursdays, the baba's special day. The smell of incense, the resonant sound of the Sufi prayers and the uplifting atmosphere would cheer me up. But the best part was the prayer ritual itself. At the mazar, a beautiful peacock-feather fan would be brushed over everyone. I would feel a cool, scented breeze envelop me.

But my mystery illness began to manifest in other ways. My initial problem of not being able to lift my leg, the heaviness in my body and the general lethargy increased.

In every home with school-going children is a parent rushing from kitchen to bedroom, multitasking to get breakfast going, corralling the children to get ready, stuffing hot parathas or sandwiches into tiffin boxes and straightening uniforms, all happening at supersonic speed. So when in the midst of all this, Mom would comb my hair and I would cry, it was easy to assume she might have accidentally been a bit rough.

But the truth was that when she combed my hair back and asked me to tilt up my chin, it put pressure on my neck and caused severe pain.

This new pain sent us back to the hospital. Once again, the X-rays showed nothing, frustrating my father to no end. Not being one to let things slide, he embarked on a relentless quest for a diagnosis. In this era before the internet, we couldn't just look up the symptoms online or type in 'best doctors for neck pain' and get a list of names. We had to rely on word of mouth, and my father left no stone unturned.

If someone recommended Vellore, we were on the next train there. Being from north India, we all knew of PGIMER Chandigarh's repute as a foremost research and treatment institute, so there we went. Jaslok and Hinduja in Mumbai, then Bombay, were our next port of call. But all these proved futile.

My memories of these trips are a haze of meeting doctors in white coats, clinical examinations, the smell of antiseptic, the chill of X-ray tables and a pervasive sense of disappointment.

But the Bombay trip was different. It was special. It was there that I got my first glimpse of the sea. Everywhere we went, my father would sit me on his shoulders. Perched there, I had an unmatched view. It was from this vantage point that I spotted the sea, much before my father did. My excitement was indescribable. Beyond the sands of the beach was an endless expanse of blue. The water near the shore was a murky grey-blue, but the farther I cast my vision, the more dazzlingly aquamarine the water sparkled, dimpled with sunlight. We spent a wonderful day at the beach and returned to Jamnagar, where we were living at the time, no closer to a diagnosis.

Still unwilling to give up, my father requested a transfer to Pune, where the Command Hospital of the Indian Army is located. He was due to write his exams for the prestigious Defence Services Staff College entrance, which require intense preparation. Papa was brilliant at his work and would have been a sure shot at getting through, but my ongoing illness meant he was unable to dedicate himself fully to studying. He was slated for a posting to a non-family station after Jamnagar, which would have led to a promotion. Instead, he sought a compassionate posting to Pune.

We moved there from Jamnagar, got a house and settled in. Then began the hospitalization. It wasn't one long hospital stay—I was in and out for months.

The first time I was admitted was also the first time I stayed overnight anywhere without family. I should have been scared, but it felt more like an adventure. Plus, bravado is in my DNA!

After a series of tests, I was sent back home. This same pattern repeated each time I was admitted. And each time the investigations became more invasive. I underwent seven lumbar punctures at the age of five, each inconclusive.

The family adapted to hospital life. Papa would stop by in the morning on his way to work, making sure he was there for the doctor's rounds. Two charts on clipboards would hang from my bed. One belonged to the doctor, the other to Papa. His chart mapped our daily routine: who would be with me at what time and who would be there for the doctor's rounds in his absence. After sending Bhaiyya to school, Mom would come with lunch and Papa's evening sports uniform. Bhaiyya would land up at the hospital after school with my schoolwork as well. Papa would come in time for lunch, and we would all eat together. Afternoons were spent playing board games, usually snakes and ladders or ludo. Then it was time for some schoolwork. Papa would change into his sports uniform and head out to his unit. Mom would keep me company, while Bhaiyya played in the hospital park. Papa's return signalled my favourite part of the day—our storytelling sessions.

So much of my personality has been shaped by those storytelling sessions. Papa generally relied on our rich mythology for the stories. I learnt about our history and culture, but the most significant lesson was the message within all these stories. Each one ended in a 'happily ever after'. There was always a situation, a crisis and, ultimately, a solution. Each one ended in triumph, in hope, in victory. The message for five-year-old Deepa was not to give up, not to despair, but to work towards that seemingly elusive 'happily ever after'. And this mindset has become second nature to me. Even at life's darkest moments, I've never let a problem overwhelm me. I've taken stock, assessed the issue and looked for the best possible solution.

The doctors tried everything. I was treated for tuberculosis and meningitis, undergoing seven lumbar punctures because they suspected an infection in my spinal fluid. The Command Hospital is expansive. The family ward I was in was on a small hill. The main building housed the emergency and the specialized care rooms, with the room I was taken to for the lumbar punctures situated towards the front. If I was taken from my ward to the main building and down a flight of stairs, it meant that I was going for a lumbar puncture. My fear of needles was born there.

Before my first spinal tap, my father carefully explained the procedure. 'The doctors want to find out what's making you sick. Just like they draw blood from your arm, they'll draw some fluid from your back.' He put his hand on my lower back to show me where the needle would go. 'It'll hurt a bit, but you mustn't move at all, because if you move, the needle may move, and that'll hurt even more. Can you promise to keep still?' I nodded affirmatively.

What happened the next day was far worse than what he had prepared me for. The room felt cold and sterile. I was made to lie on the icy operating table with my chin tucked in and my knees drawn up in the foetal position. My back was arched to widen the space between my vertebrae to make it easier to insert the needle. First came the cold, antiseptic-soaked cotton to sterilize the area. Then came the prick of the needle for the local anaesthesia. Though the area became numb to pain, I could still feel the thick lumbar puncture needle going in. I kept absolutely still, even trying to hold my breath. The needle seemed to be inside me for an eternity, though it must have been just a few moments. Once the needle was pulled out, I was asked to remain still to prevent any leakage or infection at the insertion point. I lay on my side for the next twenty-four hours, having to use a bedpan. And as the local anaesthesia wore off, the pain set in.

The next time I went for a lumbar puncture, I started screaming even before we entered the room. But each time the fluid was examined, the results showed no infection. There was nothing in the reports to explain my problem. We were all getting desperate.

In the midst of all this, inquisitive 'well-wishers' began to intrude. Each visit left my mother exhausted, overwhelmed by guilt and anger.

'Why are you wasting your whole life on this girl?' they would say. 'Whatever has happened to her is her fate. It's her destiny. By focusing all your attention on her, you're ignoring Vikram. Even if she gets better, she'll be an invalid. For her, you are playing with your son's future.'

These visits had little impact on my father. Papa had his own ways of cheering me up. Sometimes he brought dolls or board games to the hospital, but most often it was books. The gift I most prized, though, was a bright red plastic beach set, complete with a bucket, shovel, rake and mug. It didn't matter that I couldn't play with it in the hospital—it reminded me of our trip to the beach in Bombay. Those little plastic toys were a symbol of hope. I would soon be better, and we would all go to the beach to play.

While I was being treated as a test case, the doctors investigating me for any and every possible illness, change came with the arrival of a new doctor at the Command Hospital. Major C.P. Bajpayee had just moved to Pune after specializing in neurosurgery in the United States. After examining me he came to the conclusion that a nerve compression in my spine was the problem. But to find out what was causing the compression and where exactly it was located, he would have to do a myelogram, a procedure far more primitive than today's CT scans. For the myelogram, an iodized oil was injected into my spine. The journey of this oil was mapped through an X-ray. No ordinary X-ray, though—I was strapped to a table that was periodically tilted. As I was spun around, the oil dye travelled through my spine. Where the dye stopped was where the obstruction was.

It was after this intense procedure that we first heard the words 'spinal tumours'.

Maj. Bajpayee had found the culprit: a cyst growing between my vertebrae and spinal cord. Surgery was promptly scheduled, the cyst was excised and my parents waited with bated breath for the clouds to part.

3

Reborn

———◦◆◦———

THE DAY I FIRST SAW PAPA BREAK DOWN WAS THE DAY Shirdi Sai Baba appeared to me in a dream. It had been three months since the surgery; the spinal cysts had been removed and I was on anti-tuberculosis medication. Despite this, I still couldn't move.

Papa, the eternal optimist who hadn't given up hope throughout our long search for a diagnosis, was now weeping helplessly. 'Why is there no improvement even now?' I heard him ask Maj. Bajpayee, my surgeon. I don't recall the doctor's response, but that night, while settling me down to sleep, the ward nurse said to me, *'Tumko to Baba theek karenge.'*

She had just returned from a visit to Shirdi. She brought me a photo of Sai Baba and placed it on my bedside table, saying that it was now up to Baba to make me walk again.

That night, I dreamt I was walking, running, jumping—doing everything a seven-year-old should. In this dream, Sai Baba visited me in the hospital.

'Why are you lying down?' he asked.

'I don't walk,' I replied.

He held his hand out. 'Come, I'll take you to the park.'

28

Together we ventured to the park. Although I had never actually seen the hospital park, I had heard all about the swings, the see-saw and the jungle gym from my brother and the other children in the ward. Suddenly there I was, speeding up the merry-go-round by running alongside it to build momentum and jumping on as it spun, then pushing myself on the swings, going higher than the trees.

'Look, Baba, look! See how fast I'm climbing the monkey bars!' I squealed with joy. The park offered endless adventures, and I couldn't get enough.

'Don't tire yourself out,' Baba said to me gently. 'Rest now. You can come back tomorrow to play some more.'

Meanwhile, at home, Papa was having a similarly vivid dream. After his breakdown in the hospital, he and Ma had returned home, disheartened. They were grappling not only with the medical mystery of my undiagnosed illness but also with the endless jibes from insensitive 'well-wishers' who advised them to leave me to my fate. After all, I was just a girl!

Now, three months post-surgery with no signs of improvement, it might have seemed to them that perhaps the naysayers were right. Maybe it was time to accept the inevitable.

These thoughts must have weighed on my father's mind as he went to bed that night. In his dream, he saw his own father, whom, too, we called Baba.

He woke with renewed conviction the next morning. 'Deepa will walk again,' he told my mother. His father had appeared to him, questioning his tears. 'I told him how Deepa lies in bed, unmoving. I told him I couldn't bear it. But Baba told me not to cry, saying, "*Tu bekaar mein ro raha hai, Deepa to Babe naal tur rahi hai*" (You are weeping needlessly, Deepa is enjoying a walk with Baba).'

He was convinced their prayers had been answered and that I would soon start walking again. That day, he had to leave early for the office, so it was my mom who came to the hospital for the doctor's rounds.

The first thing I told her was about my dream visit to the park with Baba. At my words, she collapsed like a felled tree, overwhelmed by the alignment of my dream with my father's. It struck her as a divine message. As the nurse helped her to her feet, she began to cry, setting off my own tears.

During his examination, the doctor tested the soles of my feet for sensation. To everyone's amazement, my toes responded for the first time since the surgery. This marked the beginning of my journey to stand and walk once more.

I can't explain the dreams my father and I had, nor why I chose that particular day to move my toes. I don't believe in miracles—I know that behind what many call a miracle lies immense blood, sweat and tears. Perhaps it was my subconscious telling me that if my father was starting to lose hope, it was time for my body to respond. Call it manifestation or the power of the subconscious, but the fact is that my journey to recovery had begun.

During the months I lay immobile in bed, I learned many valuable lessons—lessons that echoed through my life when I faced similar challenges years later.

I learnt to appreciate every effort made for my well-being.

I learnt gratitude.

I learnt not to complain.

I learnt the importance of not being a burden.

Whenever my father asked if I was in pain, I never admitted it. Instead, I would say, 'It'll get better.' I didn't want my parents to feel worse. Even at a young age, I was painfully aware of how much it hurt them to see me suffer. So even when I was in pain, I kept it to myself, focusing on the future—when all this would be behind us, and I would be pain-free.

face of all odds, ingrained in me since childhood, enabled me to maintain a rigorous training schedule, waking up at 4 a.m. every day throughout my fourteen-year career as a para athlete.

Mr Fatolkar turned physiotherapy into a game, an adventure. Months of being in bed had left my muscle strength depleted. Even sitting up was tough—my weakened muscles could not hold up my torso. Like a baby, I had to learn how to crawl first, before learning to walk. And all through this, Mr Fatolkar was right with me—crawling on the floor beside me, making a game of the exercises.

The hospital's small canteen was conveniently located right behind the physiotherapy block. The window of the physiotherapy room faced the canteen, and the enticing aroma of freshly made sambar would waft in during our sessions. Mr Fatolkar would reward me for a session well done with an idli. To this day, this is my idea of comfort food—I can wake up in the middle of the night for a steaming hot idli with sambar and chutney.

Even in these rewards, Mr Fatolkar would sneak in an exercise. He had me sit in an armless chair while eating, which forced me to balance my torso, raise my arms and hold my chin upright just to take a bite.

I was finally discharged from the hospital and sent home, but that came with its own challenges. Now, either my father or my mother had to take me to the hospital for physiotherapy. Most days, my father needed the scooter to get to the office, leaving my mother with only a cycle to get me to my sessions.

With my dangling feet and weak torso, I could not balance myself on the carrier of the cycle, so she had to improvise. Her inspiration came from Rani Lakshmibai of Jhansi. Just as the warrior queen had strapped her baby to her back while battling the British on

Reborn

Before my parents visited, I made sure I was clean, fresh well-dressed. This was largely thanks to the ward assistants. T encouraged me to act bright and positive before my parents arri so that they could see me in good spirits. 'See how your mo manages all the housework, sends your brother to school, cooks everyone and comes here to be with you,' they would say. 'Do want to add to her burdens or make her feel good about being v you?'

Very early on, I learnt that I didn't want people to feel as tho they were coming to see a patient when visiting me. I wanted th to look forward to being with me, not out of obligation but beca they genuinely wanted to. This lesson has guided me ever sir Even now, I prefer to seek help from professionals for my persc needs rather than burden my family. Overburdening caregivers only lead to resentment and burnout.

My physiotherapist, Mr Fatolkar, was wonderful. Finding right physiotherapist is perhaps more important than findin good doctor. The right rehab trainer will guide you towards s sufficiency, while the wrong one may leave you worse off than best that you can become.

Somehow, throughout my life, I've been fortunate to conn with the right people. Maybe this is the will of the almighty. Ev during my lowest moments, I never felt abandoned. There v always a helping hand, and I learnt to accept that help graciously

With Mr Fatolkar, physiotherapy was not a chore. Desp the extreme pain, he motivated me never to give up. He taug me discipline. My parents, on their part, did not let me miss ev a single session. The values of consistency and carrying on in t horseback, my mom secured me to her back with two dupattas: one holding my torso in place and another supporting my legs. Strapped together like this, we would reach the hospital. Here, she would park outside the physiotherapy block and ring her cycle bell. Mr Fatolkar would come out and untie me, and my mother would dismount.

If he was unable to come out for some reason, she would not hesitate to seek help from any passersby, whom she would call out to for a hand. This is another childhood lesson that has stayed with me: if I find myself unable to get my wheelchair out of my car, I feel no hesitation in seeking help from strangers, telling them, 'Do your good deed for the day—help me get into my wheelchair.' I will never be helpless until I become hopeless.

If the diagnostic myelogram that was performed to locate my spinal cysts had been like medieval torture, the rehab was worse. I needed all kinds of equipment to help realign my weakened frame, including a chest brace. My torso was so weak and my spine so fragile that I had to be strapped into a metal frame with leather belts encircling my chest and under my arms. Any movement with this contraption on caused friction under the arms, which led to painful blisters. Every day I had to wear this brace over those blisters. Even today when I recall that pain, I shudder.

At seven years old, this would seem unbearable. But I did it. I did it because Papa showed me how. He would tell me, 'Deepa, you have to go through pain to get to your goal. Do you want to walk again?' 'Yes,' I would reply. 'Then this pain and discomfort are irrelevant,' he would say.

This became my first life mantra: to achieve your goals, you must endure pain. But the pain will not be able to stop you if you keep the bigger picture—the goal—in mind.

Along with the chest brace, I needed callipers or knee braces to keep my legs straight. I required a chin support to keep my neck from rolling. When it was time to eat, I had to remove the chin support. Every day, I would do my physiotherapy looking like this. And every day, I had to raise the bar.

Citius, Altius, Fortius.

Faster, Higher, Stronger.

It was during this time that I first heard the Olympic motto. My father encouraged me with stories of valour, victory and courage. He motivated me to consistently raise the bar—if one day I could raise my legs for sixty seconds, it had to be ninety the next. Each day was a step forward, however small.

This became my second life mantra: Raise the bar. Go a little further every day. Push the boundaries.

Throughout these years, my schoolwork continued. I had to keep up with my assignments from my hospital bed. But now I was ready to actually go to school, the Kendriya Vidyalaya in Pune. The principal, Dr P.K. John, was exceptionally supportive. I remember Papa going to meet him several times to ensure everything was accessible.

I began the third standard in a wheelchair, equipped with a chest brace, chin support, knee braces and special orthopaedic shoes. As if I weren't already weird enough, these fully enclosed boots gave me foot fungus. My ingenious dad came up with a solution: he got the tops of the boots cut off, leaving my toes free to breathe. Although this proved effective, I hated it. To this day, I avoid open-toed footwear.

This is how I entered the traumatic world of grade three. The classroom was on the ground floor, which allowed my father to easily wheel me there and settle me into a chair. During the lunch break, my mother would come to give me food and take me to the washroom.

The problem, however, was the other students. Since I looked strange, no one wanted to talk to me or be my friend. My unhappiness was evident, and my father, always attuned to my mental well-being, was quick to notice.

Concerned, he brought this to the notice of the principal.

The next day, Dr John wheeled me onto the stage during the morning assembly. He held a little basket covered in pink crepe paper frills. Inside were several golden paper stars.

'Today, I want you all to meet a very brave young girl,' he announced to the entire school. 'This is Deepa. She's in class three. She has fought with death and come back. She has braved the odds and won. We must all support her and help her.' He held up the basket. 'I am giving this basket of golden stars to her. She will give a star to every student who does something for her. And every Monday, the child with the most stars will get a special prize, a chocolate bar.'

In that moment, I became Golden Deepa. From being a scared little girl strapped into alien contraptions and trapped in a wheelchair, I suddenly became empowered. I held the power to give out golden stars. Suddenly, everyone wanted to help me. I went from being shunned, isolated and laughed at to becoming the most popular girl in school.

Dr John's initiative eliminated any shame I might have felt in seeking help. I realized that in helping me, the other students weren't just doing me a favour—they were doing their good deed for the day and earning a reward for it.

But it wasn't all rosy. While I was never overtly mistreated, there were subtle digs, especially from some of the teachers. My formative school years that should have been spent learning to write had been lost to hospital stays. Though I could read, my writing was slow. And while my storytelling and creative skills were phenomenal, my mathematical prowess lagged behind.

It was at this point that I realized how much of a difference a teacher can make. A good teacher can uplift a struggling student, while an indifferent or cynical teacher can ruin a subject for them forever. Unfortunately, my maths teacher fell into the second category. She resented having to slow down for my sake. Her impatience and sarcastic jibes left me with a phobia of numbers—a fear so intense that it later led to complications during an Income Tax Tribunal inquiry because I had avoided dealing directly with my taxes. Even now, it takes three days of mental preparation before I am able to face my chartered accountant.

While this one teacher made me hate maths to such a degree, there was another who made me fall in love with her subject.

Our Hindi teacher realized that with my neck support and chest brace, it was difficult for me to look down at the book on the desk. While the maths teacher would sneer at helping me turn the page, the Hindi teacher found a solution—in the music room.

One day she came to class armed with a music stand, the kind used by musicians to hold their sheets. She positioned the stand in front of me, adjusted the height to my eye level and placed my book upon it.

I was now in love—with both the teacher and the subject.

Her encouragement led to my first stage performance. She helped me learn Subhadra Kumari Chauhan's famous poem 'Yeh Kadamb ka Ped' for an elocution competition. I still remember every line. My love for the language had begun with my father's storytelling sessions, but my teacher helped me discover my inner writer and poet. Poetry for me has become a way of expressing my thoughts.

My favourite poem, first read to me by my father when I was battling my illness as a child, still gives me goosebumps each time

I recite it. Papa would tell me it was written just for me. As a little child, bedridden with an unfathomable illness, a child who had been so full of life, always jumping around, running like the wind, now tied to a bed, the words of the poem coming from my father would fill me with the desire to break the shackles of my illness and run once again.

The poem, 'Veer Tum Badhe Chalo' by Dwarika Prasad Maheshwari, sang to my soul.

Veer tum badhe chalo! Dheer tum badhe chalo!

It was as if the poet was talking directly to me, telling me to keep going.

Saamne pahad ho, simha ki dahad ho
Tum nidar daro nahi, tum nidar dato vahin
Veer tum badhe chalo! Dheer tum badhe chalo!

The words exhorted me to march on bravely, even in the face of insurmountable mountains and roaring lions.

Praatah ho ki raat ho, sang ho na saath ho
Surya se badhe chalo, chandra se badhe chalo
Veer tum badhe chalo! Dheer tum badhe chalo!

Whether day or night, alone or accompanied, I had to keep going forward, just like the sun and the moon do.

And so, taking the poet's words to heart, I kept going.

As I started the fourth standard, I graduated from the wheelchair to crutches. Now I was able to walk to school.

My buddy on these journeys was Shamit Biswas. We were in the same class and also neighbours. He would carry my bag, and I would hobble along beside him.

Those walks were no less than adventures. We would write ourselves into different stories, each time a new character, depending on what book we had just read or movie we had seen.

One sultry day, right when school had reopened after the vacations, Shamit and I walked along in silence, both lost in our own thoughts. I noticed a stray dog walking towards us. Initially, we paid it no heed, but it seemed agitated—perhaps guarding a litter nearby or spooked by my crutches—and suddenly it began to approach us aggressively. Soon, it was not just one dog but a whole pack of them. Shamit acted first, hurling my bag at them, then grabbing some rocks to discourage them.

I don't know what came over me, but, pumped up by adrenaline, I charged at the dogs with what I had in hand: my crutches. When I flung them at the advancing dogs, they mercifully retreated.

Thrilled by our escapade and daring, we rushed home to tell the story.

With each retelling, the danger we faced grew, as did our valour in fighting off the vicious pack of bloodthirsty hounds.

After ensuring I was unscathed, my mother started berating me in the way all mothers do.

'No more walking to school. You're taking the bus from now on,' she decided, adding that quintessential mom threat, 'Wait till your father comes home.'

Once my father was home and my mother had apprised him of the day's events, I was summoned for further judgement. But in the middle of his stern lecture, Papa suddenly stopped, 'Wait, you threw your crutches at the dogs. So how were you standing?'

Amid the turmoil of it all, we had missed the headline news: I had been standing without my crutches until Shamit retrieved them.

This marked the beginning of my journey to complete recovery. My crutches were discarded, and I was upgraded to a walking stick, and before long even that became a thing of the past.

I was reborn.

4

Fighting Fate in My DNA

———◦•◦◦———

IN 1947, FIVE-YEAR-OLD BAL KRISHAN NAGPAL, affectionately called Ballu, embarked on the adventure of a lifetime. Perched atop a camel with several of his older siblings— at that time there were eleven of them, but their number would eventually grow to thirteen—they rode in a makeshift howdah made from an upturned charpai. Turbans had been unwound and their cloth wrapped around the legs of the charpai to secure the sides so that no child fell off during the camel's undulating journey. Each leg of the charpai also had an earthen pot full of water tied to it. As night fell, the children looked up at the starry sky in wonder, unaware that overnight their destinies were changing.

They had left their home in Fort Abbas, a small town in what is now Pakistan, on the banks of the dried-up Hakra River. The Hakra is a continuation of the Ghaggar River in India, and Fort Abbas neighbours the Sri Ganganagar and Bikaner districts in India.

Partition had been thrust upon the prosperous Nagpal family, which consisted of Ballu's father and his uncle. When the two brothers realized that political developments were pointing towards a division of India, Ballu's uncle and his family had been sent eastwards with the family jewellery and as many valuables as they could gather. At that time, they had not been sure whether Partition would be permanent or not, so they did not put all their eggs in one basket.

However, as the situation worsened for Hindus in the region destined to become Pakistan, it became clear that the time had come for Ballu's family to move too. But hopeful about the future, they hid their valuables in earthen pots, sealed them, and dropped the pots into the well in their backyard. Of course, they were never able to return to retrieve them.

Now here they were, crossing the desert from what was now Pakistan to come to India. Ballu's grandfather had earned his wealth with the help of the same stars at which the children were gazing. He had been a celestial navigator, guiding travellers and traders across the desert. Not only was he skilled at reading the stars, but he also knew the safest routes to take to evade the looters and bandits who frequented this active trade route. His reputation was based on his record of never having lost a single caravan, neither to the desert nor to dacoits.

I often think that I inherited my knack for navigation from him, my great-grandfather. Perhaps it was the collective blessings of the scores of people he had safely guided that ensured my five-year-old father, his siblings and his parents safely reached India.

They found a new home in Sri Vijaynagar in the Anupgarh district of Rajasthan, just about 65 km from their old home in Fort Abbas. There, they quickly adapted to their new life.

The family secured a plot of land and turned to agriculture. But my father was keen on studying more instead of tending to the land. It wasn't the back-breaking work in the fields that put him off; rather, it was the total dependence on the weather gods for a successful harvest that bothered him. If, even after working all year long, the fruits of your labour were lost in case of a drought, it meant months of poverty. He realized that the only way to break this cycle was to get an education and a good job.

His guide on this journey was Ramesh Chandra Gupta, his teacher. Tauji, as we called him, had spotted my father's calibre early on. He had developed a fondness for his hard-working and sincere student.

My father's focus on getting an education caused some tension in the family, as some of his siblings accused him of using his studies as an excuse to shirk the strenuous farm work. He would struggle to scrape together the few annas required for his school fee. But Papa was committed to his goal and so passionate about rising up in life through education that he stuck to it. His determination is something I see in myself. If there's something I feel passionate about, there's nothing that can stop me. Even now, my wheelchair has not been able to stop me from being a biker, a swimmer—a champion.

Meanwhile, my father's guru, Ramesh Tauji, moved to Sri Ganganagar, to a bigger school, and my father followed him there. Tauji took him in, and Papa earned his board by doing the household chores before going to school. It wasn't hard work that he shied away from, as his siblings thought. He just wanted to invest his efforts in a pursuit that would provide results and better his family's circumstances.

From Ganganagar, he moved again for higher education to Bikaner, where he enrolled in the Government Dungar College. College was a whole new world for him. The imposing structure was his gateway to a new life. He didn't let his lack of smart clothes or his rusticity affect his confidence. He was a tall, handsome young man with a natural charm that attracted everyone to him. So much so that he caught the attention of his college seniors, who boisterously ragged him, resulting in his pyjamas being torn.

'I had come to Bikaner with all my worldly possessions: two pairs of pyjama-kurtas and a few books. And now, here I was, with one pyjama torn beyond repair. So I went to speak to the principal. I told him that it was with great difficulty that I had managed to reach this college with the aim of getting an education. But the rowdy students had torn my clothes,' my father would tell us kids whenever he wanted to give us a lecture on how lucky we were to have the luxuries we did.

Recognizing his earnestness and need, the principal offered him a job in the college library. There, he looked after the books and learnt a new skill: bookbinding. He would craft a glue from flour and cover the books with cloth and paper after binding them with a needle and thread, the corners especially stiffened with buckram. All through our schooling, he would protect our books in the same manner.

This earnest young man who arrived at college with two pairs of pyjamas went on to become an excellent orator, debater and, eventually, the college president.

He had taken a room in the Jail Well Mohalla, locally called the 'Jail Well wala mohalla'. It was here that he met my mother.

Veena's father worked for the Indian Railways and lived in the neighbourhood where my father had rented a room. Since he was born on Dhanteras, a day devoted to Kuber, the god of wealth, he was named Dhan Narayan Kapoor. But contrary to his namesake, he had no love for money. Instead, his passion was for books. According to family lore, he was so fond of reading that on my parents' wedding day, when it was time for my mother and father to circle the holy fire, he was found engrossed in a newspaper at the public library! His book collection was extensive and covered every topic you could think of. If he ever had to pause his reading, he would mark his place in the book with whatever currency note he had at hand at the moment.

Years after his passing, we would find these unique bookmarks whenever we opened one of his books.

My nani, on the other hand, was a real livewire and talented in so many ways—talents that she passed on to her daughters and to us. Her sociable nature made her extremely popular in the community. She and her four daughters were always in high demand during community festivities: kirtans, weddings, any celebrations. The way my nani sang bhajans, played the dholak and energized everyone ensured that she was the life of the party.

My mother and her siblings had a comprehensive education, academically from my nanaji and culturally from my nani. My mother was an all-rounder. She was active in the National Cadet Corps and a member of the Maharaja Karni Singh shooting team. She participated in theatre activities and was also a part of her college debate team. When a woman was elected as mayor of the city, my mother was at the front of a marching contingent on 26 January that year, in her honour.

In those simpler times, expressions of affection and admiration didn't require grand gestures. Silent adoration from afar was enough to form unbreakable bonds. Though my parents say theirs was an arranged marriage, their paths had crossed on more than one occasion before they wed.

My father had seen my mother perform at gatherings in the neighbourhood. They also bumped into each other at intercollege events. At one intercollege debate, my mother, as the opening speaker, delivered a fiery speech with aplomb, but she was stumped when asked to prepare a rebuttal against the opposing team. My father, ever the chivalrous gentleman, came to her rescue and helped her prepare her rebuttal.

By this time my father had become the president of his college's student body. He had grown from the tall young man in pyjamas who had been distraught when seniors had ragged him to a confident young man, on his way to bigger things. His wardrobe now included two trousers—one black and one white—and two shirts—one black and one white. His vocabulary had increased—he had taken to the habit of reading the newspaper aloud to perfect his diction. And his aspirations had grown—he now headed to Jaipur for his masters.

While attending classes, he also prepared for a government job. He wrote the police force selection exams but was unsuccessful—a blessing in disguise, as fate had different plans for him. He was soon selected for the Indian Army and in 1966 was commissioned into the Grenadiers, one of the oldest infantry regiments.

Training at the Officers Training Academy in Madras, now Chennai, added a layer of polish to my already dashing father. He had taken to horse riding and cut an impressive figure in his breeches and riding boots. On the basketball court, his height made him a standout player, towering above the rest. And when he saluted sharply in his crisp uniform, his peak cap set smartly, he looked no less than a film star.

He was the cynosure of all eyes wherever he went. It wasn't long before he caught the eye of many a mama in search of the perfect match for their darling daughters. Proposals started flooding in, some even from royal families, as army officers were considered to be quite a catch in those days.

My father, however, was a very grounded man. He wasn't looking for a princess. He wanted a partner who would be as comfortable in the army circles as she would be in Sri Vijaynagar with his family. He was the only one among his siblings to have made the move from the village to city life, but he remained committed to his familial duties—and a woman from a royal family wouldn't adapt well to his family's modest ways.

Moreover, he already had someone in mind.

Veena had made a lasting impression on him during his time in Bikaner. Once again, he reached out to Ramesh Tauji, his pillar of support, and his wife, Urmila Taiji.

During their discussions, Papa casually mentioned, 'There was this girl in Jail Well wala mohalla who sang at kirtans and sangeets, whose father worked for the Railways. Maybe someone like her. I wonder if she's married yet ...'

Taiji immediately went to work, reaching out to her old friends. After a little digging, it was discovered that Veena was still in the old neighbourhood and very much not married.

And so, the story of our small family began.

When people met my mother, they were captivated by her talents. She could sing, dance, orate. These were qualities that ensured that she was much in demand at ladies' meets and family welfares— meetings conducted for the wives of soldiers to help acquaint them with army life.

My mother was in her element when conducting these activities. Her public speaking skills, her intelligence and her ability to get along with both the wives of soldiers, who were largely uneducated in those days, as well as officers' wives, who often belonged to royal families, stood her in good stead, and she made a mark for herself.

Both my parents were fond of good food. Mom honed her culinary skills by picking up recipes from her friends and showed remarkable creativity in cooking competitions. A beloved family recipe is the one for cheese rings, something she created on the spot for a competition by just kneading cheese into the dough for namak paras and shaping it into rings before deep frying. For dinner parties, my parents would cook together, each one preparing a signature dish, my father's usually being his atta halwa.

He had a discerning palate. Every dal had to have its own unique tempering. If the ghee was not hot enough when the cumin was added during tempering, he could tell right away.

While both my parents were amazing hosts, they differed in their approach: Papa was spontaneous, always up for anything, while Mom needed to be prepared—she didn't like being surprised. In unforeseen situations, Mom would take time to adjust, while Papa would immediately go into problem-solving mode. I would wonder why Mom cribbed about sudden guests, but now I realize that it was not due to reluctance or hostility but because she liked being meticulous and organized.

Papa wanted us to be excellent students. We had our task cut out for us—every day we had to learn five new words and memorize a quote, shloka, doha or saying, much like a daily affirmation. I still remember a bhajan about Saraswati, 'Veena Vadini Gyan ki Devi'. This practice of repeating positive thoughts and inspiring quotes every day is perhaps why I've always found the resilience to persevere, even in my darkest moments.

Before dinner, he would ask my mother whether we had done at least an hour of self-study. If the answer was no, dinner was postponed until we fulfilled this requirement.

As I progressed to more senior classes, I often saw him working on his office files at home. From him I learnt the art of concise writing: how to draft notes and present information logically and clearly. This skill has been invaluable in my communication with corporate houses and government departments while seeking sponsorships or advocating for policy changes to benefit para athletes.

He also nurtured our village roots. Not only did we spend holidays in the village, but we also brought some aspects of village life back with us to our city homes. We kept a cow in the yard for fresh milk. When the yard was in bad shape, we would plaster it with fresh cow dung and mud. We were never hung up on material wealth; we found happiness within our means.

I have subconsciously filtered out the minor flaws of both my parents and imbibed their best qualities. But I may be more my father's daughter than my mother's.

Vacations were also an important part of our childhood. Initially, holidays meant just the four of us going to the village. But soon we became a big group of uncles and aunts, cousins and pets. Often, it was my mother's siblings and their families who joined us. We would also holiday with my bua, my father's sister, and her family in Jaipur. With so many of us, getting a cab was out of the question. So my father would hire a mini truck. We had a stool to climb in and out, and the back would be made as comfortable as possible with mattresses and cushions. Singing and playing games, we travelled from one destination to the next: Vaishno Devi, all of Maharashtra, Agra, Akhnoor, Gulmarg. Cooking was easy—Papa had a wooden box with all the essentials, including a stove and utensils. We'd stop anywhere, cook in the great outdoors and enjoy our picnic meals.

Life was one big, joyful journey in my childhood. I probably caught the travel bug early on. Even my wheelchair has not been able to put the brakes on my love for travel and adventure.

5

The Wonder Years

FTER I THREW AWAY MY CRUTCHES, THERE WAS NO stopping me. I was running, cycling, swimming, playing—I had to make up for lost time. Amidst these activities, I stumbled upon a new passion, which came from an unlikely source.

In school, our Hindi textbook had a chapter on Nadia Comăneci. Her story fascinated me: a girl just a few years older than me was standing before the world, receiving applause, bowing to be awarded medal after medal. I wanted to be her.

At home, I fashioned a gymnastics outfit from my white stockings and my brother's vest. I would climb onto the dining table and jump off, landing on my feet and rising on my toes, body arched and arms outstretched. I could almost hear the applause, feel the surge of adrenaline that every athlete feels when they stand on the winners' podium.

While Papa indulged my fantasies, he also grounded them with reality. He took me through Nadia's story in my textbook but highlighted the grit and discipline behind her iconic perfect ten score and gold medals. Nadia's tale, he explained, wasn't just about elegant movements and graceful flourishes. It was about dedication and determination. The endless hours of practice. The unmoving focus.

He told me that for her to reach the Olympics at the age of fourteen, she must have started training very early. At age six, she was already part of a local gymnastics team. At seven, she had been hand-picked for Romania's centralized gymnastics training programme.

The seeds for focused hard work were sown in me with Nadia's story.

After the two years I had spent waiting to walk, every day that I ran, cycled and played was special. I had picked up swimming at the Rajendra Sinhji Institute while we were still in Pune after my surgery. I was like a fish in the water. Exercising in the water also helped in my recovery.

My bicycle became a defining symbol of freedom during my childhood. When I was eleven years old, we moved to Binnaguri, a small cantonment town in the Jalpaiguri district of West Bengal. Papa was stationed in Hasimara on the Bhutan border, where families couldn't reside, about 40 km away from us. He would be at work during the week and home on the weekends.

At that time, we had two cycles in the house: one my mother's and the other, Bhaiyya's. I had to wait for my turn on Bhaiyya's cycle, which would come only after he had had his fill. This was usually at sundown—our signal to head home. Instead of waiting for his mercy, I started saving my pocket money to rent a cycle. While he would spend his pocket money on treats and candy, I was happy to invest in the freedom of a rented cycle. The rush of the wind, the thrill of the speed and the sheer joy of it all were worth so much more than a few toffees.

In Binnaguri, we lived in army accommodation meant for the families of officers stationed elsewhere. Initially called the Separated Family Accommodation, the name was later updated to the more politically correct Forward Area Family Accommodation, to refer to homes for families of personnel posted in forward areas—those close to the borders.

In this colony, with most of the men posted away, the ladies formed a tight-knit group, not just to share happy times but also for support. Everyone would go together to the weekly haat, or market, to shop. While sometimes we children went along, more often we were all packed up in one person's house, and what a blast we all had.

The weekly market was not just for necessities like vegetables and fruits, but also for dresses and trinkets. I still remember a pink frilly top with a ruffled collar that my mom got for me—I felt so grand when I wore it. Recently, I bought a similar top, which my younger daughter, Ambika, has dubbed my 'clown top'.

As I grew older, our familial harmony began to wane. The once-indulgent Papa, whose favourite I was, soon became Papa, the Disciplinarian. Mom, who had been a fount of unquestioning love and succour throughout my illness, now seemed to have reduced her expansive vocabulary to a single word: 'no'.

Now, as a mother myself, I understand many of their concerns, but back then, these shifts in our family dynamic nudged me towards rebellion.

In Binnaguri, we had a first-floor house and I was easily climbing the stairs. This was taken as a good sign, as it meant I was physically fit again. The struggle now was keeping me home. My tomboyish inclinations did not sit well with my mother. She wanted me to stay home, study and 'be a good girl'. But for me, the call of the wild was irresistible—I had to have that last round on the cycle, outrun the boys, be the last one to be found in a game of hide-and-seek.

And my struggles with maths didn't help matters.

Consequently, when Papa came home from Hasimara every weekend, there was a litany of complaints about me. 'She didn't do well in her unit tests', 'She was out till dark', 'She took Vikram's cycle too far from the house', 'She doesn't listen to me': the complaints varied little in tone. And my loving father now began to lay down the law.

Alongside all these remonstrations came the constant comparisons to my brother, who always stood first in his class. The refrain became: 'Why can't you be more like your brother?'

Yet, in the midst of all these growing pains, a memorable moment of joy emerged unexpectedly. My brother, the ideal son, the good student, the responsible beta, was poised to receive a reward for doing so well in school. On his birthday, my father got him a brand-new maroon cycle from Jalpaiguri.

While everyone fawned over the shiny new cycle, my focus was on his old cycle, which did not have any claimants. Finally, I had a cycle all to myself. It was old and battered, but it was more precious to me than anything else.

Soon it was time to move again. This time we headed from east to west, from the lush humidity of West Bengal to the arid desert of Rajasthan. The terrain change, however, did not bring about much change in my situation. I continued to suffer the comparisons to my brother in academics.

The good thing in Nasirabad was that I started finding school interesting, not so much for the studies but for the variety of other activities. One of my favourites was the Socially Useful Productive Work (SUPW) class. Here, we were taught skills like embroidery, knitting, sewing and other crafts. I loved this: working with my hands, transforming simple materials like thread and cloth into artistic creations.

I was fascinated by embroidered handkerchiefs, how they looked so pretty and delicate. They appealed to my softer side, despite my athletic interests.

Inspired, I planned a surprise for my mother's birthday. I had seen a set of six dainty hankies in the local shop, each a different pastel shade with a small floral motif embroidered in one corner. Convinced my mother would love them, I raided my piggy bank, collected all the coins and a few currency notes and marched off to the shop. With the leftover money, I bought a cake—my favourite, Black Forest—layers of chocolate sponge, whipped cream and tinned cherries, topped with more cream and cherries and little bits of shaved chocolate.

Excited to surprise my mom, I rushed home. But she was the one who ended up surprising me. Instead of the hugs and praise I expected, I got an earful. 'Why did you break your piggy bank without permission? Whom did you ask before going to the market alone?'

My plan had backfired badly. This reaction to what was an expression of pure love left a deep mark on me.

In hindsight, as a parent now, I can understand that her anger was probably the result of concern. But at that time, it felt as if it came from a desire for control.

Now, however, both my daughters and I are big on gestures, whether it's through a card or a bouquet, maybe a cake or finding just the right gift. I love making the people who matter to me feel special.

The 1982 Asian Games that were held in Delhi marked a watershed moment in India's sporting history. Appu, the chubby elephant mascot for the games, was everywhere, and sports fever had afflicted everyone. I was especially hit because my overactive imagination got so much fodder.

I was fortunate to be in the stands at Jawaharlal Nehru Stadium during the opening ceremony. Watching the Indian contingent march past us filled me with an immense sense of pride. In my mind, I envisioned myself among them, holding the national flag high, thunderous applause surrounding me. Years later, this vision came true: I found myself wheeling along the same track with the Indian para athletic contingent, my daughter cheering from the stands.

Not content with having watched the opening ceremony in person, I also watched the repeat telecast at home.

It was courtesy my bua, my father's sister, Suchitra, that we were able to witness this historic event. Her father-in-law was a member of Parliament, Chaudhary Kumbha Ram Arya. He had been a freedom fighter and was a respected leader of farmers in Rajasthan. After serving two terms in the Rajya Sabha, he was a Lok Sabha member for Sikar, representing Chaudhary Charan Singh's Lok Dal. During Charan Singh's caretaker government, the Asian Games had been dismissed as a wasteful luxury. However, when the Congress returned to power in 1980, the games were back on track, though the Lok Dal protested against them. As an MP, my bua's father-in-law got passes, but owing to his party position, he decided not to attend, which meant the passes came to us.

We stayed at the home of Chaudhary Kumbha Ram on Pandit Pant Marg in Lutyens' Delhi, a huge, white-painted official bungalow. It was an especially happy time because I was with my cousins Tinnoo Bhaiyya, Belu Bhaiyya, Baby and Bittoo, my bua's children. Unlike my more serious brother, Vikram, my cousins were always up for an adventure.

The opening ceremony was spectacular, but I was particularly eager to watch the gymnastics events, given my admiration for Nadia Comăneci.

While the events were thrilling, what truly captivated me was the winners' podium. Even at that age, from a distance, I could feel the adrenaline rush that athletes feel when they stand on that podium, draped in their country's flag, their national anthem playing as they gracefully bend to accept the medal.

I was fascinated by this ritual.

As kids do, I began to replicate this ritual in the games we cousins played in the huge lawns of the Pandit Pant Marg bungalow.

Back in those pre-liberalization days, our options for branded snacks were limited to Parle-G and KrackJack biscuits. It was a common practice to get biscuits baked for the family from local bakers. We would supply the raw ingredients—atta, ghee, sugar—and receive in return healthy atta biscuits neatly packed in big cuboid tins known as pippas. These 15 kg pippas, previously used by us kids as drums, were now stacked to become our winners' podium.

Each cousin picked a sport, and after a well-contested make-believe competition, the winners would be declared. I was, of course, a gymnast. Once again, my stockings came out and combined with a t-shirt, became my leotard. I showcased the cartwheels I had mastered and finished with my trademark flourish: standing on my toes, back arched, arms outstretched. I was always able to bully my way to the top of the winners' podium, always wanting to be first, always winning gold.

The medals were an integral part of our game. They had to be because the entire purpose of the game was victory, symbolized only by a medal. I crafted them by braiding ribbons around bangles foraged from my bua's dressing table. With great ceremony, one of the cousins would play the chief guest and come to the podium, congratulate us and garland us with the medals.

The next few years at home were not as idyllic. As academics intensified, so did the expectations of my parents. Bhaiyya was still the ideal student. He had a knack for memorization and was able to score well in his exams because he would reproduce the answers perfectly. While he was a hard worker, I was a smart worker. I knew the concepts well enough to answer exam questions, but rote learning was never my thing, which meant my results, though solid, never matched his. So while Bhaiyya always stood first in his class, I was second or third.

Our family was united once again, and our daily routine became more structured. Papa would work almost fourteen-hour days, while Mom was busy with housework and her duties as an army officer's wife. 'My job is the army. Mom's job is ensuring there is healthy food on the table and keeping the house in order. Your job,' Papa would tell us, 'is to focus on your studies.'

Bhaiyya diligently followed that dictum, but I was unable to focus on just one thing. I wanted to make little dresses for my dolls. I wanted to go out and play. I could not sit in a chair for long. My restlessness made me constantly want to move. Even after my paralysis at twenty-nine, though I ended up in a chair, I have ensured that my chair has wheels.

Our sibling rivalry came to a head during an inter-house debate at school. Bhaiyya and I, in different houses, faced off on a topic related to democracy. I was the youngest contestant. We went on one after the other. Even before the results were announced, everyone knew who had won. I had defeated my brother and all the other contestants to clinch first place.

Co-curricular activities and sports were my forte. While Bhaiyya coming first in class was a given, my academic performance was always held back by maths. That year, tragedy struck when Sanjeev Choradia, the class topper, suddenly passed away from an inflamed appendix. His death brought an overwhelming mix of grief and guilt, as his absence led to me coming first in class.

The mixed emotions were tough, but my achievement brought joy to my father. He handed out boxes of mithai to everyone in the school, saying, 'Both my kids have come first in school.'

We lived a simple yet rich life, devoid of luxuries but full of comfort. The intense heat of Rajasthan's summers was unbearable, but we could not afford a cooler. So my father fashioned one for us by placing khus grass mats in the window and creating a sort of drip irrigation system with a pipe to keep the grass wet. When the hot winds passed through these moist barriers, they transformed into cool, fragrant breezes. This aroma of khus is as embedded in my childhood memories as the smell of agarbattis. On some days, we would place a table fan in the garden and sleep under the stars. Our beds, each enclosed by a white mosquito net, would be laid out in a row.

These outdoor nights satisfied the nomad in me and deepened my love for camping. As a Bulbul with the Bharat Scouts and Guides, I also experienced real camp life. Dressed in our indigo blue multi-pocketed tunics with military-style shoulder flaps, we'd set off for Khetadi for our annual camp. What an adventure that was!

My competitive streak made me want to win all the competitions: best tent, neatest bed, best campfire song. My creativity shone when I found some round river stones and arranged them in neat designs outside our tent. Of course we won the best tent prize.

As I began to develop a strong independent personality, my brother grew more controlling, with my parents often siding with him. I thrived on being the centre of attention, while he wanted the opposite. Everything I did was to stand out from the crowd. I wanted to be the star. I needed to be the best. And this irked Bhaiyya. If all the cool kids on the bus ride home were standing and singing songs, I had to be not just the loudest singer but also the first one to start dancing. During our evening cycle rides, I had to race the boys and win. If curfew was at 6.30 p.m., I was the one sneaking in an extra round. Every day, Bhaiyya tattled to Mom, and every day, I was scolded for my mischief.

Tensions escalated when I was off-roading on my cycle one day. The smooth road was too tame; I always went through uncharted terrain. Pillars had been erected in one area for an upcoming fence. Emulating professional drag racers, I would zig-zag between the pillars. I took off to go off-road—I ran into an almost invisible obstacle. Overnight, labourers had started constructing the fence and had strung up a length of wire connecting the tops of the pillars to get their measurements right. No one spotted the wire. It hit me across the torso and I tumbled from the cycle and lost consciousness.

Despite getting grounded, having my cycle taken away and sporting a bruised shoulder from the fall, I still managed to sneak rides. As my parents' restrictions increased, so did my defiant streak.

Deepa, the Rebel, was born.

By the time I was thirteen and we moved to Kota, I stood tall at 5'5". Bhaiyya and I joined the Kendriya Vidyalaya there. Kendriya Vidyalayas, or Central Schools, are a chain of government-run schools primarily for the children of government employees who are constantly on the move.

On my first day, my height and appearance drew immediate attention. The most notorious boy of the school decided to make my acquaintance. As I climbed the stairs to my classroom, I found him posed a few steps above me, likely attempting to appear taller.

'*Aapka mere baare mein kya khyal hai?*' (So, what do you think of me?), he asked.

He was unprepared for my answer. Without a thought, I impulsively slapped him hard across the cheek. The echo of that slap was heard by the entire school.

From that day onwards, I was nicknamed Tataiya Mirchi (stinging wasp). Every morning I'd find a green chilli on my desk.

It was during this period that I became conscious of my looks, which drew a lot of attention. We were in our adolescent years and teenage pairings were happening. Somehow, any romantic whispers were termed my fault. Despite not being the one to initiate a cheesy pick-up line, I was scolded for it. My parents suddenly became even more strict. Previously, restrictions were to curb my boisterous play; now I was held responsible for how other people reacted to me.

I rebelled.

Ankle socks were forbidden, but the minute I boarded the school bus, they were rolled down. Expected to blend in, I stood out— literally, as I towered over most of my male classmates. I was now an inch-and-a-half taller than when I had joined the school. My height made me equally sought-after on the playing field and I was naturally drawn to sports. Soon I was in all the teams that the school had—including basketball and track and field.

We were living in a civil area next to a doctor's house. As always, my father had found a house that was dilapidated, but with a lot of time and effort, he had managed to make it shine. It was an NRI doctor's house and had fallen into disrepair. Papa and I would spend hours on the repairs, supervising the labour as well as getting our own hands dirty. I learnt how to fix leaky taps, get bloated doors into shape and landscape a garden—all this fostered the special bond I shared with my father.

But my adolescence was not easy on them.

Dramatics was another area that attracted me. Our neighbour, Dr Tandon, was a Rotarian, and his daughter, Milli, became my best friend. We created our own code language and would spend hours after dark sitting on the small wall between our homes chatting about everything teenage girls talk about.

The Rotary Club in Kota was known to put on plays, and when they needed fresh talent, I was a natural choice. It was a three-act play with only two characters, and I played the boy. I still chuckle recalling one of the jokes. The other character said something about illustrious forefathers and my character responded with, 'Oh, you have four fathers?' This line had the entire audience in splits.

My fan following had increased by now. On our way to rehearsals on our cycles, Milli and I would be followed by a boy on his Luna moped. He never said a word, simply escorting us to rehearsals and back. Over time, we became friends, and I even attended his wedding. Tragically, we later lost him to alcoholism.

Diwali that year was one that taught me a big lesson. We lived in an affluent neighbourhood. The corner house in the lane opposite our house belonged to a rich businessman known as Bamboriwale

Sethji. His bungalow was huge, with two cars parked in the porch. His sons, around my age, were known for their extravagant Diwali fireworks. Before the days of anti-cracker campaigns, wealthy families would celebrate Diwali by literally burning money in the form of pathaka ladis. Milli and I obviously had to be there.

After the fireworks, an impromptu party started with the sethji's two sons, Milli, her brother, Bhaiyya and me. The brothers brought out a music system and placed it on top of one of their cars and we all danced. As the music faded, someone suggested a car ride. All of us piled into their car and drove around, revelling in the colony's festivities, and before we knew it, it was 9.30 p.m. Realizing we were late for the Lakshmi puja, Bhaiyya and I rushed home.

We were greeted by the front door, firmly bolted from inside. Despite our knocking and pleading, Papa did not budge. 'You like your moneyed friends so much, go live with them,' he said from behind the door.

We had missed the puja entirely. Papa was unmoved by our apologies and begging. We stood outside for almost two hours before Dr Tandon noticed and pleaded on our behalf.

But the lesson was firmly embedded. I became conscious of our financial situation. I realized that my father's reaction stemmed more from hurt than anger. He did so much to give us everything he could on a tight budget, and we had spurned our family traditions and values for a few crackers and a car ride.

In Akhnoor, our family dynamics shifted. Bhaiyya had been sent to the Army Public School in Delhi. Papa was in a forward location. Mom and I were in a one-room outhouse belonging to a self-made Dogri businessman whom we all called Shahji. He lived with his family in the main house.

With Bhaiyya away at boarding school and Papa only visiting on weekends, I became the man of the house. My cycling, once frowned upon, now became our lifeline. In fact, I was upgraded to a moped so that I could run errands and do odd jobs.

It was in Akhnoor that I received my first marriage proposal. Despite only being in the tenth standard, I looked more grown-up because of my height. During a Raising Day celebration for one of the local army units, I acted in a skit, which was followed by a dance party, my first dance with young officers. I must have left a lasting impression because soon enough my parents received a proposal for me. They turned it down, of course, but I later learnt that the officer who had sent the proposal eventually named his daughter Deepa.

Socially, I was doing well, but academically, maths and science were a nightmare. Every time Papa came home, it would be like being marched up to a senior. He would look at my grades and frown. 'You're not making her study,' he would say to my mother. In turn, she would spend the entire week badgering me: 'Do your work or I'll be held accountable.' I took to writing poetry to express my teenage angst.

Meanwhile, Bhaiyya was also not faring well in Delhi. The pressure of boarding school took its toll, and after a fellow student in the hostel died by suicide, Papa confronted the school's administration, holding them responsible for Bhaiyya's falling grades. Bhaiyya came back home with him.

That was an extremely stressful time for us all. Education had been the tool my father had used to rise up out of life as a farmer. Education had been my mother's biggest asset. Now, when it was time for us to carry the baton forward, both Bhaiyya and I were lagging.

Calcutta (now Kolkata) might have been the City of Joy for Dominique Lapierre, but for me, it will forever be the City of Friends. During the two impressionable years I spent there, I not only forged lifelong friendships but also met the most enduring love of my life: the motorbike.

After having lived in the smaller cantonment towns of India, Kolkata was no less exciting than New York or London to me. There were two parties a week at the club, we could go to watch movies in proper cinema halls, not open-air army theatres, the shops were fancy and the city buzzed with life.

Our school was in Salt Lake, a suburb some distance from Fort William, the military station where we lived. While most army children went to school inside Fort William, there were five of us who went to Salt Lake every day. There was no school bus, so we all went in an army jeep. Those jeep rides were the highlight of my day. The battle was for the front seat, usually bagged by Tapan—he pulled rank because his father had arranged our transport.

Turmoil continued at home. Whatever I did was scrutinized: the way I dressed, the way I behaved in the club, whom I spoke to, the amount I laughed, the length of my socks and skirt. The list felt endless. This censure, typical of the '80s in India, drove me to seek external validation.

I had a good group of friends who were my steadfast support, but for my parents, they were a sore point. We often hung out as a big group, Bhaiyya included. Naturally, pairings began to form. I was linked with another boy only because we matched each other in height—there was no romance brewing. Unfortunately for me, Bhaiyya faithfully reported all this information to my parents.

My brother did not approve of my friends. They didn't fit the mould of 'good boys', though they were genuine friends. Poltu, who looked like a gangster back then, is one of the kindest people I know to this day. Shamit, who had fought off the pack of dogs with me when I was on crutches in Pune, was back now, but did not meet my brother's approval because, after a stint in Bombay, he had become a breakdancer. Raj Mohanty, despite being academically gifted and coming from a reputable business family, did not pass muster with Bhaiyya.

I, on the other hand, was always looking for the best in people, overlooking superficial judgements that pegged them as 'bad influences'. This open-mindedness planted the seeds of my rallyist spirit. I never judge a book by its cover, which helped me strike gold when it came to making lifelong friends. When challenges were thrown my way, it was this group of friends from Kolkata who stood by me and were my rock.

My family's disapproval of everyone and everything was stifling. I wanted to soar, yet instead of being the wind beneath my wings, my parents—who had fought so hard for my survival—were now trying to chain me down. Fortunately, fate intervened: my brother was selected for the NDA, the National Defence Academy, and I no longer had a policeman hovering around me.

With this newfound freedom, I totally came into my own. The weekly club events had me hunting New Market for danglers in all hues and belts to refresh my outfits. At the pool, I was in my element, earning the nickname Miss Long Legs. My social life was vibrant.

I was also doing well academically. The dreaded maths, physics and chemistry felt like a bad dream. I now had subjects that I was good at, where I could excel effortlessly. My popularity soared as I was elected head girl of the school. The vice head girl was Swati Gautam, who went on to launch her own brand of customized lingerie. All my friends who were thought to be a distracting influence on me turned out to be extremely successful in their own fields.

My friend Tripti and I often led our gang on escapades. We'd go on tram rides and get off at a place where a new fast food joint had come up. One day, Shamit showed off his breakdance skills, drawing a crowd and inadvertently boosting the restaurant's business. Out of gratitude, they gave us free softies. When my parents came to know of this, they were horrified: 'You're performing on street corners and begging for food!'

That summer we went to Jaipur. Suchitra Bua and all my cousins were there. Jaipur had an active underground drag racing scene near the airport. My cousins would go often, so I was invited to join them. I quickly became addicted to the thrill. Motorcycles were the natural progression in my love affair with wheels. That summer in Jaipur was a major turning point in my life. Not only was I getting to ride, but also there were no judging eyes, no tattling to my parents, no one stopping me. This was what freedom felt like.

On our return to Kolkata, just as a junkie can find a dealer anywhere, I was able to find the local biker gang. The city's vacant lots became our playground for riding and stunts. The first time I went there, no one took me seriously. But when I got onto a bike and showed off some of the stunts I had learnt over the summer, I secured my place within their ranks.

My dad's official charter of duties included handling land encroachment cases where army land had been illegally taken over. One day, he was on his way to inspect one such lot of land in his official jonga. I happened to be on the same road with my gang, performing stunts on a bike. It was like a scene from a movie: his jonga approaching from the opposite direction and me standing on the moving bike with my arms outstretched, similar to the now-famous Titanic pose. Our eyes locked as we passed each other. There was a screeching of brakes as both of us stopped. The next thing I *heard* was the bang of the jonga door slamming shut. And the next thing I *felt* was a stinging slap across my face.

I don't know who was more shocked—me upon seeing my dad, or him witnessing my antics.

The hell that awaited me at home that day paled in comparison to my next big scrape.

Bhaiyya was away at the NDA, and with him was the tall boy from our group with whom I had been loosely linked. India was just waking up to displays of affection, and we embraced it with Giggles, the country's answer to Hallmark, which also sold teddy bears and cards for all occasions. I decided it would be harmless to send the boy a good luck card, written in my favourite pink pen. As luck would have it, it was Bhaiyya's turn to distribute the mail in his squadron that day. Recognizing the pink ink and my handwriting, he intercepted the card and mailed it straight back to my dad.

That was the last nail in my coffin. I was grounded. It was decided: as soon as my board exams were over, I would be sent to the village. That would keep me away from the boys. Once the results were out, I would go to an all-girls college.

In the interim, I was enrolled in grooming classes under a franchise of the famous Shahnaz Husain. This contradiction baffled me—on the one hand my parents wanted me to learn how to look more attractive, while on the other they did not want me to attract male attention!

What was intended as punishment unexpectedly turned out to be the best thing that could have happened to me. Papa and I reached the 68–66 chak markings on the Gang Canal, where my cousins from the village were supposed to meet me. But no one was there. Papa had to rush back to catch his train to Kolkata, as he hadn't been able to get more leave. My adventure began from that moment itself: he made a quick decision, leaving me alone on the highway.

There I stood with my bags, the Gang Canal flowing by. I felt the thrill of it all, but I couldn't shake off the apprehension: was this the punishment? What if no one came to get me? Perhaps I was being abandoned. However, before my overactive imagination could spiral further, a jeep arrived with my cousins, and off we went.

My parents had thought that I needed to be kept away from boys. What they had not understood was that my interactions were based on shared interest, not romance. I was hanging out with them because they loved what I did: wheels.

I wish my parents had given me more credit; not every boy I talked to was a potential boyfriend or husband. They were my buddies, my gang—my go-to friends.

Many years later, when I asked these 'boyfriends' from that time why none of them asked me out, they said they had been too scared of losing me as a friend. I was the dream girl—confident, funny, beautiful and a biking enthusiast! But there was a clear line never to be crossed. Our bond was because of a shared passion for wheels, and I was essentially one of the boys in that regard. I wish my parents had understood this as those adolescent boys had.

I didn't miss boys when I was in the village—it had almost everything I loved.

The farm had a dairy, and every morning, milkmen would come to collect milk for delivery. They carried big milk cans, which were saddled across the pillions of their bikes. Did I say bikes? I meant motorbikes—sturdy Rajdoot motorcycles, to be precise. I was like a kid in a candy shop. So many bikes to choose from and no one to stop me.

Every morning I found myself racing across the farm on those milk can-laden motorbikes. When the milkmen left for the day, my attention turned to the jeeps and tractors—anything I could drive. Long before dune bashing in Dubai became a thing, I was mastering the skill in the deserts of Rajasthan.

Next on the daily agenda was swimming. The clear waters of the Gang Canal beckoned me, and I would spend hours there, swimming with my cousins in the open water.

Farm life started early. We would be up at 4 a.m., and by 9 a.m., all the chores were completed: the animals had been fed and milked, the crops tended to and the milk dispatched with the milkmen. What remained was feeding ourselves. Food for everyone was cooked together—community cooking in the *dhani*. I learnt the art of cooking on an open flame there.

For me, it was like being on a vacation, but I also learnt a lot—practical things that helped me later in life. Maths had always been my nemesis, but observing my father's elder brother, who never went to school, running a successful wholesale vegetable business offered a new perspective. He would buy vegetables by the truckload and sell them to retailers. He used mental maths all day long.

By watching him, I learnt the nuances of managing a business and negotiating—he'd get the best deals at the vegetable auctions. I learnt empathy from him—he'd give away unsellable but perfectly edible vegetables to the needy who lived near the mandi. I saw their gratitude. I learnt survival—people making a living out of what others were just throwing away. This experience reinforced my attitude of always being able to make the best of the worst situation. And everything I learnt in the village helped me when I later ran a restaurant in Ahmednagar.

Luckily, when the exam results came out, I had exceeded everyone's expectations. I had scored the second-highest marks in the school. Now it was off to college: an all-girls one.

Life at Sophia Girls' College in Ajmer wasn't a dull, lacklustre existence as I had expected—it was fun, despite the restrictions. The nuns there were strict, but nothing could quell the rebel in me. I had tasted freedom in Kolkata, and nothing could stop me. My defiant spirit made itself known right from the first week.

I had barely settled in, when I was accosted by a gang, led by two girls, Tubby and Hina.

Tubby, a fellow fauji kid, with fair skin, curly hair and big eyes, confronted me. 'You, fresher, what are your subjects?'

'English literature and geography,' I replied.

Hina, who has since transformed from the tomboy of our college days into a picture of sophistication, chimed in. 'I have the perfect job for you, English Literature.' She thrust a well-read Mills & Boon romance novel into my hands.

'Translate this into Hindi,' she said, opening the book to a dog-eared page.

The passage described the heroine quivering at the first fevered touch of the hero, his lips poised just above hers before going for a long, lingering kiss.

Always up for a challenge, I gave it my best and turned my ragging into a performance that surprised and entertained the girls so much that I was asked to repeat it on several occasions.

I quickly found my gang—the five of us are close to this day. We were ordinary girls, not from royal families, not the children of big businessmen. No luxury cars came to fetch us from college, nor did we have fancy tuck boxes or big trunks full of expensive clothes. But we were arguably the happiest lot, getting up to mischief and finding happiness in activities that did not cost much.

I discovered that the way to get permission for outings from college was through the sports ground. I was fond of basketball, volleyball, athletics—but I found my space among the cricket players. I was soon in the college team, competing in the district finals against Savitri College.

The Dharmendra-starrer *Ghulami* was playing in theatres, focused on the inter-community rivalry between Jats and Rajputs. Savitri College was a Jat-dominated one. As we faced off on the Government College grounds, our focus shifted from the pitch to some commotion near the main gate. Suddenly, a mob of angry young men charged towards the pitch. Instinctively, we ran in the opposite direction, towards the Ajmer Pavilion, an all-glass viewing gallery at one end of the field. Once inside, we realized the glass walls placed us in even greater jeopardy. A quick-thinking teacher hurriedly draped us in blankets for protection. That day, we all had a narrow escape.

Yet, cricketing did not stop. We were selected to be a part of the Ajmer district team and, with our rivals from Savitri College and other teams, we reached the state finals against the Railways team. The match was in Bhilwara. Our collective talent led us to triumph. Upon our victorious return to Ajmer, I stopped the bus and urged all the girls to climb atop it. Perched there, we sang and danced, hooted and shouted, wielding our trophy, as the bus wound its way through the city roads towards our college. We were the talk of the town for days to come.

This spectacle didn't amuse the good nuns. Needless to say, we were grounded.

Cricket wasn't the only arena where I excelled. I also won the Sushila Pathak trophy for Best Speaker in the Hindi debate and saw my articles and poems published in the college magazine. I was an all-rounder. My middle-class background never dampened my confidence. I had my mother's genes, after all. Despite my rebellious attitude, I was very much my parents' daughter.

From my father, I had taken the attitude of being able to make the best of the worst situation. Even with our limited resources, my gang of five managed to have a lot of fun. On Sundays we'd conjure up whatever excuse we could to leave campus, usually heading to the Ajmer Sharif dargah, where devotees come from all over the world. Thursdays and Sundays were special because famous qawwali singers would duel with each other. And there was the added attraction of the meethi sevaiyyan (a sweet dish). The challenge, however, was the distance. A direct tonga ride from the college gate exceeded our pooled budget of Rs 10. So we'd walk to a bus stop, cover some distance and then hire a tonga from there.

Our other small joy came from eating kachoris, which we bought for 25 paise, unable to afford the burgers and pizzas that were gaining popularity among the wealthier students. We would often hire cycles and ride around the Sarovar.

No college experience would be complete without bunking classes to go watch a movie. Our film of choice was *Qayamat Se Qayamat Tak*, the film that launched Aamir Khan and Juhi Chawla.

In the hostel, we were notorious for waylaying the tuck boxes of the wealthy boarders. In the scorching Rajasthan summers, at a premium were bottles of Kissan orange squash and Rooh Afza rose sherbet concentrate. But our thievery was more akin to Robin Hood's—we would pour the contents of the bottles into the common earthen pots that were our water dispensers, so that all the girls could partake.

The fun and games of college life came to an abrupt halt when riots broke out in the city. I still remember it: it was around dinner time, and we were all in the dining room, under the nuns' watchful eyes. Suddenly, a mob barged in. They upturned furniture while shouting slogans and hurling stones. That was the end of the term. We were all sent home.

6

Love, Bikes and Marriage

H OME AT THAT TIME WAS BABINA, A SMALL cantonment town in Uttar Pradesh, where Papa's unit was posted. After the riots disrupted the end of my college term, here I was, in this sleepy town.

Surprisingly, I didn't find Babina boring at all. Having played district-level cricket, I was keen on a career in sports. I developed a disciplined routine to fulfil this ambition: mornings began with a run, followed by basketball, and early evenings were reserved for swimming. Babina, being home to several military units, was the hub of a lot of sporting competitions. I would attend these games: basketball, handball, hockey, cycle polo—often the only young girl in the audience. My days usually wound up with an outing to the club. In between all this, I would squeeze in some hours of studies.

Though my father wanted me to pursue a career in law or write the civil services exam, I was steadfast in my pursuit of sports.

In another instance of their dichotomous expectations from me, my parents were simultaneously looking for a suitable match for me. On the one hand they wanted me to pursue a career, and on the other they wanted me to 'settle down'.

71

During my morning jogs, I would bump into a cross-country running contingent of a particular unit. Among them was a tall but unremarkable-looking officer. At the handball and cycle polo games, he was always the top scorer.

This young officer seemed to be everywhere, and without realizing it, I found myself looking for him if he was missing from any sporting event.

This distant appraisal went on for some time, till one day, we finally made contact. I was on the basketball court after my morning jog, when we all heard the roar of a motorbike. It was the latest model of the Ind-Suzuki. The bike stopped. The rider, dressed in the typical army sports rig of white shorts and a white T-shirt, parked the bike, removed his helmet and placed it on the seat, before putting the keys in his pocket. He walked over and joined in, effortlessly sinking a few baskets.

After the game, just as he was about to insert the key into the bike, I said, 'Nice bike.'

He turned towards me, but before he could respond, I asked, 'Can I take it for a ride?'

His surprise was evident, though he masked it well, countering, 'It's a big bike. Will you be able to manage?'

'Just give me the keys,' I said, holding out my palm.

He dropped the keys into my hand—and I was off. What a ride it was!

Our first interaction opened the door to more frequent encounters, either at club events or on the sports field.

About a month into these casual meetings, my father had an accident. His vehicle had overturned, and though he wasn't severely injured, he was sent to the Command Hospital in Lucknow, accompanied by my mother.

Alone at home, I seized the opportunity to plan a longer ride on Bikram's bike. He suggested that he should come along, for safety.

When I agreed, he proposed we make it a day trip with a spot of fishing at Sukma Dukma Dam, around 30 km from Jhansi.

And so our first date took shape. I drove his bike, clad in a parrot-green and rani-pink embroidered salwar kameez, while Bikram sat on the pillion, holding on to his fishing pole and the backrest for dear life. That day revealed another talent of his: he was a singer. He had a guitar for which he had got a customized case so that it could fit on his bike. After fishing—though I can't recall if we caught anything—we settled down to enjoy the sandwiches he had packed for us. Then, he began to croon.

When he sang Kenny Rogers' 'Lucille', I was floored. I learnt later that his entire repertoire consisted of four Kenny Rogers songs, this being one of them.

When he dropped me home that evening, I invited him to lunch the next day.

My culinary skills were basic: I made a simple dal, a sukhi subzi (pan-fried vegetable dish) and rotis. As I cooked, he sat on a chair in the kitchen. We talked and ate, and by the time he left, we both knew that this was it.

On the third day, my parents returned and soon after, I returned to college in Ajmer, as things had calmed down in the city. We never got a chance to say a proper goodbye.

I had told Bikram not to write to me—the good nuns were known to steam open the letters that came for us.

I missed him, but I wasn't heartbroken. Life at college continued as usual. During the Republic Day weekend, while a lot of the girls went home, I stayed behind. While tidying my room, I received word that someone was waiting for me at the gate.

Curious and a little anxious about this unexpected visitor, I reached the gate. An almost alien-like figure awaited me. He was dressed in sand-coloured overalls that were stuffed with newspaper—which I later found out provided insulation and protection in case of a fall. He wore a space-age helmet and biking gloves, and was coated head-to-toe in dust. But when he took off his helmet and smiled, that's all I could see. It was Bikram. He had left Babina the previous evening and ridden 535 km through the freezing night to reach Ajmer. Officially, he was visiting his father in Jodhpur—a convenient cover story.

We headed to Fun 'n' Food, where he bought me burgers and fries, a luxury compared to the 25-paise kachoris, which were our usual fare. After a few hours with me, he drove all the way back to Babina and was back on parade before he could have been missed.

That was when I fell well and truly in love.

Meanwhile, my parents continued looking for a match for me. A 'suitable boy' in their mind was an army officer from a family similar to ours. The compatibility of the families was as important as the credentials of the boy. First the families would meet; if they got along, the potential couple would be introduced—though they'd have to meet in the presence of the parents. It was expected that these brief interactions would be sufficient to decide on a lifelong commitment.

When I returned to Babina to prepare for my exams, I faced this exact situation. The 'boy' was an army officer. That ticked one box. His father was a general. That ticked another. The families had met and got along. Now it was our turn.

I met the prospective groom. All he could talk about was his father. His entire identity seemed to stem from his father's reputation, not his own character.

Perhaps I'm being this harsh because I was already in love with Bikram at that point. Bikram had never boasted about his father. He was his own man.

My refusal to accept the proposed match led to some tension at home. However, Papa told me to focus on my exams for the time being. Although they didn't say anything, I'm certain they had caught a whiff of my brewing romance—they insisted that I stay home and study, no outings. My father meticulously created a study chart for me, breaking down my syllabus—twenty-two books of literature as well as my geography study matter—and calculated that I could afford only fifteen minutes per book, given the time until the exams.

So it was nose to the grindstone for me. But how could I put my heart in my studies when my heart was already taken?

The main exams started and I was almost done with the practicals. There was a gap of free time between the end of the practicals and the beginning of the main exams. I was at college when Bikram unexpectedly showed up for the weekend.

He had started his drive after office hours, arriving on Sunday, and planned to return the same night to be on duty by Monday morning, with no one in his regiment missing him.

However, he *was* missed.

Bikram had been commissioned into his father's unit: the renowned Scinde Horse armoured regiment. His father, Maj. Gen. Balbir Singh Malik, was the senior-most serving officer of their unit and held the designation of Colonel of the Regiment. He happened to be in Jhansi for an official visit and decided to surprise Bikram by visiting him in Babina. Bikram's regiment was located in Babina, which was operationally under the higher command located in Jhansi.

But Bikram was nowhere to be found—not in his room, not with the troops, not at the officers' institute. His bike was gone and so was he. The search parties came back with nothing, and the Colonel of the Regiment was not amused.

Bikram made it back by midnight and faced his superiors on parade the next morning. His evasive answers didn't convince any of them. They suspected a romantic entanglement but did not know that the girl in question was in Ajmer.

By now Bikram and I were fairly certain that we wanted to be together forever. There were no 'I love you's exchanged, but we were both certain this wasn't just a fling.

With him, I never had to pretend. He loved me as I was—messy hair, jeans, no make-up, always ready for the next adventure.

Our love grew from our shared passion for bikes and the great outdoors. He was the first person to not only accept this about me but actually encourage me. He was completely at ease riding pillion, his confidence unshaken by me taking the driver's seat.

I half-jokingly told him I'd leave him if he ever asked me to give up riding. He told me he'd leave me if I ever gave up riding.

That sealed the deal.

Papa was surprised to find Bikram in his office one day. Dressed in his uniform and sporting his black beret, he smartly saluted. 'Good morning, Sir,' he said.

'Good morning,' Papa replied, slightly puzzled.

'Sir, I'm Capt. Malik from Scinde Horse.'

'What can I do for you?' asked Papa.

'Sir, I'd like to buy a bike for your daughter. I need your permission to marry her.'

Papa told him that this was a private matter and should be discussed at home, inviting him over in the evening.

As soon as Bikram left, Papa was on the phone with Col. Goel, Bikram's commanding officer. The report was positive. He said that Malik was a second-generation officer, well-regarded and liked in the regiment. Papa requested to see his dossier since it was a question of his daughter's future. Col. Goel readily agreed and invited Papa to his office.

But on reviewing the file before him, Papa was perplexed. 'This isn't the same boy who came to meet me earlier,' he said.

Col. Goel was momentarily flummoxed before it hit him. Scinde Horse had two officers with the surname Malik, both general's sons, both carrying a good reputation. He had accidentally shown my father the file of the other Malik, not Bikram, whose unassuming nature made it hard for Col. Goel to imagine him as someone who would court a woman, let alone speak to her father about a proposal.

After this misunderstanding was cleared the correct dossier was presented.

'What sports does he play?' Papa asked.

Col. Goel responded that he was a good sportsman and played all the troop games—a plus for my father, as this meant he was well-liked by his troops, was physically fit and had leadership qualities.

Bikram's performance in his service-related courses got him a grade of B. This was another positive indication for my father. B was an 'officer-like' grading to him. He was neither a C-grade dunce nor an A-grade workaholic.

Hesitatingly, Col. Goel ventured, 'The youngster does enjoy his rum on the rocks.'

'But has he ever lost control, misbehaved in the mess or been carried out of any parties?' Papa asked.

The response was reassuring—nothing like that had happened. Bikram could hold his drink.

That evening, Bikram came over. He wore a white silk shirt, his pack of cigarettes visibly outlined in his translucent shirt pocket.

He spoke with a distinct Punjabi accent, having studied at DAV College, Chandigarh, and by virtue of belonging to a regiment with Sikh troops. This endeared him to my Punjabi father, who had been with Jat troops.

Soon after, both of our parents met, and just like that, my future was settled.

When I returned to college for the final term, my hands were adorned with henna and my wrists decked with glass bangles. My friends were shocked—I, the tomboy of our gang, was the first to get engaged.

The college authorities were very strict about any correspondence we received. Our parents had to provide a list of approved names. Bikram's name was duly added to the list and our romance blossomed through love letters.

Bikram's name being on the approved list didn't stop the nuns from steaming open the envelopes to read the contents. I'm sure my creative and literary letters—as behoved a literature student—entertained them, till the outpourings of two lovelorn hearts made them blush.

Scandalized, they sent for my father and presented him with the letter, heavily underlined in red pen.

He refused to read it. 'In our culture, it's a sin for me to read the private conversations between my daughter and her future husband. An engagement is like a Gandharva vivah, as good as marriage. I will not invade their marital privacy. In any case, I have sent her to this college to get an education, not become a nun,' he thundered.

The sisters were taken aback but unwavering. They claimed that letters like this had the potential to corrupt the other students. To date, I think their belligerence stems from one line. In full literary flow, I had written, 'I am impregnated with joy ...', which I'm assuming they took in the literal sense.

Ultimately, they insisted on my removal from the hostel. That's how I found myself in Ma'am David's PG. She was a delight to live with, and the PG was not only more affordable but also less strict. My parents' home in Jaipur was in the final stages of completion. I could easily go down to Jaipur every weekend and help oversee the construction work, along with doing a spot of wedding shopping while there.

So all in all, the ordeal with the love letter ended on a happy note.

Our wedding was unlike any other. In those days, before *Band Baaja Baraat* made wedding planners de rigueur for all weddings, I had my fairy tale wedding. The famous Jai Mahal Palace had just been renovated and was yet to throw open its doors to the public. Thanks to my father's people skills and Ramesh Tauji's connections, who was then the tourism commissioner of Rajasthan, we were able to host the wedding here.

Since Bikram's father was a highly respected general in the Indian Army, our guest list included several dignitaries, from state governors and prominent politicians to high court judges. The stress on my parents to put up a good show and ensure Bikram's family felt well-cared for was immense.

While we were able to get the venue at a discounted rate, we still had to worry about accommodations for the groom's party.

Ramesh Tauji was able to book rooms in the tourism department's newly commissioned bungalows. Since they'd just been built, many lacked amenities like buckets and curtains. Undeterred, Papa went and bought these himself.

The only problem now was the road from the tourism bungalows to Jai Mahal Palace, a short but neglected and poorly lit stretch. Papa cajoled the municipal authorities into maintaining the road, particularly appealing to their sense of patriotism by highlighting that the road would be leading to the wedding of an army man and that the guests included high-ranking army officers. Sure enough, before the wedding, the entire road was not only cleaned and lit up but also resurfaced.

The wedding was truly royal. Being an Armoured Corps officer's wedding, a chariot came from 61 Cavalry, the only cavalry regiment to still have horses. The Grenadiers' band played, since that was my father's regiment. Ramesh Tauji ensured that the baraat was greeted by bedecked elephants and the sound of nagadas (drums).

I was dressed in a red lehenga. While I had not been too particular about much else, this was one thing I had definitely wanted. My cousins and college friends surrounded me, our laughter and their teasing filling the air. The sangeet was a whirlwind of dance and joy.

It was all like a fairy tale. I had found my Prince Charming. Now all that remained was our happily ever after.

Life as an army wife was all I had envisioned and more. After a brief stay with my in-laws in Jodhpur right after the honeymoon in Udaipur, we settled into our own little house in Babina, adorned with thoughtful housewarming gifts from my parents. We had beautiful blue floral curtains, plenty of potted plants, and our cherished bike and cycle.

Soon we welcomed our first pet—Sable. A labrador and cocker spaniel mix, she was gifted to us by friends, Ranjana and Col. Vineet Tiwari. Jet-black Sable came to us wearing a red bow and instantly became a part of our family.

We soon fell into a steady routine, one that was different from that of other couples around us. Instead of him driving me places, I was driving him to work and bringing the bike back home. Instead of him going for runs alone, I would go jogging with him.

There were eleven bachelors in the unit, who would joke that with my arrival, they had their twelfth man. My unofficial role, just like the twelfth man on the cricket team, was to take care of the food and drinks for our frequent trips. And there were so many places to visit: Jhansi, Orchha, Sukma Dukma Dam, Matatila Dam, Gwalior and Khajuraho, where we went to celebrate my first birthday after marriage.

Power outages were common back then, leaving us without electricity for up to forty-eight hours at a time. But we turned even those days into fun. The officers' mess had a generator, and we would all go there for marathon movie sessions.

I found mentors among the other ladies in the regiment. Ranjana Tiwari and Anuja Mehta were master bakers and taught me the secrets to their fancy desserts. They also gave me good tips on how to prepare for raids. Raids were conducted on a regular basis by the unit's bachelors. They would arrive at any ungodly hour, generally very late at night, and demand food. They especially targeted newlywed couples. The trick was to have a lot of half-prepped food in the freezer.

The bonds forged during this time remain strong. Capt. Idris, Bikram's former roommate, was now married. When he came to Babina with his wife, Tabassum, they could not get accommodation. Without thinking twice, we gave them a room in our house. As we prepared to move to Ahmednagar for a course at the Armoured Corps Centre and School, Tabassum and Idris stayed on in our house.

In Ahmednagar, we were allotted accommodation in Ghora Barracks, aptly named, as once upon a time they had been stables. Partitions—that didn't go all the way to the ceiling—had been installed. This meant conversations and odours drifted freely from room to room. If someone three rooms away decided to have a smoke, I'd instantly know—a sensitivity heightened by my pregnancy. Yes, we were expecting our first child.

Sanjeev and Virma Gupta were our neighbours. Virma was the paragon of orderliness and efficiency. She managed every inch of her home, with her five-month-old, Sakshi, glued to her hip the whole time. From her I learnt valuable lessons in motherhood and how to organize myself in a tiny space. When the smell of cooking overwhelmed me, she would push me out and do the cooking for me. We'd push our TV into the veranda in the evenings, so that all of us could watch it together.

That stint in Ahmednagar also marked my debut in the beauty pageant circuit. I participated in the May Queen Ball there, wearing my pink engagement lehenga. I loved the experience of walking the ramp, of impressing the judges with my witty answers to their questions and of walking away with the crown.

After Bikram completed the course, we returned to Babina, but not for long. It was time for the regiment to move to Jodhpur. In the short span of my marriage, I had already moved from Babina to Ahmednagar, then back to Babina and now on to Jodhpur. Each move meant packing, unpacking, decorating the new house and turning it into a home. I was putting to good use all the skills I had learnt from watching my father.

Our journey to Jodhpur was special because we went by a military special train. It was my first time, and I was fascinated by what went into it, from the loading of the tanks onto the flatbeds to the transformation of bogeys into a mess hall and accommodation for the officers and their families.

Travelling with us was another expectant mother, Sabi. While Sabi and Maj. K.J. Singh were expecting their second child, I was navigating my first pregnancy. Both of us had to be fed well. Bhupi Bhaiyya, our inventive cook, had to rely on tinned peas in the name of green vegetables. We had peas in our egg curry, peas with potatoes, peas mashed in spices and made into parathas. Sabi and I had to draw the line at pea sandwiches. Finally, our pleas were heeded, and fresh green vegetables were procured whenever the train stopped.

My parents were in Nagpur when Devika was to be born. I travelled from Jodhpur to Nagpur for the delivery. Devika arrived ahead of schedule and was in the NICU by the time Bikram arrived. Once both Devika and I were fit to travel, we went to Ahmednagar, where my father-in-law had taken over as the Commandant of the Armoured Corps Centre and School, a position of honour for Armoured Corps officers.

7

Children's Ward—Redux

I ALWAYS WANTED A DAUGHTER—NOT JUST ONE, BUT two. Call me a rebel, call me reactionary, but I wanted girls to bring up without the patriarchal influences that had bound my adolescent years. When Devika was born, I was the happiest in the family.

Though she was premature, she was born with a full head of hair. She was born in Nagpur, where my father was posted at the time. My tiny baby spent the first few days of her life in the NICU as not only was she premature, she also developed jaundice.

As soon as she was well and we were able to travel, we moved to Ahmednagar where my father-in-law was posted. My in-laws lived in a huge, historic bungalow that was no less than a palace compared to the barracks and modest homes we'd known. The spacious, high-roofed rooms and cool verandas were a luxury. I would sit there with baby Devika and marvel at the beautiful little being I had created.

I took to massaging her with ghee, gently applying it to her fontanelles. This was based on the traditional belief that ghee feeds a baby's brain cells. Whether it was the ghee or something else entirely, Devika grew into a remarkably bright girl.

My days in Ahmednagar with my in-laws were idyllic. I set up a workspace for a local tailor right on our veranda. My sister-in-law, living in the United States, would bring back fashion catalogues for me when she visited. Using these for inspiration, I worked with the tailor to make frilly frocks, colour-coordinated swaddling clothes and bassinets with cartoon cut-outs, embellished with lace and contrast piping. My creativity was at its peak.

By the time we moved to Bikaner, where Bikram had been posted, Devika was old enough for me to manage her, my own postpartum health, Bikram, our two dogs and the responsibilities that came with being a mother and an officer's wife. My parents were still in Nagpur, but Bikaner was special to the family—it was where they had met and got married, and was like home. In fact, before we moved, my father travelled there, found us a small two-storey house with an indoor staircase, and got it ready for us to move in.

At fourteen months old, Devika was taking her first unsteady toddler steps, keen on exploring everything. Maybe it was because of the years I spent confined to a bed in my own childhood, but watching my daughter walk was a magical experience. I bought her silver anklets adorned with tiny bells, so I could hear her tinkling footsteps no matter where I was.

One morning, Bikram left for the office and our maid busied herself with cleaning the house. I was on the terrace, hanging the laundry to dry. I could hear the dogs playing out in the yard. The maid finished her work and called out to let me know she was leaving.

Every day, a cow would amble up to our gate. She would nuzzle her nose against the iron bars, and the sound would alert me to come out and give her something to eat.

That day, when the maid left, she somehow missed closing the gate properly.

When the cow arrived for her daily bread and nudged the gate, it swung open, allowing her inside. This enraged the dogs, who began barking furiously and charged at her. Spooked, the cow retreated, but the dogs chased after her. Amidst this chaos, I rushed down.

In the brief moment it took me to run downstairs, Devika had followed the dogs out to the main road. As she toddled after them, a motorcyclist struck her.

By the time I reached the road, she was lying in a pool of blood. I immediately shifted into crisis-management mode. My first priority was to stop the bleeding. The towel I was going to put out to dry was still draped over my shoulder. I wrapped it around her head and, lifting her in my arms, rushed to my Luna. Holding her between my knees, I somehow managed to drive to the nearest hospital.

The doctors managed to stop the bleeding, but the damage had already been done. As Devika lay in the hospital bed, I noticed her left hand clenched in a tight fist, her left leg motionless and her left cheek drooping.

The doctors told me that there was internal dilation of the brain. Already she was showing symptoms of hemiplegia—paralysis of one side of the body. At that time, they couldn't fully assess the extent of the internal damage.

The biggest concern was whether her cognitive abilities would be affected.

Against everyone's advice to stay in Bikaner until the brain swelling subsided, I decided to take her to Pune. My old doctor Col. Bajpai was still at the Command Hospital, where I had recovered from my own childhood illness. Guided by instinct, I was certain that Devika would also get better there.

While in the throes of crisis management, I managed to ward off negative thoughts. But in moments of solitude, the thought that history was repeating itself would creep into my mind.

'*Chhoriyan to bhagwaanon ki marti hain …*' (Blessed are they whose daughters die).

'*Aise shareer ke saath jeene se to behtar hai ki bhagwan utha hi le …*' (Rather than live in a paralysed body, it may be better if God takes you).

'*Abhi to iski maa ki umar hi kya hai, aur bachhe ho jayenge … abke chhora hoga …*' (Her mother is young, so she can have more children … and next time it will be a boy).

As my baby fought for her life in the hospital, these were the remarks whispered by visitors. No one said anything to me directly, but everyone who came by had something to say.

A distant relative told me that my mother-in-law had also lost her first-born, a baby girl, to an intestinal blockage at just a few months of age. Despite being rushed to AIIMS, the child did not survive. Sharing this story was perhaps, in her own convoluted way, meant to give me strength.

Through these stories and comments I began to understand why my own mother had wept so much after every visit by 'friends and family' to see me in the same hospital.

Just as my parents had stood by me during my illness, I was determined to get the best treatment for Devika. If my parents could help me walk, run and play state-level sports after my bedridden childhood, I knew I could do the same for my Devika.

After about a month at the hospital, we moved to Ahmednagar, just a few hours away, where my in-laws were, so that we could keep bringing Devika back for regular check-ups and therapy.

Over the next three months we went through a gamut of treatments. It seemed everyone was a doctor and everyone had a suggestion. Instead of wasting my energy in debating the pros and cons of alternate and faith-based treatments, I focused on physiotherapy. Meanwhile, we heard it all: 'You need to go to Dr V.K. Habbu for homoeopathic treatment', 'You need to become vegetarians', 'You need to pray more'. I continued with her physiotherapy, occupational therapy, hand exercises and making her stand using calipers.

Devika was getting better physically, but concerns about her cognitive development lingered.

We returned to Bikaner with the now eighteen-month-old Devika, and I went into Super Mom mode, echoing the dedication my parents had shown me.

Making a toddler exercise regularly was a tough job. There were times she resisted and moments I felt like giving up. But my father came to my rescue. He drew parallels to the trials in the Ramayana and Mahabharata. He reminded me that we all have to go through our own versions of vanvas and comforted me by saying that when god seeks parents for special children, he chooses the most capable.

In moments of frustration, I screamed about the injustice of it all. Why was I the chosen one? Why was I being made to relive my childhood with my daughter? It felt like a cruel repetition of the past.

After my battle with the spinal tumours and physiotherapy as a child, I had subconsciously been fighting all my life to prove that I was not only equal to but better than my peers. I had spent my post-surgery childhood seeking validation for my body. Now I was back again where it had all started.

My father understood my angst. His words to me were a challenge: 'Deepa, it's your turn now to show everyone how good we were as parents.'

In that moment, the strain that had developed in our relationship during my adolescent years melted away. In my desire to break free from them, the parents who had stopped me from biking and sent me away to the village, I had forgotten to appreciate the effort my parents had put in just to keep me alive.

Gratitude overpowered me. I recognized this as my moment of redemption. It was time for me to give back. They never gave up on me, and I wasn't about to give up on Devika!

As Devika grew, I began devising ways of keeping her interested in physiotherapy and intellectually engaged. She couldn't run, so we played board games. I got her memory flashcards to work on her vocabulary and recognition. I read to her a lot. At night I would put her in stretch bands to keep her leg straight.

We found joy in her kindergarten years, especially during fancy dress competitions. I'd hand-stitch her costumes myself to give her a sense of victory despite her challenges. But here, too, we encountered insensitive comments from intrusive moms.

'Oh, she still cannot walk?'

'How old is she? My son was running around at that age.'

Devika was cautious, preferring not to use her left side, but she was meeting most of her growth milestones. She was toilet trained earlier than many of her peers, and she started speaking at a young age.

But these constant comparisons and probing questions about Devika made me realize the need for us to respect others' medical privacy. Why should someone's health challenges be public fodder?

During a family visit to my parents in Jaipur, when Devika was around three years old, we went out for dinner to a popular new Mughlai restaurant. As we got up to leave, I was suddenly overcome with severe pain in my abdomen. I made it to the footpath before having to sit abruptly. I threw up, waves of nausea gripping me.

This pain was not new. I had experienced similar episodes over the past few months, each marked by a pain so intense that I would have to lie down and curl up.

However, once it passed, I would be fine. Like so many Indian mothers, I put my health on the back burner, focusing all my energy on Devika. And since I wasn't taking my health seriously, no one else did.

My father was deeply concerned—actually, he was furious that we hadn't sought medical advice earlier. He dragged me for a check-up, which revealed I had gallstones and needed surgery.

Laparoscopic surgery wasn't available at the Jaipur military hospital, so we decided on the Command Hospital in Pune. It was close to Ahmednagar, where my in-laws were, and it would also give us a chance to get Devika a check-up.

Once again, I was back in Pune, back in that hospital. This time around, even the ward sahayikas remembered me from the time we had spent there with Devika.

My cholecystectomy was one surgery that I went in for in style. I checked into the hospital wearing smart slacks, a T-shirt and fluorescent sneakers. Each evening before the surgery, we would walk along MG Road. We ate ice cream sundaes, shopped for Devika's upcoming birthday and enjoyed the big city lights—it was like a holiday. I even went and got my hair permed the day before my surgery, wanting to look like the glamorous ghazal singer Penaz Masani.

I prided myself on being a model patient, in stark contrast to another woman undergoing the same procedure. Despite my eighteen stitches, I was up and walking soon after the operation, while she refused to get out of bed. I was discharged within six days—a record for the hospital as the fastest recovery.

After driving to my in-laws' house in Ahmednagar, as I triumphantly got out of the car, a friend's reaction was: 'Did you go to get operated or to get electrocuted?' My beautiful Penaz Masani perm had succumbed to the rigours of the hospital stay. Instead of glamorous curls, I now had hair that stood on end, as if I had stuck a finger in a socket.

When Devika was three and a half, we travelled to Pune for her IQ test.

The doctor's office featured a window positioned unusually high on the wall. After we sat down, he asked Devika to go and open the window.

Perched on a shiny metal swivel stool, she turned towards the window, then back to look the doctor directly in the eye, and said, '*Aap ko pata nahin main kitni chhoti hoon? Khidki kitni oopar hai. Mera hath kaise jayega?* (Don't you know how little I am? The window is so high. How will my hand reach it?)

With that, any doubts anyone might have had about Devika's IQ flew out of the window.

It was around this time that my tumour had returned, unbeknownst to me. It would still be years before it would be detected.

In the days leading up to Devika's IQ assessment, I found myself subconsciously stress eating. The overwhelming fear of raising a child with a disability led to disordered eating. Once we got positive news about Devika's cognitive development, we felt encouraged to consider having a second child.

I began putting on weight rapidly, which we all chalked up to the pregnancy. A persistent, dull ache developed on my left side, dismissed as just another pregnancy side effect. I gained 30 kilos over the course of the pregnancy. My back hurt. I grew irritable and short-tempered.

All the while I prayed fervently. My earlier prayers had been solely for Devika's recovery: 'God, please make my child better. May all my child's problems come to me. I will bear them.' Now that I was going to have another baby, I had a similar prayer: 'Please, god, let my baby be healthy. Let anything happen to me, but please make my baby healthy.'

Perhaps the return of the tumour was the result of my prayers.

Ambika came into the world with a bang. We were in Hisar, Haryana. We still had a month to go for the due date. It was a sweltering day in May when my mother and I, after running some errands and eating a Chinese lunch, decided to go for a routine prenatal check-up. The doctor immediately admitted me, and within two hours Ambika was born—a tiny, wrinkled, bald, pink baby, wailing at the top of her lungs.

I had already picked out her name, wanting my girls to have rhyming names that also meant the same thing. Hence, Devika's sister had to be Ambika, both names of the Mother Goddess, symbolizing Shakti.

Ambika's arrival was heralded by silence in the ward—the hospital staff assumed we wouldn't be celebrating a second girl child. This quiet was shattered by Bikram's entire regiment landing up with balloons and champagne within fifteen minutes of getting the news. My family was complete now.

The bad news was that Bikram did not clear the Defence Services Staff College entrance exam—a critical step for advancement in the Indian Army's hierarchical promotion system. Papa had missed the same exam when I had fallen ill as a child. While no one said so, I felt that maybe my cholecystectomy had kept Bikram from getting enough time to study. Burdened with guilt, I threw myself into being the perfect wife, mother, daughter-in-law and hostess.

The good news was that with Ambika's arrival, Devika began to develop faster. She would play with the baby and want to do things for her. She started using her left hand more, something she would shy away from earlier.

I committed myself to my fitness, and within six months I lost all the excess weight. We had moved to a bigger home and frequently hosted parties, often barbecues. I was actively involved in the community, participating in all the theme parties at the club. I was crowned Basant Queen in the spring and Saawan Queen in the monsoon at the club's seasonal pageants.

But my back pain was constant now, and I started to drag my left leg, although it was hardly noticeable. I restricted my physical activities, opting to drive instead of walking or cycling. I was too tired to even stand for too long. The doctors advised me to slow down my weight loss. My gynaecologist's husband, an orthopaedic surgeon, sent me for an X-ray, which showed nothing amiss. I came back from the hospital with calcium tablets to counter the post-pregnancy calcium depletion.

Meanwhile, Bikram was preparing for his second attempt at the Staff College entrance exam. I wanted him to make it this time, so I provided the kind of home environment he needed to study. I kept my health concerns to myself.

Bikram cleared the exam, and we began our twenty-day road trip from Hisar to Wellington, Tamil Nadu. The rear seats of our Tata Estate were pulled down to create a flatbed for the children and the dogs, the luggage was piled on top, and off we went.

We first drove to Jaipur to meet my parents, then on to Mhow, where my brother was. Our final pit stop was Ahmednagar, so that we could spend some time with my in-laws.

The drive worsened my pain. Now it was getting difficult for me to even get out of bed in the morning. My head would spin.

I decided to go to Pune and consult with my old doctor, now a brigadier, C.P. Bajpai. Based on my backache and dragging left foot, he sent me for a lumbar spine MRI. This would prove to be the biggest missed opportunity of my life. The results showed nothing. Had Brig. Bajpai asked for a dorsal spine MRI, maybe the tumour would have shown up. But he was so confident of his previous surgery, in which he had removed the tumour from my dorsal spine, that he did not consider the possibility of it returning on the same site.

With the all-clear report, I headed back to Ahmednagar and tried to follow my in-laws' suggestions: I woke up early, I started yoga and I tried homoeopathy for pain management. I tried to ignore myself. I did not want to be labelled a 'defective piece'. I wanted to fit in. I wanted to be accepted. I sought validation.

Wellington is a beautiful hill station in the Nilgiris. Life here was a dream. It was like being back in college. All the officers were students and we, their spouses, made up a vibrant community full of camaraderie and esprit de corps.

The officers had a busy schedule. That left us young wives and mothers to find our own amusement. I explored self-improvement and self-expression, though I paid no attention to self-care.

I ignored the growing pain in my leg. I wore boots for support and drove as much as possible. Whenever someone commented on the foot drag, I would pass it off as stiffness from sitting too long, the cold weather, wrong shoes—anything except the possibility that it might be a bigger medical issue.

Socially, I was everywhere. I wrote for the college magazine. I was a part of the angling club. I further honed my baking, making cakes, loaves of bread and pizza. We had the biggest car, which not only would take my friends around but also doubled up as a school bus for the kids whenever required. We had theme parties, barbecues, ladies' meets. I was in my element.

Devika was also thriving, making friends and excelling at school. This was the affirmation she needed. One day, a friend of mine showed me an ad in the local paper. An ad film was to be shot in Ooty for a men's perfume. They needed a child actor. The ad depicted a bride drawn away by the scent of another man's perfume, leaving her groom at the altar. The child would then look at the jilted groom with a particular expression. I sent in Devika's pictures, and she was called for the audition. Her extremely expressive eyes won her the role.

I took part in the Staff College amateur dramatics activities. I even competed in the Navy Queen pageant conducted by the Staff College.

As we prepared for the pageant, I overheard a conversation between two other contestants. One of the ladies, confident of her chances, remarked on how fortunate she was to perform right before me. *'Arre, Deepa to tedhi chalti hai. Uski to walk hi nahin hai. Vo to langdi hai.'* (Deepa walks crooked. She will never be able to score for her catwalk. She is lame.)

It was at that moment that the extent of my foot drag first hit home. But my competitive streak kicked in—I now wanted to win.

I got an orange-and-gold outfit couriered to me from Jaipur by my mother, along with matching jewellery. I knew the foot drag would be an issue, so I focused on my strengths. For the talent round I performed a stand-up comedy routine in the deadpan style of the famous Hindi poet Surender Sharma. My skill in crafting came to the fore in another round, where we had to create a costume and jewellery from newspapers.

I made it to the finals. Now came the question-answer round. One judge asked me a question based on my interest in angling. 'One day, you go fishing with your friend, but fail to catch anything. You both go your own way. But on your way home, you decide to buy some fish and pass it off as your catch. While your mother is cooking the fish, your friend lands up at your place. Your mom invites her to stay for lunch and enjoy the fish you caught. Your friend looks at you questioningly. What do you say to her?'

'I'd say to her, "Nothing fishy about this,"' I replied.

My response got me not just applause, but also laughter. However, the next question, this time from a different judge, touched a nerve.

'Why are you limping? You're not walking properly. Why are you in a beauty pageant if you're not well?'

'I'm in this beauty pageant because no medical condition is going to stop me from feeling beautiful,' I replied.

Once again, my wit and my spirit won me thunderous applause.

I got the first runner-up crown.

That was the last pageant I walked in.

PART 2

8

Wheelchair-bound

FTER A MARATHON TWENTY-HOUR OPERATION, I was brought out of the operation theatre. I had an intense pain, concentrated in my chest and all along my left side. The doctors thought that this was the point of paralysis and didn't address it further.

I was moved from the ICU to a regular room in no time. Despite the pain, my spirits were high. I even asked the ward attendant to wash my hair, happy to be recovering as expected.

On the third day, the doctor came to check up on me. He cheerfully asked me how I was doing. As we chatted, I suddenly found myself speaking without hearing my own voice. I went quiet. My eyes glazed over. But I must have been somewhat coherent because the doctor turned to leave.

As he headed for the door, he turned back, paused and then looked under my bed. 'Nurse, please check under the bed. The urine bag is leaking,' he said, pointing to a puddle.

After taking another step towards the door again, he hesitated. The urine bag was near my leg, but the puddle was under my shoulder.

He rushed to my side and turned me over. I felt myself falling, as if through water, trying to swim but unable to.

Fluid was leaking from my surgical wound.

The doctor's face fell. He screamed for the nurses, who came running. A stretcher was brought swiftly. As they wheeled me once again to the operation theatre, I heard the doctor's words to me: 'I'm so sorry. I'm so sorry. I tried my best. I warned you. I knew this could happen. Please stay with me.'

Even in this chaos, my sense of humour flickered briefly, because later he told me that I had said, 'So, you get to see me naked again.'

I awoke nearly two and a half weeks later, after the doctors had performed a second surgery and kept me in a medically induced coma to aid my recovery.

My cerebrospinal fluid had leaked. This was a complication the doctors had hoped would not occur. Now there were concerns that along with the paralysis, I might have suffered brain damage.

The day they were taking me off the sedatives, they informed my parents, who rushed to be there with my daughters.

Everyone was anxious. What if I had lost my brain function? What if I had amnesia? What if I couldn't speak?

The first thing I remember seeing upon waking was a pair of eyes. While I lay in bed, peeping at me through the gap between the mattress and the metal tubing of the bed, were the pretty eyes of my little Ambika. I shifted my gaze a little and saw Devika next to her, and then my parents.

'*Kya karte ho aap, Mom? Meri ladkiyon ko tel laga kar namuna bana rakha hai.*' (What is this, Mom? You have oiled my girls' hair and made them into such specimens.)

These were my first words.

My mom's reaction was, 'I do so much and this is how you thank me!'

My dad was just relieved, muttering, 'She's okay, she's okay.'

I spent another week in the ICU. This was the toughest time for me—it was when the paralysis was setting in. I constantly felt a burning sensation in my lower back and spasms in my leg as spasticity increased. I would go into a spasm while passing urine. I desperately wanted to pull up my knees or turn over but couldn't. I kept asking my mother to rub my feet to ease the burning sensation or the spasticity, yet I would feel nothing. I would yell at her, asking why she wasn't rubbing, even as she was.

The constant beeping of the machines drove me to the brink. The sound seemed amplified. I kept my eyes shut to try and escape it. One day, I opened my eyes slightly and saw something shiny at eye level. Reaching out, I grabbed it. It was the metal belt buckle of the hospital commandant, who had come on his rounds to check my progress.

'How are you? What can I do for you?' he said.

'Make the noise stop,' I responded.

'That noise is from the machines that are keeping you alive,' he explained.

'But it's driving me crazy. I can't bear the beeping anymore. Can't I have some music?' I asked, trying to find a solution even in my weakened state.

With the commandant's approval, I got a Walkman. The music drowned out the beeps—it even seemed to drown out the pain. My father got me a big bowl of batteries so that I would not have to go without music for even a minute.

To this day, I can't be without music.

When I was shifted to the ward, I got an unfiltered account of how the outside world perceived my condition. Until this point I had been focused on just getting through the surgery, getting out of the ICU and getting used to being dependent on others for every little thing.

My bed was next to the ward window, which overlooked a corridor. The window was fitted with a screen, blinds and a one-way glass pane. Right outside was a bench, where visitors could sit.

One day, as the attendant was helping me with my routine care—sponging me, changing my urine bag and helping me pass stool—some of Bikram's relatives from his village arrived. They were asked to wait a while and unknowingly chose to sit on the bench right next to my window.

Although the glass pane was open, the screen was drawn and the blinds were down. As the attendant sponged me, I heard them talk.

'*Kati kandam ho gayee.*' (She is totally beyond repair now.)

'*Tatti-peshab bhi nahin kar pati.*' (She has no control over passing urine or stool.)

'*Beta bhi nahi hai. Do chhori hain. Ek beti bhi kharab hai.*' (She has no son. Only two daughters, and one of them is also damaged.)

Their words swept over me, not as the gentle lapping of waves at a seaside resort but as the tumultuous surges of a stormy sea, each word like a slap across my face, each sentence a reiteration of the harsh judgements of the world.

The attendant, an elderly woman who had been at the neuro ward for years, noticed my distress and consoled me, telling me not to pay heed to what people say. Later, she gave me a mantra that has since guided me.

'*Maine sirf potty-susu dho-dho kar apne bachhe paale hain.* (I have brought up my children with what I have earned by cleaning urine and poop.) But I can share something with you that may help. You are now in a condition where you will need help all the time. You will need to keep people close to you. Stay calm, be nice and maintain a positive outlook. Stop talking about your condition all the time. *Sar pe baraf aur mooh mein chini rakhna, zindagi aaram se kat jayegi aapki.* (Keep your cool and remain positive.) You have to think of your two girls.'

I deeply appreciated that wise, compassionate woman's advice. I learnt to remain level-headed and positive and kept my frustration away from my conversations. Even now, when I have visitors, I hardly talk of my condition.

For every relative who showed me a lack of basic compassion, I had multiple well-wishers who visited often and were my pillars of strength.

Among them was my friend Kamla Rathore, whose husband was from my father's unit. She bought me a collection of colourful loose frocks made of the softest cotton from the export surplus market in Sarojini Nagar. These dresses kept me cool and comfortable, and they provided decent coverage, even with my catheter. My husband's regimental officer Kunwar Narpat Singh and his wife, Anjana, also visited me regularly, as they lived nearby. Amar Chacha and his family not only visited me but also opened their doors to my mother and my daughters, who used Chachaji's kitchen for meals and slept at the home of a neighbour who was away for the summer.

My in-laws visited too. My mother-in-law gave me a long list of things to donate to appease the gods.

Bikram's visit was especially poignant. It felt like a lifetime since we'd last been together, back when I was still on my feet in Gurez. The last time we'd spoken, he had promised to carry me in his arms forever. He had come for just one day—our anniversary. We celebrated by cutting a cake in the hospital, which we shared with all the attendants and nurses who had been taking care of me. For that one day, I was happy.

❧

It took a month in bed before the doctors even attempted to make me sit up. Lying there, I had become exasperated with just staring at the ceiling. I would plead, cajole and demand to be taken out of the room. They obliged by rolling the entire bed out, giving me a chance to look at something new. Even the frequent trips for MRI and CT scans were a welcome change.

I had given myself two years for rehab to get back on my feet, so I was in a hurry to start physiotherapy. But the doctors kept telling me to take it slowly. I had undergone two major surgeries between the T1 and T7 vertebrae levels, known as a laminectomy. There was now a big gap in my spine. This meant that my surgery site, which had been cut open three times, was very soft. A titanium plate could have provided reinforcement, but it was not recommended in my case due to the risk of the tumour recurring.

The first day that I was made to sit up, I kept falling over. I found it hilarious. It reminded me of Prabhu Deva in the song 'Mukkala Mukkabala'. With his incredible flexibility, Prabhu Deva would bend his body almost as if it were fluid. Like him, my lower half remained static while the top half flopped around.

A few months into physiotherapy, I got a brand-new motive for getting better quickly. It was November 1999. The hospital's physiotherapy room was next to the parking lot, where one day I saw a Maruti Gypsy. This was no ordinary Gypsy. It was decked out with stickers, banners, a chequered strip along its side, and the names of the driver and the navigator emblazoned on it, topped with huge fog lights. It was the fanciest Gypsy I had ever seen—it was a rally car.

I was going through the paces with the physiotherapist, when the owner of the Gypsy strolled in, dressed in bright dungarees.

After consulting the physiotherapist, he began his exercises nearby, while I gathered the courage to speak to him.

'Hi,' I ventured.

'Hello, ma'am,' he replied. As luck would have it, he was from the Armoured Corps, the same as Bikram, and knew about me. His name was Shakti Bajaj, then a captain. We got chatting, and the pictures he painted for me had me hooked.

I visualized vehicles speeding along dirt tracks through mountains. The terms he used—road book, extreme category, TSD category, odometer, calibration, black ice, sub-zero temperatures, gruelling, dangerous—had me enthralled.

Lost in his description, I forgot for a moment that I was paralysed.

Mentally, I added rallying to the top of my wishlist. Just as I had refused to acknowledge that death was a possibility before my surgery, I now dismissed paralysis. I told myself that the minute I got my legs back, I would rally.

I must have articulated this desire because Capt. Bajaj was saying, 'The Army Adventure Wing will help you if you are keen.'

'Can we do it together?' I asked.

'Ma'am, in our next life, we'll do it together,' he replied.

I stored all this information carefully. I had two vaults in my mind: one for treasure and one for trash. All the unpleasant experiences were locked away in the trash vault, never to be thought of, and all the things that had the potential to bring me joy went into the treasure vault, to be retrieved and savoured during tough times.

The moments I looked forward to most during my hospital stay were when my girls would come to see me from Jaipur.

I stayed in the hospital in Delhi for two reasons: one, I needed rehabilitation and physiotherapy; and two, moving home without a support system of attendants and physiotherapists would have been a financial burden. Bikram was still stationed in Gurez. My father discussed the possibility of him getting a compassionate-grounds posting to Jaipur, but that would have been detrimental to his career. We decided to wait till the position of squadron commander of his unit's independent recce squadron in Jaipur opened up. I was determined to get better by the time Bikram moved to Jaipur. Why spoil his career graph? I was the brave, dutiful wife.

For the girls, coming to visit me in the hospital in Delhi was like a picnic. They travelled by the Shatabdi train, which had aircraft-like amenities: in-train catering and reclining seats. Each visit, I would try to compensate for the time they had been away from me by pampering them. We celebrated both my birthday and Devika's in the hospital. Remembering how my parents had ensured that my hospital stays as a child were not depressing, I did the same for my daughters. I would play with them, share stories and update them on the daily happenings in my small world in the hospital, making it seem as though I were having the time of my life.

My physiotherapy had progressed to where I could sit up unaided and shift to a wheelchair. Using the strength of my shoulders and arms, I would push myself from the bed to the wheelchair. When I put weight on my legs, they would spasm and stiffen for a few seconds, providing a weight-bearing mechanism that I used to shift into the wheelchair.

The physiotherapists had taught me all they could. Before I moved to Jaipur, my father replicated the hospital infrastructure at home, a daunting task given the scarcity of readily available information at that time. He personally visited hospitals, connected with attendants and calculated the expenses involved to find the right balance between skill and cost-effectiveness.

With everything finally in place, we were ready to go to Jaipur in the winter.

My recovery was fuelled by my maternal instincts. In full mama bear mode, I was prepared to do everything for my two darlings. I did not want them to feel even for a moment that their mother was incomplete in any way.

I found myself in a paradoxical situation. On the one hand, I wanted to be with them constantly, never feeling my absence. On the other, I wanted to prepare them for a future that might not include me. I wanted to smother them in love and hugs; I wanted to keep them at a distance to make them independent.

This energy kept me alive, filled me with love. At the same time, it kept me emotionally distant so that they would not miss me if I died.

Once I was home in my own bed, I felt I was back in control. My staff was there: the maid Lali Bai, the cook Anil and the maid's son Amar Bhaiyya, who cared for the dogs.

My first project was Genie, the German shepherd puppy we had got just before I went to Delhi for the surgery. Though she had been fed and walked in my absence, her forelegs were weak from insufficient calcium, she was infested with ticks, her ears were full of wax and her teeth had tartar deposits. In Genie I found my purpose. She needed me. With every day that I sat her on my lap to groom her, remove her ticks, clean her ears, feed her supplements and play with her, I realized more and more that there was a lot I could do from my bed.

I started asking Devika and Ambika to sit by me so that I could oil their hair, creating a family tradition that still continues. This is the time we feel closest to each other.

We developed a symbiotic relationship at home. The girls learnt to be gentle around me, avoiding jumping and climbing on me. The cook would fix my meal tray and the girls would bring it to me. Ambika would sit in front of me—I would feed her and then she would feed me. The microwave came in handy now. Meats and vegetables prepped by the cook would be easily finished by the girls under my guidance.

I had to go to the hospital for physiotherapy twice a week, but transportation was an issue. I had thought that Bikram would be posted to Jaipur by now, since the officer he was to replace had received his relocation orders. Unfortunately, someone else from the regiment came to Jaipur instead of Bikram. Now it was up to my father to find a solution. He bought a Gypsy. It felt like a manifestation of my desires—although I had hoped for one to go rally driving, not to go to the physiotherapist. He modified the back to have a pull-down ramp and clamps so my wheelchair could be rolled into the car and strapped into place.

After four or five months, I no longer needed the specialized equipment at the hospital, and we found a physiotherapist to come to the house instead. By then I had become stronger and had also learnt more ways of efficient transfers.

One afternoon, I was alone at home, waiting in bed for Devika and Ambika to come back from school. Suddenly I heard a sharp crack. I looked out of the window and saw that a high-tension electricity cable had snapped and was whipping around the front yard like a snake. It was a deathtrap. I had to act quickly. I reached for the landline next to my bed and dialled 100, the police emergency number.

The police responded with impressive speed. They alerted the nearest station, the beat constable arrived promptly and he called someone from the electricity department. Before the girls came home, the live wire had been neutralized, rolled up into a big bundle and kept to one side. Devika and Ambika were none the wiser of the drama that had preceded them.

This incident bolstered my confidence—I knew then that I could still handle a crisis.

This was followed by another incident that could have been disastrous but instead revealed a silver lining. The girls and I had settled into a comfortable routine. They would fix trays with everything I needed for different activities. To get them ready for school, they would fetch a tray with a hairbrush, hair ties, ribbons and clips. I would style their hair while they sat in front of me. For homework projects, the tray would have cardboard, glue, scissors, tape, paint, glitter—the works. Meals would also be brought on trays.

From my bed, I even crafted beautiful costumes for them for school events. Devika was a magician and Ambika was Shakuntala, complete with dance steps I taught her using just my fingers.

One day, I needed hand lotion from my dressing table, which was in the next room. Ambika dashed off to fetch it. The dressing table was a mirror with wrought iron brackets and a loose glass shelf fixed to the wall. Ambika climbed onto a stool to reach it. In her eagerness, she knocked askew the glass shelf and it fell, shattering into sharp pieces all around her.

The crash and Ambika's panicked screams reached my room. I shouted out to her, urging her to calm down. The only other person in the house was Devika. Though she had overcome her hemiplegia to a great extent with physiotherapy, she was still slow to move. I told her to go to Ambika but to first wear her shoes to protect herself from the glass. Until now, someone had always helped lace her corrective shoes. But that day, faced with an emergency, she not only did up her own shoelaces but also walked into the room strewn with shattered glass, lifted her little sister in her arms and brought her out to safety. My little hero had risen to the occasion and saved the day.

We were all finding hidden reserves of strength within ourselves. We were all heroes in our own way. We had to be. This was the only way we could have a regular life.

Bikram finally came to Jaipur for three months. While he hadn't received the posting we'd hoped for, he was able to come on an official assignment—what we call an attachment in the army.

I had still not accepted the wheelchair as my fate, hoping to be able to walk again. To help with my mobility around the house, Bikram repurposed the snapped electricity cable that was lying in the front yard. He rigged it like a guidewire from my bed to the bathroom and the dining room. He installed handles, the kind you see in buses, and I would hoist myself up using my upper body strength and drag myself along these paths. Initially, it gave me a sense of independence, but the effort of dragging myself around left me in pain. This pain made me irritable, and I found myself lashing out at everyone.

Often, I found myself alone inside while everyone was outside. I longed to join them, but the effort of dragging myself and the subsequent irritability it brought on made me stay in bed. And I was afraid that I might have an accident with the urine bag or if I was wearing a diaper, that it might leak and cause me embarrassment.

It was around this time that my brother and his wife came to see me for the first time since my surgery. Vikram had been in Wellington, doing the same course Bikram had completed, and had been unable to make the trip earlier. A year had gone by.

During this visit, his wife, Anupma, offered me insights that literally and figuratively opened the world to me. She had worked with British Airways before marrying my brother. She brought a fresh perspective to our family, one of a modern, working woman who had an identity of her own. When I first met her, I was already married and had Devika. Talking to her then, I had wondered what might have been had I not married Bikram right out of college and had taken up a career instead.

Now, when Anupma saw me dragging myself around, she asked why I was not using the wheelchair.

'I don't want to be confined to a wheelchair. I want to walk,' I said.

'I use spectacles for my weak eyes. Why aren't you using a wheelchair for your weak legs? It's all the same. It's just an assistive aid,' she told me.

The meaning of her words dismantled the stigma I associated with the use of a wheelchair, with being labelled a cripple. I thought about what she had said the whole night. The next morning, I saw my chair differently. The wheels on their own were a symbol of movement and progress. Human civilization evolved after the discovery of the wheel. The wheel finds place of pride in our national flag and our national emblem, representing progress. I wondered why people using a wheelchair were called 'wheelchair-bound'. The moment I sat in it and moved around the house, I felt 'wheelchair-liberated'.

Anupma's next piece of advice opened up a new world for me. 'Stop wasting your time watching television soaps. Get a computer and use the internet to research your condition,' she said.

With these two insights, she more than made up for their year-long absence. The resentment I had held towards Bhaiyya and Bhabhi for not visiting me for a year vanished.

In those days a desktop computer cost about Rs 50,000, a significant sum. When I spoke about it to my in-laws, who were also visiting me after a year of my moving to Jaipur, they immediately wrote me a cheque for the amount. They had seen how much time and money my parents had invested in my recovery. Perhaps this was their way of contributing. Once the computer was installed, I needed to learn how to use it. My mother stepped in here. Her friend's son was running an Aptech computer centre, so he volunteered one of his students to teach me. Every week, this young man, an IIT graduate and an ISKCON devotee, dressed in a dhoti and kurta, with a bright chandan tilak on his forehead, would come to teach me all about computers. Interacting with him, I learnt to be able to distinguish between appearances and reality. No one would have guessed this young man in his dhoti would have that depth of knowledge about computers. He was confident enough not to care about how other people perceived him. From him, I learnt to forget about how I looked on my wheelchair and focused on gaining knowledge.

The summer before Bikram left, we made a trip to Delhi, to celebrate Devika's school results and to get my check-up done. This trip was memorable for two reasons: we celebrated Devika's academic success—remarkable for a child once doubted intellectually—and we welcomed a new family member, Leila the boxer.

Devika's achievement—scoring over 95 per cent in school and winning the best student award in the entire primary wing of the school—was her way of proving herself to everyone who had questioned her abilities after her accident. For me, it was also a validation of my abilities as a mother. I was able to show all the relatives and so-called well-wishers who had called me kandam that my paralysis in no way compromised my skills as a mother.

Devika's prize was that with her report card, she would get a free ice cream sundae at one of Delhi's iconic fast-food chains. Ever since her result had been announced, she had been brimming with anticipation. For her, it was a sundae that tasted the sweetest because she had earned it with her hard work; but for me, it was a trophy for my achievement as a mother. That was the best day we all had in almost a year. We were together as a family, on an outing to the big city, celebrating our achievements. Though I was in a wheelchair, it wasn't the end of the world—it was a roadblock, but it was something we would overcome together.

While driving through Neeti Bagh, we spotted an adorable boxer puppy and, swept up in the dreamlike quality of that day, we decided to add Leila to our family, taking her home to our two other dogs.

More than a year after my surgery, Bikram finally got posted to Jaipur. While he had been away, I was forced to give up the house I was in and move to a smaller house as I was no longer entitled to that scale of accommodation.

We moved into army housing in the cantonment and swiftly set up home. I put up parallel bars in the garden to strengthen my upper body. Embracing my role as the squadron commander's wife, I went about meeting the families of our troops, seeing to their well-being and attending army events, all on my wheelchair.

With Bikram's return, our social life blossomed, and we frequently entertained guests. Among those whose company I enjoyed was Ranjana, a college friend I had serendipitously bumped into at a bakery in town. She was a teacher now, and because her daughter had a cleft palate, we would share notes and got along well. Through her, I was introduced to a new group of women, and together we went away on weekends and for picnics when the weather permitted. The bonus was that our husbands also got along.

But this idyllic life did not last long. Bikram's squadron was moved to Jhansi. Just when we had got our rhythm going, the move happened.

Initially, I stayed on in Jaipur to continue with my physiotherapy, but before Diwali in 2001, I had made up my mind that we would spend the festival together as a family. Fate, however, had other plans. We had barely been in Jhansi for a month or so, when the terrorist attack on the Indian Parliament occurred, and the entire Indian Army was mobilized for Op Parakram.

Suddenly I found myself alone once again, bearing the responsibility of caring for not only two daughters and three dogs but also the thirty families of our troops. Fresh out of the tragedy and loss of Kargil, we were now in another potentially critical situation. Many of the women in my care were newly married or had young children. I visited them in my wheelchair, organized potlucks, kept spirits high with games and activities, even attended parent-teacher meetings on their behalf, as most of them were unable to read or write.

With the army personnel deployed, our usual support system was unavailable. But Bikram's network of local connections from having studied in Jhansi proved invaluable. It was these friends who were there for us, and I could call on them if I needed anything.

But by and large, we were a band of women who looked out for each other and handled whatever was thrown our way while the men served on the front.

I immersed myself in the welfare of the families of the troops under Bikram's command. This served a dual purpose: it kept up their morale and it ensured that I did not have the time to dwell on my condition. Despite going everywhere in my wheelchair, I felt empowered because I was able to contribute in a meaningful manner to the lives of others.

My efforts did not go unnoticed. When the soldiers returned at the end of Op Parakram, the general officer commanding of the army division our squadron was a part of, Maj. Gen. D.S. Shekhawat, learnt of how I had looked after the families of our troops. He presented me with a certificate of appreciation for my efforts. His gratitude must have stayed with him, because some years later, when our paths crossed again, he was able to help me in a big way. Life comes full circle, and no good deed goes unnoticed.

9

Breaking Walls

M Y MOTHER-IN-LAW DID THE HONOURS OF cutting the ribbon. Having her inaugurate Dee's Place symbolized the cutting of the umbilical cord between me and my years of dependence. Dee's Place was my answer to everyone who had pitied me, everyone who had ridiculed me, everyone who had made me feel like my life was over. Dee's Place was my way of standing tall, even while sitting in a wheelchair.

We had been in Ahmednagar for about a year. Bikram was posted here as instructor in the Armoured Corps Centre and School. Living in our makeshift home brought back memories of living here as students at the beginning of our marriage.

There was a lot of socializing, mainly because I often called people over. I would set up my barbecue and position my wheelchair right next to it, so that I could serve richly marinated and grilled foods. My egg rolls were a hot favourite. Everyone from our course mates to regimental officers to student officers, all tired of the lack of good restaurants in the city, raved about my cooking.

I participated in all the army community activities, like ladies' meets, where I often emceed. At the club I would call out the tambola numbers, and I also participated in cooking competitions.

It was during this time that I became aware of the judgement around me. For a Christmas baking contest, I made a yule log and created a complete festive scene with a Christmas tree, a fireplace with little hand-knitted stockings and even a miniature Santa. I was overjoyed when I won, but my achievement came with a bitter aftertaste. 'She has magic in her hands,' I overheard one of the ladies at the event say. 'The magic is not in her hands—it's in her feet,' said another, ascribing my winning to sympathy rather than skill.

The snide remarks extended to how I was bringing up my daughters. I take pride in the fact that they were always well-dressed, neatly turned out and doing well in school. I ensured they didn't miss out on anything. They had already learnt how to cycle in Jaipur under my supervision. Now, I would make a road trip out of my check-ups in Pune, clubbing them with trips to the mall and movies. We would come back from the big city laden with goodies. After one trip, we brought back the latest chocolate chip cookies—they'd become wildly popular because of their ad campaign. When my girls took these cookies to school in their tiffin box, I had to hear remarks like, 'Poor girls—their mom is in a wheelchair, so they don't even get homemade food in their tiffin; they're surviving on biscuits.'

The reality could not have been more different. I not only ensured they had nutritious food but also helped them with their studies and projects that won prizes. I had helped Devika create a diorama on freedom fighters, using medicine boxes to create pedestals topped with printouts of the heroes stuck to each one.

Gradually, I noticed a decline in my social activities—I stopped getting invited to parties that weren't wheelchair accessible. Perhaps out of concern for me or perhaps because people generally feel uncomfortable around differently abled persons, I would be left out of picnics, pool parties and events in places with stairs. This brought home the reality of how blind so many are to issues of inclusivity and making public spaces accessible.

However, amidst this gloom was a ray of sunshine: Mezbeen Sayyed. Her husband, like Bikram, was in the Armoured Corps. Mezbeen was amazing—while I was in a wheelchair, she was zipping around on an 80cc Bajaj bike. One day, she simply showed up at the house and said, 'Both my boys are in the same classes as your girls. They have school projects coming up, so I'm going to the market to get some stuff for them. I'll get the same for your girls too.' Just like that she became the friend I so needed at that time. She seemed to know everyone and everything, and kept me updated on what was going on around us. We even worked on an editing project together. She was always there for me.

Meanwhile, Daulat Bhaiyya, one of the older cooks at the club who remembered us from our earlier stay there, came to me. He wanted to set up a restaurant and asked me to help him by putting in a word with my father-in-law, who had retired now but whose word was still respected. I heard him out but let the matter slip from my mind.

Soon after, my in-laws had to travel to the US to visit Bikram's sister, and were planning to be away for about six months. It was decided that we would shift to their home in their absence. Shifting meant that my world was now restricted to one bedroom, a mere 10x10 space. The house had too many barriers for me: entry steps, a sunken drawing room and dining room, and two steps to get to the rest of the house. I didn't have any freedom to move around within the house and it was difficult for my friends to visit me as well.

Moving to my in-laws' house also created issues with the household staff. My daily schedule was different from that of the rest of the family. I couldn't leave my room until my attendant came to help me with my morning routine, which included helping me with passing stool and urine using the pressure method. Only after being bathed and dressed could I have my breakfast, served around 11 a.m. I would skip lunch and have an early dinner before the rest of the family. These special meal timings must have irritated the domestic help because she would feed me leftovers from the previous night's dinner for breakfast and then lunch leftovers for dinner. As a house-proud lady who loved socializing and setting the table beautifully with the right crockery and cutlery, cloth napkins and flower arrangements, being given my meals on an old steel thali was disheartening. When it came to giving meals to my daughters, the domestic help would leave before they came back from school, so they would have to serve themselves cold food.

All this irked me no end.

One day, something snapped in me. Ravi, a local contractor, was working on fixing the compound. I called him to my room and told him to knock down the wall, extend it towards the rear of the house and install a big window.

Without asking anyone, without telling anyone, while my in-laws were out of the country, I not only opened up my bedroom but also added an outside kitchen and constructed a ramp entry to my room from the side of the house.

I broke the walls.

With this act of breaking out I was just testing the waters. This was just the beginning, to see what I could achieve. Encouraged by this success, I decided to support Daulat Bhaiyya's venture. I knew my cooking was popular, and coupled with the lack of quality restaurants nearby, it seemed like the perfect opportunity.

Ravi used the leftover materials from the compound renovation work and my bedroom expansion to build a tin shed and a tandoor on a plot of land Bikram and I owned.

And thus, Dee's Place was born. It was never just a restaurant. It was my way of showing the world what I could do.

We started Dee's Place without any formal background in catering or running a restaurant—we were guided purely by instinct. My team comprised Daulat Bhaiyya, three cooks and a few boys from the nearby village of Nimbodi.

While my room at home was being renovated, I had taken to helping the children of the labourers with their studies. These young men, needing to retake their English exams, benefited from my tutoring and got good results. This prompted the sarpanch to seek my help with other kids as well. One day, one of the boys I had tutored was picked up by the police for questioning in a case of stolen sandalwood. Without thinking twice about it, I went to the police station and was able to convince them that the boy was innocent, securing his release.

This boy and some of the others I had taught became my staff at Dee's Place.

We were open from 5 p.m. to midnight. Initially, business was slow, but we soon saw an increase in home delivery orders. As the restaurant started breaking even, it offered me more than money—it was an opportunity to socialize; it was where I was in control; it was the reason I was able to get through the lonely morning hours at home.

From three cooks we grew to five, and soon I had eighteen young men serving tables and handling deliveries. They were my community. I was their go-to person for whatever they needed: from college admissions to job placements. I even helped a girl who had a hole in her heart with a job at Dee's Place. Draupadi is still a part of my life—I had given her a cycle back then, and recently I gave her a scooter. She remains a steadfast presence in my life, someone who will come and stand by me whenever I call. Sangram, nicknamed Don, and Deepak were two boys I put through driving school. The day they got their licences, I got wheels—one of them would be at my doorstep whenever I needed to go anywhere. Even now, on my trips to Ahmednagar, I call them when I need to go anywhere.

Dee's Place gave my girls and me a free space to create our own little world. I made a giant-sized snakes-and-ladders board on a concrete patch there, set up swings and also made a miniature Grand Prix track with toy cars for the kids to enjoy.

We began to do better and better. As Dee's Place flourished, so did I. I've seen over the years that my life seems to oscillate between phases of subservience and those where I emerge as a super-positive and confident version of myself. These phases are dictated by my health. When I was ill at five years old, I strove to be the model child—obedient and untroublesome, compensating for taking up everyone's time and energy by being the best I could be. When I recovered and entered adolescence, I became the rebel because I began to seek things that satisfied me, that did not conform to what 'good girls' were supposed to like, such as biking on the sly. When my daughter had her accident, I again took up a more passive role because I somehow felt responsible for her condition. My own illness kept me on the defensive. I took whatever everyone wanted to give me, without expressing my own needs or desires in any way.

With Dee's Place, I once again became the person I was destined to be: a vivacious, confident go-getter, always ready to tackle problems head on, always seeking new challenges and excelling in everything I undertook.

Tuesdays and Thursdays were quieter at Dee's Place, with most of my army clientele busy. But there was a group of local lawyers who had started visiting the restaurant frequently, and when they saw that these two days were slow, they came to me with a request.

'Can you let us use this space every Tuesday?'

'For what?' I asked.

'We want to hold our musical evenings here,' they said.

It turned out that these lawyers, with their black coats and stern demeanours, were actually music buffs. Someone played the harmonium, someone the flute. Another sang, and one played the tabla. So began the musical evenings at Dee's Place. I laid out white mattresses for them, creating a cosy concert setting for their private performances.

This group of talented lawyers quickly transitioned from patrons to my friends.

Diya Chaudhary, a journalist friend who worked with *The Indian Express*, noticed one key element missing from Dee's Place: publicity. She suggested hosting a press conference to announce that I, a woman in a wheelchair, was doing something different to create a space for myself in the community.

I organized a small press event at the restaurant, inviting the local media.

My message was that society had different expectations from a woman in a wheelchair, but here I was to prove all those notions wrong.

The impact of this event was unimaginable. A local Marathi newspaper carried the headline—'*Jiddi lach pankh futale*' ('When a new bird wants to fly, it sprouts wings').

As the news spread, the local Rotary Priyadarshini group gave me my first award, a nod to the impact the restaurant was having on the community.

The Hotel Management Institute of Ahmednagar also took notice. Their students began to intern at Dee's Place, stepping in whenever we hosted events like New Year's parties, Diwali melas and other special functions. For these big parties, we would set up a dance floor, bring in a DJ and print discount coupons in the local papers.

Dee's Place became a sought-after spot for anniversaries, birthdays, even proposals. I had made a makeshift thatch-roof hut and would do it up according to the occasion: hearts and pink colour for Valentine's Day, candles and soft music for date nights.

My growth was mirrored in the growth of my team. My band of boys began to get opportunities for better jobs. Deepak and Don learnt to drive and got daytime jobs as drivers. Deepak became a recovery vehicle driver with the regional transport office. Santu Mama, our butler and usher, went on to run a gym and a car wash. Asif, who was an orphan, learnt the trade with us. He took me with him when he went to see a prospective bride, as he had no other family. When I shut down Dee's Place, I passed on my equipment to him, and he now runs a stall in Bhingar. Mehra Bhaiyya, our Chinese food cook, had come to us after running away from debt. One day, the loan sharks tracked him down, ready to extract their pound of flesh. I intervened and settled his outstanding amount. Pintu was our cashier. Mohsin, the neighbour's maid's son, waited tables for us. Rafiq, a freelance contractor for party equipment, would do our events without making a profit on what he charged us.

The local management institute conducted a study on Dee's Place as a successful business model. The students analysed how a place like ours could thrive despite the challenges: operating in a remote location with poor access roads, employing local men who weren't trained formally, being led by someone without professional expertise. That a place like this, which ran six days a week with peak sales for only three hours a day, could turn a profit was a matter of research. They later invited me to their college for an interaction.

This brought me in contact with the local hoteliers, who, without any sense of competition, shared their professional practices with me: where to go for wholesale purchases, how to tweak my menu to suit local tastes, how to reduce wait times by having fast-cooking items.

Through Dee's Place, I made friends with people from all walks of life—lawyers, hoteliers, jewellers—and my networking skills grew stronger.

I was everywhere—in the news, winning Rotary recognitions and attending their events, being awarded the Swavlamban Puraskar by the government of Maharashtra, speaking at school events. When I went into town, I would run into ten different people who either knew me or knew of me. It was a new high. I was known for my own achievements, for what I had created for myself, not for being an army colonel's wife or for being an army general's daughter-in-law.

But success tasted the sweetest when a teacher at my daughters' school, who had peeked into their tiffins earlier and commented on my parenting skills for giving them biscuits, asked me to cater the picnic lunch for their class group.

Along with the growth, all this attention also brought with it a slew of complaints. The first was that I was running a commercial establishment on agricultural land.

Since Dee's Place was beyond the city limits, the only permission I needed was from the village sarpanch. This approval I already had. My bond with the villagers was strong—they were almost like family. The sarpanch and residents of Nimbodi were grateful to me for all I had done for the community—teaching them, getting them vocational training, helping with college admissions, hiring them myself and guiding them towards better jobs.

In addition to this permission, to be doubly safe, I also got a soil analysis conducted. The results showed that the land was unsuitable for agriculture.

Subsequently, a new complaint emerged, alleging that I was serving alcohol without a licence. This led to the excise department carrying out a surprise raid at Dee's Place, where they found nothing—no alcohol bottles, not even bottle caps.

Despite the lack of evidence, I was summoned to the local Excise Department office in Ahmednagar town. Frustrated by the obvious targeting, I sought help from the local Shiv Sainiks. I shared the details of the raid and the summons and how the office, located on the second floor of a building, would be totally inaccessible for me on my wheelchair.

When the day came, I reached the building and was greeted by a large group of Shiv Sainiks, all tall, well-built young men with saffron turbans and tilaks. They literally carried me up the two flights of stairs, wheelchair and all. I felt like a queen being taken up on my palanquin.

The officials were taken aback when they saw me. They had not expected a woman in a wheelchair. I laid out the circumstances surrounding the complaint, the findings of the surprise raid and the summons. They realized that the complaint was rooted in mischief more than legitimacy and dismissed it.

However, that was not the last of my problems. When complaints failed, those jealous of my success began spreading rumours. One that took the rounds was that the restaurant was haunted.

Whispers began of eerie noises, like shrieks and groans, and of an apparition in a tree nearby. *'Raat ko bhoot aate hain'* (Ghosts visit at night), they said.

I took this as a challenge. 'If there's a ghost, I'll meet it myself,' I declared to whoever would listen. That night, I stayed at Dee's Place well after closing. It was a moonless night, chilly and windless. There I sat, alone in my wheelchair. At first, I was kept company by the sounds of the neighbourhood settling in for the night and the lights that flickered in the nearby homes. But slowly, as the night progressed, the sounds stopped and the lights were extinguished. I was shrouded in darkness. My rational mind mocked the superstitions that fuelled the rumours. I would prove everyone wrong.

Creeeeeak.

Clang!

Groaaan.

The sounds startled me. Had I not been paralysed, I might have jumped out of my wheelchair in fright!

I looked around, fully expecting to confront the ghost. But as the sounds continued, I recognized their distinctly metallic quality.

The case of the ghostly sounds was solved. The culprits were the tin shutters of the sheds. Due to the heat from the clay oven, the metal was expanding during the day and then, on cooling at night, contracting and producing ghostly sounds.

With that, the rumour was put to bed, and news of my having spent the night there and surviving to tell the tale went around.

If Dee's Place gave me my community from Nimbodi, it also gave me a friend for life from Mumbai. Sushant Divgikar was just a thirteen-year-old when we first met. He was a part of a group of affluent Mumbai kids who would come to Ahmednagar for a camp during school holidays. The camp, run by a retired army officer, aimed to expose these privileged children to the realities of life.

They would come from Mumbai by bus—not in luxury cars—and would stay in the army camp instead of hotel rooms. They would go through a boot camp of sorts, where they did things themselves and learnt the value of hard work and discipline.

Dee's Place got the catering contract for them. Our menu was nutritious and wholesome, rather than a five-star spread. For breakfast we served eggs, poha, upma or parathas. Lunch would be a nice chicken curry, dal, seasonal vegetables, salad, curd, chapati, rice—what most of India eats. At teatime we gave them healthy sandwiches and biscuits. Dinner was similar to lunch.

Most of the kids enjoyed the food, maybe because they were hungry and tired from the different activities or because it was so different from the elaborate meals and junk food they were used to. But as in every group, there were some kids who pulled faces and tried to create a scene.

In this situation, young Sushant stood up and gave the troublemakers a stern lecture on the value of food, telling them to be grateful they were getting such good food to eat. This worked—the troublemakers were silenced.

This young boy, so different from his classmates, would later embrace his identity as a woman and is a well-known activist in the LGBTQIA+ community. Back then, he took on the biggest bullies in his group and silenced them. We immediately connected. Both of us different from the norm in our own ways. Both of us with the courage to take on whatever challenges came our way. Both of us ready to fight the world for our convictions.

We became friends, and whenever I'm in Mumbai, we make it a point to meet. He always offers me his guest house when I need a place to stay, and he has been with me for many significant events in my life.

'Ma'am, we have a special tradition,' the youngster began hesitantly.

'What tradition?' I prodded.

'We'd like to celebrate our course senior's birthday,' said his friend.

'Sure, everyone likes celebrating their friends' birthdays. We have special arrangements for parties. We can do theme-based decor, a special menu … let me know what you have in mind,' I said, slightly amused by their hesitation.

'No, our tradition is a little different,' said the friend.

'So what exactly *is* your tradition?' I pressed, now a touch impatient.

'We break glasses,' they said in unison.

It turned out that the young officers of this particular batch of YO's doing the Young Officers Course followed a tradition of toasting their course senior and then smashing their glasses.

I couldn't help but smile. 'As long as you pay for the damage, you can smash anything you like.'

That was how my bond with this particular bunch of youngsters grew. They loved that I was allowing them to follow their tradition, free of judgement. They not only paid for the glasses they broke but also generously tipped my boys who cleaned up after them.

This batch included some officers who were almost like family. There was Arjun Patil, who had been born in front of me when I was in school in Akhnoor. There were some second-generation officers whose parents were our friends. There were also two officers from our regiment.

Our bond was cemented the day I let them break the glasses, but it had started to form at a New Year's Eve party at Dee's Place. Due to the tsunami in 2004, the official parties and celebrations had been cancelled, and these youngsters had headed to Dee's Place to unwind.

While my laid-back attitude had quickly made me their friend, there was another reason they felt comfortable in my company. They had a course mate from their time at the National Defence Academy, Shubhjit Mazumdar. He had been the star of their course: cross-country running champion, academically bright, very popular. Unfortunately, an accident had left Shubhjit paralysed while still in the academy. His friends, now training in Ahmednagar, were still in touch with him and consequently were familiar with disability. This made them empathetic in their behaviour without making me feel awkward or pitied.

Shubhjit was still in the Command Hospital in Pune, and on long weekends, some of the course mates would go visit him. One day, they invited me to join them.

Initially hesitant, I eventually decided to go and meet this young man who was so admired by his friends.

That decision turned the course of my life.

We drove to Pune in my car, my girls accompanying us.

Our first meeting was profoundly emotional for both of us. We had each lived active, sporty lives before being paralysed. Unlike those who may have never walked, we had experienced life with full mobility, so we knew what we were missing. Our first meeting made us both cry—we had each found someone who truly understood the extent of what we had lost.

Once our tears had been wiped away, we decided to have lunch together. Packing both our wheelchairs into the car, we went to E Square Mall. Before heading to the restaurant, we stopped at a new music store there, where you could listen to songs before buying the album. The song we heard that day, '*Yaaron Dosti Badi Hi Haseen Hai*' (Friendship Is Beautiful), brought home the beauty and value of friendships. That afternoon, I was among friends. No one was judging me. I was their age. No one saw me as different. I was a part of the group. I belonged.

After lunch we returned to the hospital and parted with plans to meet again in the evening. We left the girls with the maid in the guest room and went out to a disco.

Ironically, my first visit to a disco came at a time when I couldn't dance. But that didn't stop me from having a great time.

That weekend changed me. I realized that my life did not need to be limited by my wheelchair.

Shubhjit showed me the path to greater freedom. He told me about a six-week workshop being conducted in Delhi at the Indian Spinal Injuries Centre. Led by Arun Sondhi, a Swedish powerlifting Paralympian of Indian origin, the workshop would focus on active wheelchair living.

Intrigued, I dove headfirst into researching Arun Sondhi online. The moment I saw him on a modified trike, I was hooked. Further research brought me in touch with a support group for those with spinal cord injuries.

It was after meeting Shubhjit that I finally accepted the wheelchair as integral to my life. I now wanted to focus on living the best life that I could. Shubhjit himself progressed remarkably—he went on to complete his MBA at the Indian Institute of Management and is now working with an MNC in Bangalore.

As for me, I headed to Delhi to find out more about the six-week workshop at the Indian Spinal Injuries Centre.

10

Wheelchair-liberated

———◦•◦———

ONIKA AND I BECAME FRIENDS WHEN WE WERE AT
Sophia College. She was endearingly goofy, experiencing
hostel life for the first time, which drew out my maternal
instincts. I took her under my wing, and we made sure to remain
in touch.

She had visited me in Ahmednagar, and when I went to Delhi to
explore the rehabilitation programme at the Indian Spinal Injuries
Centre (ISIC), she generously invited me to stay at her home.

Two of the young officers who were finishing their course in
Ahmednagar were from Delhi, and they offered to escort me to the
city.

Monika's home was beautiful. Immaculately kept and stylishly
decorated, it was straight out of a home décor magazine.

She showed me around the house, decorated with large,
glamorous photographs of her. But one wall in particular made me
stop in my tracks. I wheeled myself closer to the hanging framed
certificate—it was a Limca Book of Records award.

Monika had set a record for the fastest weight loss. Her success
had propelled her into celebrity status. She was now the brand

ambassador for a nationwide weight loss clinic and a fixture at high-profile parties.

Her story, marked by a dramatic transformation and success, resonated with me. I stored this information in my mental vault, and one corner of my brain kept ticking, thinking of what record I could create for myself.

After settling in, I went to the ISIC and met Shivjeet Raghav, a peer counsellor there. His life had been drastically altered when, as a young MSc student, he was paralysed from the neck down, all thanks to a case of mistaken identity. A gang of thugs had been instructed to target a man in a red jacket. As luck would have it, that day, Shivjeet wore a red jacket. For no fault of his, except being in the wrong place at the wrong time, wearing the wrong colour, Shivjeet was attacked and ended up paralysed. Since 1996, he had been working at the ISIC, motivating others who were similarly wheelchair-bound.

The ISIC was in the process of creating a programme for active wheelchair living, in collaboration with Arun Sondhi. Arun, paralysed in an accident during his college years, had rehabilitated in Sweden and had since become a Swedish citizen. He represented Sweden in the Paralympic Games and was the world champion in Paralympic powerlifting. He was also a computer professional and had a strong interest in biking.

Shivjeet encouraged me to enrol in the programme. The attendance fee was nominal, something like Rs 200 per day, although the cost went up if you opted to stay at the hospital. I knew I could arrange army accommodation for the six-week duration, so financially the workshop started to look quite doable.

The challenge, however, came from a condition: participants had to attend alone, without family members. The idea was to teach us independence. Having someone at our side to handle our tasks could hinder our willingness to step out of our comfort zone and learn to do more things for ourselves.

To support us, though, the ISIC offered the services of an attendant while we were there.

After thinking about it for a bit, I signed up.

At that time, Devika was staying in her hostel and Ambika was with my in-laws in Ahmednagar. Leaving her behind, I arrived in Delhi for the workshop after a gruelling twenty-hour train journey. My father had made arrangements for my stay in an army hostel and also sent his car for me from Jaipur to use for the six weeks of the workshop. I hired a local driver, and Sandeep, one of my employees at Dee's Place, accompanied me to help me with the wheelchair.

I arrived at the ISIC for my first day. It was a different world. Instead of being the only person in a wheelchair amidst able-bodied people, I found myself among many like me. Shivjeet, whom I had met earlier, was in a wheelchair. Mohit, who was working in the IT cell, was in a wheelchair. All the other participants were in wheelchairs. Notably, I was the only woman.

A cheerful young man with a ready smile greeted me. This was Virendra Vikram Singh, the physiotherapist assigned to me. 'How are you today?' he asked.

'I am well,' I replied.

'May I examine you?' he asked, before carefully examining my paralysed leg. 'You didn't sleep last night, did you?' he asked.

Virendra's skill was remarkable. With a single touch, he was able to assess the stiffness and spasticity in my leg and pinpoint the reason. 'If you don't sleep, your spasticity will increase,' he said gently.

I began to weep. It was his kindness, his genuine concern, his understanding that touched me to the core. For the first time, I felt truly seen and supported by someone who understood what I was going through, who knew how to help me and who inspired faith.

Soon after, Arun arrived. He started our session with a round of introductions, allowing each of us to share our journeys so far and our expectations from the workshop. Arun then told us his own story, beginning with a video of the opening ceremony of the Paralympic Games in which he had won his medal. That moment took me back to 1982, when I had attended the opening ceremony of the Asian Games at Jawaharlal Nehru Stadium. I was filled with possibilities. The world was slowly opening up before me. I was excited to see what all could be done.

His trike rekindled my passion for biking. I was overjoyed to know that biking could still be a part of my life. At that moment I knew what record I would create: I'd be the first woman with chest-below paralysis to ride a bike.

The workshop began with a structured routine. Each day started at 8.30 a.m. with warm-up exercises while seated in our chairs. This was followed by forty minutes of occupational therapy. To counteract our stiffness from prolonged sitting, we would do stretching exercises. Practical lessons included how to transfer ourselves from our wheelchair to a bed, a toilet or a shower. We were taught how to roll over in bed to use a bedpan. Then we would work on strengthening our arms and upper bodies, using medicine balls, Therabands and hand cycles. Mechanical stationary bikes kept our leg joints supple. We would sit on the bikes with our feet fixed in the pedals. The pedals would move mechanically, exercising our knee joints. To maintain dexterity and flexibility, we were trained to pick up small objects, and for posture balance, we performed kneeling and balancing exercises.

Maj. H.P.S. Ahluwalia, the founder of the ISIC, frequently joined us for our sessions. As a veteran who had scaled Mt Everest as part of the first Indian team to do so, he was a towering figure of inspiration. During the 1965 Indo-Pak war, he was shot in the spine, leaving him paralysed. This did not limit him in any way, and he continued with his adventures. He had set up the ISIC to help other paraplegics live more meaningful lives. He would play table tennis with us, the bat firmly secured to his wrist. It was a treat to watch him play, seated in his wheelchair, and it was even better if you got to play with him.

This approach to rehabilitation was very new to me. It was so different from my previous physiotherapy. I discovered that physiotherapy could be fun, not just going through the paces in a single room. We were playing games, catching and throwing things, keeping our reflexes sharp. With a belt around our knees, we were stable, there was no fear of spasms or of keeling over. I had never felt so free or had so much fun since my surgery.

I felt a renewed sense of independence. I was doing things on my own, interacting with people twenty years younger than me—a new generation who taught me so much. The time I spent there served as a reminder that we have to embrace change. Unlike the army hospital physiotherapist who, because of my husband's and father-in-law's ranks, was hesitant to push me, here I was being challenged every minute.

I experienced a profound sense of lost time—I wished I had come here six years earlier.

One of the biggest limitations for a person in a wheelchair is managing the daily routine of voiding the bladder and bowel. Things which are so normal for everyone are a big challenge for us.

My lack of knowledge about proper bladder management had caused considerable social anxiety. I would avoid socializing for fear of an accident. Anything could cause a leak: loud noises, pressure on my abdomen during transfers, even the sound of flowing water. I tried not to attend pujas with my mother-in-law because the sound of the bell would trigger a leak. Before travel, I would avoid drinking water, and this in turn would leave me vulnerable to infections.

At the workshop, Shivjeet taught us bladder management techniques, tailored to different levels of disability.

Some people prefer to use a catheter and a urine bag, especially during periods when access to a toilet is uncertain. I personally use a catheter with a urine bag fastened to my leg during my sports competitions and on long journeys. When the bag is full, there is a stopper that can be opened, and I empty it into a bottle to discard later. Generally, I save plastic water bottles for this purpose.

Those who have adequate upper body mobility are able to use the toilet like able-bodied people. They wheel up to the toilet, lock the chair and then, using their arms, slowly hoist themselves onto the toilet seat. I can do that if I have somebody to hold my shoulder because I do not have torso control. If I were to try this on my own, I could end up falling forwards and landing on my nose.

Another technique I learnt at the ISIC was how to use the bedpan myself. I've learnt to recognize when I need to use the toilet because when my bladder is full, I get a leg spasm. I also now know how many minutes it takes after drinking something for my bladder to get full. I generally lie on a protective sheet in case of accidents. My bedpan is lined with an absorbent sheet, similar to the pee pads now so easily available for pets. I roll over and position the bedpan. I have two buckets next to me: one with clean water and one with water mixed with some fragrant detergent. I empty the bedpan into the bucket with the fragrant water to prevent a foul smell and wash myself with the clean water and a washcloth. I keep Dettol and a bottle of sanitizer near me and use these as well. But most of the time, I rely on a diaper for convenience and assurance.

We have a routine to manage bowel movements, too. With a proper diet and adequate fluid intake, we can have regular bowel movements. Most people with paralysis use the pressure method, which involves gently massaging the abdomen for about fifteen minutes to stimulate a normal bowel movement. In some cases, the person can wear gloves and stimulate the rectal region, while others use enemas. Some also get a colostomy, where an opening is surgically made in the abdomen and a bag is attached to empty the bowel.

At the ISIC, I had sessions, both individual and group, with Namita Bhutani, a psychological counsellor. After my surgery, this was the first time I was meeting someone for my mental health. Up until then I hadn't considered the importance of psychological healing in the process of learning how to live with paralysis. Within the whirlwind of trying to normalize life for my daughters in the absence of my husband, I never got a chance to think of how this life-altering change had impacted me. But in my own way, without even realizing it, I had found a solution to my unacknowledged mental health issues: Dee's Place had provided a feeling of acceptance, a place where I could talk to and joke around with people, a sense of being seen as a person, not a wheelchair-bound person.

In the group sessions we spoke about our common challenges. We discussed how to be most comfortable in our chairs, the best gel cushions to get, whether we had pooped properly, which method worked best for us, which foods helped and which didn't.

We opened up about our deepest fears and shared our darkest experiences. Someone bared their soul about a betrayal; another confessed to thoughts of ending their life, another about job loss. We became agony aunts for each other—who else could understand us better?

One day, I felt ready to discuss an issue that had been bothering me for the last six years—an issue I had been avoiding, that I had been running away from. The issue of sex.

In the months following my surgery, I had been alone in the hospital. Bikram had been able to visit me for just a day. After my hospital stay, I had been alone in Jaipur. When Bikram came to live with us for three months, I avoided the issue of intimacy. Though he never made me feel any less, the doubts came from within me. Was I still attractive? Was I still complete? Did he still find me sexy? How could he, when I felt anything but? This was when Bikram had installed guidewires and handles in the house for my mobility. Using these to drag myself would tire me out, leaving me extremely irritable. My focus was on being able to walk again. And the longer we ignored our lack of physical intimacy, the more difficult it became to discuss it.

I had one-on-one sessions with Namita to talk about sex. She explained that sex for people living with paralysis depends on the degree of mobility they still have. But she clarified that sex is not limited to physicality. She told me about the different ways partners can satisfy each other, the different erogenous zones of the human body. Physical intimacy, she said, is a natural and necessary aspect of human life, wheelchair or no wheelchair.

Through these discussions, Namita helped me see that sex is less about the physical act and more about the emotional connection between partners, and how that can offer solace and comfort.

I had never had these conversations before, and they opened my eyes. I had been grappling with feelings of inadequacy. The grief I felt at being paralysed was akin to that of losing a loved one. Just as widows often wear white to symbolize their sorrow, wiping away colour from their lives, being paralysed made me feel I had to forfeit my right to feel beautiful and wanted.

If Dee's Place was my answer to my need to feel relevant, it also became an excuse to avoid intimacy. I would stay there till 1 a.m., returning home to find everyone asleep. Then I would be up early to rush to the wholesale market to stock up on vegetables for the restaurant.

Bikram had started sleeping in a separate room, partly because his loud snoring would trigger my bladder, making me leak urine. Sharing a room meant I'd need to wear a diaper constantly, which was impractical and could lead to rashes.

When Namita asked me about romance, I was reminded of Bikram's tender promise before my surgery: that he would carry me in his arms for the rest of my life.

Now, Namita encouraged me to rekindle romance in my life, suggesting I express my romantic feelings through the written word. After a long time, the poet in me awoke and I poured out my feelings in poems and letters that I never sent to anyone.

One part of our rehabilitation was standing practice, with our knees locked in a brace. Kaushal Kishore was a master craftsman who made these knee braces in his workshop. For some reason there was a delay in making my brace. I had asked him repeatedly to hurry up with my brace, but he was in no rush.

'Why is your brace taking so long?' Virendra asked me for the umpteenth time.

'I don't know!' I replied exasperatedly. 'Kaushal keeps giving me some excuse or the other.'

'Let's make him do an express delivery,' he said with a twinkle in his eye.

By now we had all become friends, and Kaushal, despite delaying my brace, was well-liked by everyone.

'How good of an actress are you?' Virendra asked me.

'Try me,' I replied, the actor in me awakening.

Cut to Kaushal's basement workshop.

Virendra: Malik Madam was saying her brace is still not ready.

Kaushal: Yes, I'm getting to it. So many pending orders.

(Me at the top of the stairs leading down to the basement, looking down with a stern, almost angry expression.)

Virendra: If I were you, I would do madam's brace before doing anything else.

Kaushal: I'm on the job. I'll get to it in a day or two.

Virendra: You don't want to annoy her. See how impatient she's getting?

Kaushal: Everyone must wait their turn.

Virendra: You say this because you don't know who she is.

Kaushal: Who is she?

Virendra *(glancing up at me, and whispering)*: She's Dawood's sister. She was injured when her car overturned during a gang chase. She's already come to you twice with a reminder. She's not used to having to wait. I overheard her saying that she's losing patience and is going to call her brother tonight. Don't blame me if the underworld comes knocking on your door.

That did the trick.

Kaushal came up the stairs to me, sweating bullets—and it wasn't from the effort of climbing up. He apologized profusely for the delay. Wiping his brow with a grease-stained hanky, he promised me my brace by the next morning.

That night, the shutter remained up in the workshop and Kaushal worked overtime. He did not go home till my brace was ready.

'This standing exercise is so boring,' I complained to Virendra one day during physiotherapy. 'I wish we had some music.'

'I'll take you to a disco,' he replied.

And so began our outings.

As our mobility and control had increased, so had our confidence, transforming us into a vibrant, fun-loving bunch. In fact, our exercise sessions brimmed with such joy and camaraderie that it felt like being in a college canteen, joking and having fun in between classes.

Our first disco outing was to We2, a nightclub in M-Block Market in Greater Kailash. We unloaded our wheelchairs and rolled towards the club. It was on the first floor. By this time, I had discarded my 'patient-wala' wheelchair and got a more agile chair. We entered the club and found an empty table and chairs for the whole group. There wasn't enough space to keep our wheelchairs close, so we folded them up and tucked them aside.

Settled in and vibing to the music, I was really enjoying myself, when I felt someone tap me on the shoulder. I turned and looked—it was a stranger. His words totally floored me, 'Would you care to dance?'

He hadn't realized that we were wheelchair users. He had found me attractive and come to ask me for a dance. I felt so beautiful in that moment.

'I'd love to, but I can't stand,' I replied.

But that did not deter my admirer, and Virendra Vikram found a solution. The bar counter had a metal handrail running along its outer edge. He got my knee brace calipers, strapped me in and made me stand next to the bar counter, where I could hold the handrail. Cinderella had her glass slippers, and I had my calipers.

I asked the DJ to play my favourite song at the time: '*Dus Bahane Karke Le Gaye Dil*'. Then he played a song dedicated to me: '*You Are My Superstar*'.

That evening, I really did feel like a superstar.

The owner of the club came over to meet our group, and we all had drinks on the house. The DJ became a friend and regularly invited us to his gigs. Of course, we went, and of course, everywhere we went, we got at least one round of drinks on the house.

Our outings began to include picnics and movies. We became our own little family, celebrating together, working out together, going out together and, most importantly, learning together.

Virendra and Namita asked us to make a wish list of all the things we wanted to do but felt we couldn't because of the paralysis. For some of us, these were new adventures; for others, these were things we used to do and missed dearly: having kulhad chai at the nukkad-wala tapri or going to a dhaba and sitting on a charpai there for a meal of dal makhni and tandoori roti. Virendra and Namita went to great lengths to make as many of these possible for us as they could.

What they were doing was preparing us for the real world. They wanted us to enjoy life's simple pleasures without limitations. Sitting on a charpai at a dhaba may have seemed impossible for us—charpais don't have a mattress, and the rope webbing could cause rashes and spasms. But they showed us that with some foresight—carrying a gel cushion with us and a backrest frame—everything was possible.

This is what the workshop aimed to do: equip us with the skills we needed not to miss out on anything, ensuring our lives remained as uninterrupted by our paralysis as possible.

I was a quick learner and picked up all the tricks they taught us. To use a motoring analogy, I had a high-performance battery, but the surgery had left my battery low. All I needed was a way to jump-start it again. That's what the six weeks at the ISIC provided: a jump-start to my life.

At thirty-five, I felt like the eighteen-year-old Deepa, for whom the whole world was her oyster.

11

Swimming Against the Tide

W HEN I RETURNED TO AHMEDNAGAR AFTER MY six weeks at the ISIC, I settled into my old routine: beginning my day with shopping trips to the local wholesale market for fresh produce for Dee's Place and ending it by shutting for the night.

The difference, however, was in my attitude. I now knew that there was a whole world out there beyond our small town of army officers and retirees, and I felt compelled to break away from the easy routine that defined my life.

I made changes at Dee's Place, starting with incorporating my exercise routine into the daily operations. Instead of finding a gym, I turned Dee's Place into my playground. Before we opened for customers, we would spend an hour cleaning the place and setting up. The boys would wash and wipe down every glass, plate and piece of cutlery, and then lay the tables—an admittedly tedious job. To keep things interesting, I incentivized the process—whoever did the best job could skip this task the next day and help me with my physiotherapy instead. My focus was on building my upper-body strength. We'd start by playing a game like catch. I had a set of parallel bars and would need help while I did pull-ups. This, too, we turned into a competition among customers to see who could hold a pull-up for the longest time, rewarding the winner with a free milkshake or juice. My Formula 1 racetrack with toy cars and toy cycles had already become a big hit. I offered a lot of freebies for kids—my mother would buy handmade wooden toys in bulk from Jaipur, and I would hand these out with the food.

The time I spent at Dee's Place saved me from losing my mind. My days were filled with work, physical activity and ample social interaction—far from an isolated, bedridden life. What gave me the most satisfaction was knowing that despite being in a wheelchair, despite being 'disabled', I was making a difference to the lives of all my employees. These young men might not have had such opportunities otherwise. My customers knew that the staff ate at the restaurant, so they often donated rations for their meals. Some even organized medical check-ups for them—this was how we discovered Draupadi had a heart condition. And they received more than charity, also getting training opportunities and job interviews.

As the summer months came upon us, I decided to get back to swimming. I had done hydrotherapy at the ISIC, which had dispelled any shyness. I no longer hesitated to seek help from complete strangers to get into the pool. The pool I frequented was also used by the Mechanised Infantry Regimental Centre (MIRC) swimming team. Often, I would ask them to lower me into the water. Initially, they hesitated—I was an officer's wife after all. But they got over their hesitation and even mentioned my swimming, despite my paralysis, to their own coach. Talk of this spread through the MIRC and reached a clerk posted there. This was LDC Vilas Dhawane, who lived with polio. He was a para athlete who competed in powerlifting.

One day at the pool, the MIRC swim coach told me that Vilas was keen to meet me. I told him that he could come to our house any time. But Vilas was apprehensive about going to the house of a general. We decided to meet at Dee's Place instead.

It was that evening at the restaurant that Vilas showed me the path that would eventually lead me to Rio. He told me to connect with the District Paralympics Committee and prepare for the upcoming nationals that were to be held in July.

This was exactly the opportunity I had been waiting for. I promptly registered with the District Paralympics Committee and learnt their requirements for the swimming nationals. I had to swim for 50 m at a stretch, doing either a breaststroke or backstroke. This was a challenge, but I was determined.

I could not be in cold water for a long time. To work around this, I began to go to the Cavalier Lagoon Swimming Pool at the Armoured Corps Centre and School in the warm afternoons, around 3 p.m., when the pool was far less busy.

I soon realized that I didn't have enough stamina to complete 50 m without a break. Fortunately, I met and trained under the late Coach Ramdas Dhamale, who taught me the breathing techniques to help increase my stamina.

This marked the beginning of my journey in para sports.

While I was embracing new challenges and forging a new path for myself, there was a big upheaval in my personal life. Bikram was commanding his regiment and needed to attend a course in Mhow. Mhow was also where my brother's in-laws lived, with whom I shared a close bond.

For me, this move meant a potential escape from the stagnation I felt in Ahmednagar.

One day, a regimental officer mentioned to me in passing that now that Bikram was going to the Indian Institute of Management, he would begin to earn in crores.

This piece of information hit me like a ton of bricks. I had no inkling that Bikram and I would not be going to Mhow. I had absolutely no idea that at a time when we needed money, he was thinking of leaving the army and going to management college.

Before we could even discuss this, Bikram resigned from his command halfway through his tenure. He came home, and I left for the Nationals.

At the Nationals I qualified for the 9th FESPIC Games (Far East and South Pacific Games for the Disabled) to be held in Kuala Lumpur, Malaysia. This was a major multidiscipline event for para sports in the Asia-Pacific region, and the 2006 edition was to be its last. There were very few participants in my category, chest-below paralysis, and I was the only Indian woman.

The trials were overseen by Dr V.K. Dabas, who pioneered the National Para Swimming Championships in India in 1996, starting with just four children with polio. He was based at the Lakshmibai National Institute of Physical Education (LNIPE) in Gwalior. He was the one who told me that qualifying for the FESPIC Games was just the beginning; I would now have to attend the camp at the LNIPE to prepare seriously for the FESPIC Games, which were just a few months away.

Eager to take on this challenge, I returned to Ahmednagar and promptly got my passport made in anticipation of going to Malaysia.

Back home in Ahmednagar, there was another surprise awaiting me. Bikram's name was not in the list of retiring officers selected for the executive MBA programme at IIM Ahmedabad, a part of the Indian Army's resettlement initiative.

Our hopes of financial security in the future went up in smoke. Just as I felt ready to fly, I found weights tied to my feet. After the initial shock, I shifted into problem-solving mode.

I found the phone number of the officer in charge of allotting seats for the resettlement courses at the Directorate General of Resettlement. I called him and explained that despite being a Staff College-qualified officer, my husband had stepped down from command as I was a case of repetitive tumours. I requested that the least the Indian Army could do was give him the opportunity to be equipped to support me and our daughters.

Something I said to the officer must have had an impact, because when the final list of officers going to IIM Ahmedabad came out, Bikram's name was on it, albeit written in pen at the bottom of the list.

We now prepared for Bikram to go to Ahmednagar and for me to go to Malaysia.

There was, however, a cost to this opportunity.

The history of para sports in India is full of stories of struggle. Just as para athletes struggled with their individual challenges, the Paralympic Committee of India struggled to find official recognition. Despite significant achievements, like Devendra Jhajharia's gold medal in javelin at the 2004 Athens Paralympics, recognition remained elusive. Devendra, whose left hand was amputated after a childhood accident, was propelled into sports by the Dronacharya awardee coach R.D. Singh in 1997. India had won its first Paralympics gold in 1972 when Murlikant Petkar created a record in swimming. Yet the national body for para sports, created in 1992, was still not treated at par with the federations associated with able-bodied sports.

As a college student, my mother Vishna Kapoor (extreme left), popularly called Veena, was in the National Cadet Corps and even commanded her college's NCC contingent in the early sixties. I get my confidence from her and the upbringing she gave me.

My parents Col. Bal Krishan Nagpal and Veena, a few days after their wedding.

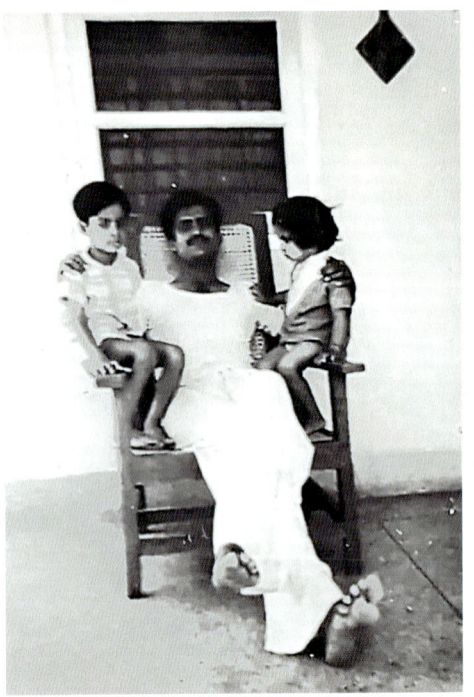

My elder brother Vikram (left) and me (right) with our father, spending an idyllic afternoon in one of our regular storytelling sessions which helped build my moral fabric and form the fondest memories of my time with him. This was a few years before I fell ill in my childhood.

Vikram and me (on the tricycle). My love for bikes was evident even as a toddler.

1986 was the first time in Kendriya Vidyalaya, Fort William, Calcutta (now Kolkata), that I, a girl, that too from the humanities stream, was elected school captain. It was at this school that I formed some of the most enduring friendships of my life.

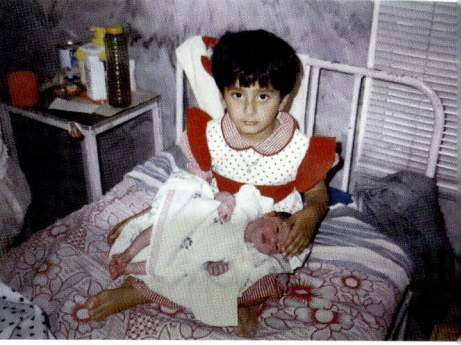

Devika holding baby Ambika. Devika, whose left side was paralysed after a childhood accident, would not use her left hand much. But with the arrival of Ambika, her recovery became faster as she willed herself to use both her hands just so she could hold her baby sister.

Posing for Bikram's camera on our first date at Sukma Dukma dam near Babina

As newly weds, we explored the tourist spots around Babina, the first place we made our home after marriage. Here we are on a trip to Khajuraho to celebrate my first birthday post marriage. Bikram is wearing the trademark khaki dungarees he usually wore on long rides and had been wearing when he surprised me at Sophia College, Ajmer, in the early days of our courtship

In Wellington, my severe backache meant that I could not join the ladies for walks. But my driving the Tata Estate became a boon for them as I would take them around in the hills and drive their kids to school when the buses were not plying.

In the last pageant that I walked in, I won the first runner-up award. It was at the Defense Services Staff College in Wellington during the Navy Queen pageant. Here I am accepting the sash at the crowing ceremony.

One of the prizes I won in the Navy Queen pageant was a holiday in Kovalam. This is a picture of me with Devika, Bikram and Ambika at Kovalam Beach, my last holiday walking. The pressure from the undetected spinal tumour made me favour my right leg and I had taken to standing with my left leg bent like this, not wanting to put weight on it.

Dee's Place in Ahmednagar was more than a restaurant—it was where I was able to create a new identity for myself after paralysis; one that was not restricted to a bed in a 10x10 room.

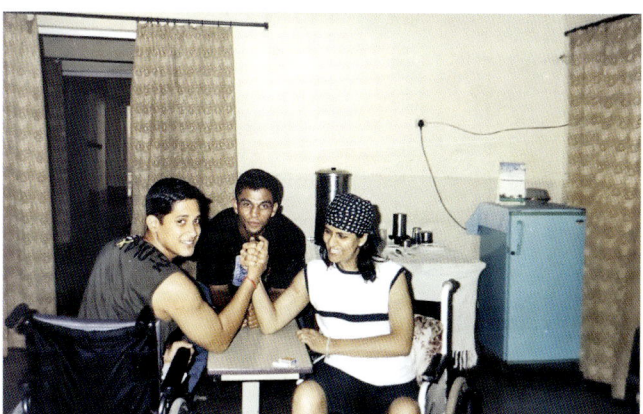

Shubhjit had become a paraplegic while in the National Defence Academy and his course-mates, who were now in Ahmednagar as part of the ACCS YO-115 course, connected us. Shubhjit (left) told me about the Indian Spinal Injuries Centre in Delhi and the advanced physiotherapy methods available for active wheelchair living.

With Rajesh Lathia, a fellow para athlete affected by polio, at the FESPIC Games in Malaysia, the first international games that I participated in. Though I placed second in my swimming event, I did not get a medal, only a certificate. On our return to India, Rajesh, who had won a silver medal in his field event, presented his medal to me, marking the beginning of a lifelong friendship. He later trained Devika as well.

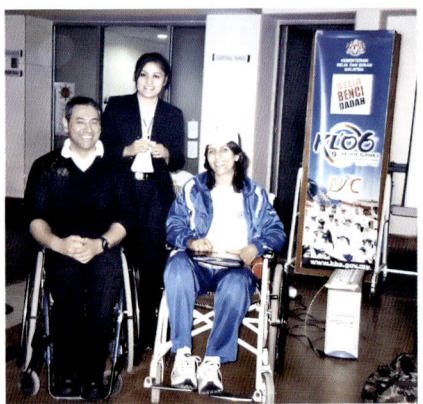

Arun Sondhi, an Indian-origin paraplegic who had migrated to Sweden, had represented his adopted country in the Paralympics and rode customized bikes there. After meeting him, I pledged to do the same in my India. In the centre is psychologist Namita Bhutani, whose sessions shattered the myths around professional psychological counseling, and I became more comfortable in my skin. In this picture, I am meeting them again after my return from the FESPIC Games, to thank them and deliver a lecture to spinal-cord–injury patients at the Indian Spinal Injuries Centre. It is important for our tribe to pass on the baton of experience-sharing.

At Gau Ghat in Prayagraj (then Allahabad), others do a victory lap, but I got to do a victory lift. Soon after creating the record for being the only woman with chest-below paralysis to swim upstream in an open river, I am being carried out of the Yamuna in my wheelchair.

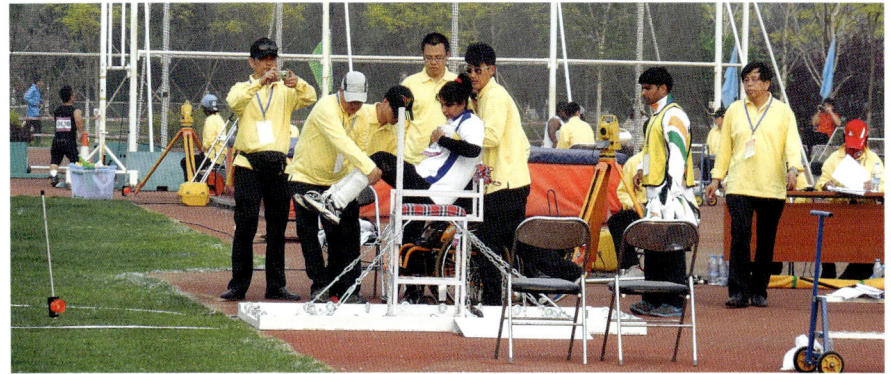

The effort that it takes to move from the wheelchair to the throw frame. I am being lifted by four volunteers as Rajesh looks on from behind (in the tricolour sleeve). Later, a new rule was introduced and now only the para athlete's competition partner can assist the transfer.

Perseverance was the key to getting my 'dream bike'. KRP had to give in and customize a bike for me.

The record-making bike ride was shifted out of Mumbai due to the 26/11 terror attacks to Nashik.

I am a firm believer in manifestations. When I worked towards being a biker again in paraplegia, I had targeted being on MTV Roadies, riding along with John Abraham, being part of motorcycling fraternities like xBhp and with my hard work, achieved all of it.

At the Opening Ceremony of the Commonwealth Games 2010 in Delhi at the Jawaharlal Nehru Stadium. Devika is wheeling me as Abhinav Bindra leads the Indian contingent. It was at this same venue in 1982 that I had witnessed the Opening Ceremony of the Asian Games as a child and the seeds of a desire for sporting greatness were sown. This was another occasion when life came full circle for me.

I was adorned with the pink turban generally reserved as a mark of respect for men, at the award ceremony of the Shiv Chhatrapati Maharashtra State Sports Awards in Balewadi, Pune. My mother-in-law Satya Malik, husband Bikram and father-in-law Maj. Gen. B.S. Malik are with me, along with an official of the Maharashtra Government Sports Department.

With Prateek Gahlaut (standing second from left) as my competition partner at the Asian Para Games in 2010. Prateek, recovering from his own biking injury, had found a lot of inspiration from my journey. After CWG, Devika had to go back for her college exams, and he volunteered to accompany me.

The pain of missing the London Paralympics was somewhat mitigated when I was presented the Arjuna Award by then President Pranab Mukherjee in 2012.

With Sanjay Sharma, popularly known as Hardy Sir (JK Tyres Motorsports). He helped me in battling the challenge of the exorbitant entry fees for the Desert Storm car rally and subsequently, with media coverage to help spread my message.

I dared to dream and challenge myself to prove that it is mind over body. Every high altitude pass I drove across during my record-making drive left me on a high of self-worth.

Aiming for the sun. Learning the skill of javelin throw at forty years of age made me not only the first Indian woman to win the Asian Para Games para athletics medal, but also a para athlete to win three consecutive Asian medals creating a new Asian record each time (Asian Para Games 2010, 2014 and 2018). Practicing my javelin throw at Jawaharlal Nehru Stadium

Though I created a new Asian record in my F-53 category, I still had to settle for a silver medal as we were competing in combined category class. At the podium in the Incheon Asian Games in 2014.

No medical problem can stop me from feeling beautiful. I may not have walked the ramp after Wellington, but I have wheeled myself down the ramp in many a fashion show since. Here I am, as a showstopper for jewellery designer Akkash K. Aggarwal at the India Runway Week in 2015, making a statement for inclusion.

I always choose to be with those who help me stay positive and emotionally robust. Devika and Sarandeep do just that. This photo is from the day my biker friends did an all-the-best rally for me just before leaving for the Rio Paralympics.

The silver medal–winning throw at Rio. I was in the zone, internalizing the thought of safeguarding my integrity and honesty to my preparations of shot-put, and threw with all my might to cross the 4.48 m mark for which I had been taken to the high court. I won my Paralympic medal with a throw of 4.61 m.

With Prime Minister Narendra Modi at the celebratory reception for the Paralympic contingent at his residence, on our return from Rio in 2016. The reception was a moment of transformation for para sports in India—it was the first time in the history of Indian sports that a prime minister was meeting the Paralympic contingent on par with the Olympic contingent. It marked the mainstreaming of para sports in India.

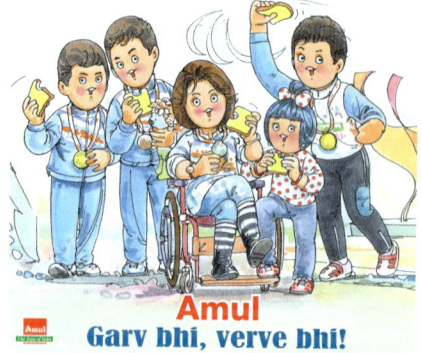

The Amul billboard that greeted me after I won silver at Rio 2016. Another full circle in my life—I had made an Amul girl cake for my daughter on her sixth birthday and now here I was, in my forty-sixth year, featuring next to the Amul girl herself, on billboards all over India.

The cake I made for Ambika on her sixth birthday inspired by the Amul girl.

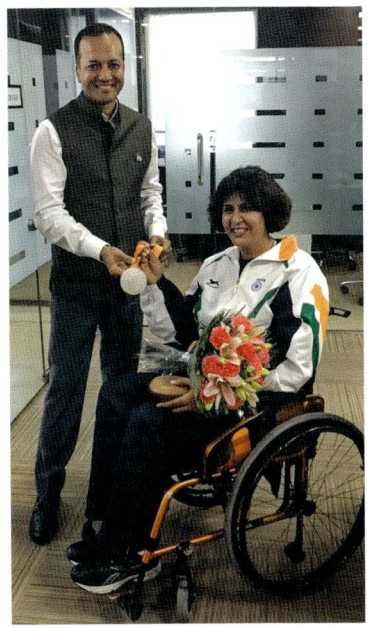

It was an emotional moment when my father Col. Nagpal welcomed me at Indira Gandhi International Airport after my victorious return from Rio. It was due to his untiring efforts that I recovered from my childhood illness and grew up to be the woman I am.

With member of parliament and industrialist Naveen Jindal. Jindal Steel supported me when I was at my lowest financially, by offering me regular motivational speaking assignments.

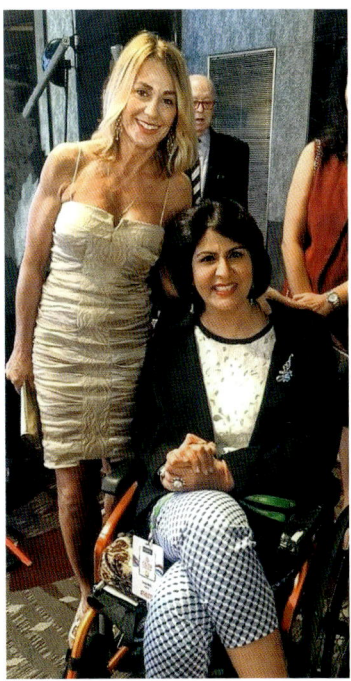

Mr Satyanarayana (in pink shirt), athlete and sports administrator, was one of the first to see the spark in me. He made me the torchbearer at the IWAS World Games in Bangalore in 2009 when I was still a relative newcomer.

With my childhood inspiration Nadia Comaneci. As a fifth-grade student, reading about her perfect ten in my Hindi text book had lit the fire within me and meeting her during the Times of India Sports Awards ceremony in 2017 was another full circle in my life.

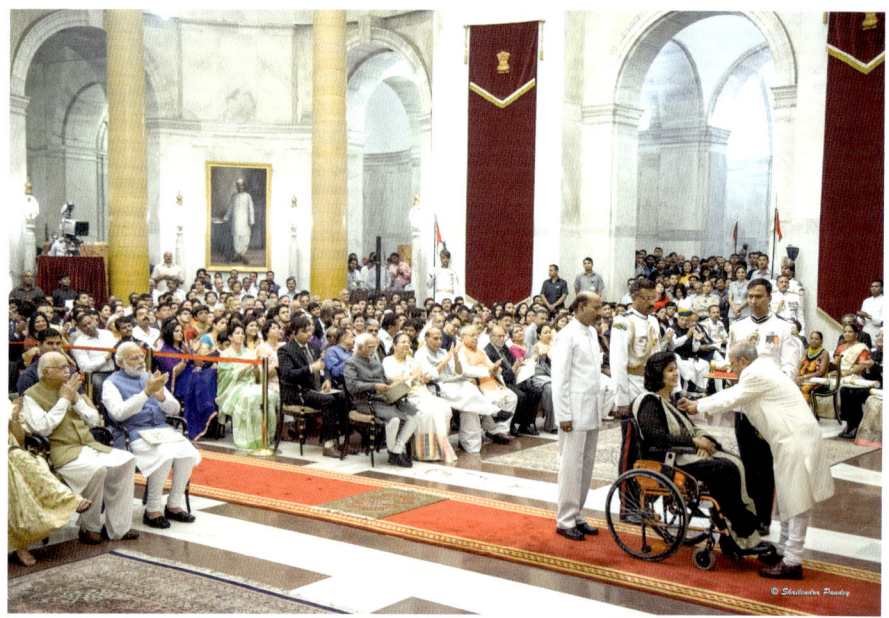

I received the Padma Shri award in 2017, for service to sports and society.

I received the Khel Ratna in 2019. My father had hoped to see my name—Deepa Malik—alongside Sakshi Malik and Deepa Karmakar in 2016 post Rio. To fulfil his dream, I had to continue to work hard and win more medals for my country, finally receiving the award in 2019, post his demise. I know he smiled from the heavens above.

My daughter and I are giving back by enabling underserved people with disabilities through our NGO Wheeling Happiness, a Deepa Malik foundation. During COVID lockdowns, we arranged food packets to be regularly distributed to people in need.

As NDMC brand ambassador, I have used every platform to spread awareness about ability beyond disability. I continue to collaborate with physiotherapist Dr Virendra Vikram Singh (in beige suit) and Shivjeet Raghav (in wheelchair) regularly to empower many more people with disabilities. Also in the picture is Dr Ramesh Kumar, senior NDMC official.

Standing tall even in my wheelchair, as the first female president of the Paralympic Committee of India with Prime Minister Narendra Modi, former Sports Minister Anurag Thakur and heads of the various sporting federations of India, including Mr. Adille Sumariwalla (president, AFI). Mr Sumariwalla had helped to get media attention to my appeals for disability inclusion in the early days. I'm proud to have shared the same platform of sports-administration responsibilities with him over a decade later.

The first Indian woman and para athlete to be unanimously nominated by the Asian Paralympic Committee governing board as the representative of South Asian countries in the APC executive board.

I couldn't have ended my active sporting career on a better note than at the 2018 Asian Para Games, Jakarta, with both my lovely daughters Devika (left) and Ambika (right) beside me. I won two medals and dedicated one to each, symbolizing my gratitude for their unconditional love and support.

Though we were a strong contingent going for the FESPIC Games, we had to pay some component of the expenses ourselves. I was expected to pay Rs 49,000. Meanwhile, Bikram was to leave for his MBA, and had to spend Rs 60,000 for a laptop. His retirement paperwork remained incomplete, and we found ourselves without any income or Bikram's pension.

With all these concerns playing on my mind, I reached the LNIPE, Gwalior, for the preparatory camp. With the help of Vice Chancellor Maj. Gen. Shibnath Mukherjee, I was able to get a guest room to stay in for the duration of the camp. I had with me Sandeep, my employee from Dee's Place who had also gone with me to Delhi for the six weeks at the Indian Spinal Injuries Centre.

Dr Dabas, the dean, oversaw our swimming training. His journey into para sports training was born from a personal tragedy. His daughter suffered from cerebral palsy due to a severe bout of jaundice suffered as a newborn. While on a two-and-a-half-year government-sponsored fellowship to study the science of sports training in East Germany, he learnt about para sports and specifically about aqua therapy and its benefits in the rehabilitation of amputees, people with cerebral palsy, visually impaired people and those with paralysis. When he returned to India, he tried the techniques he had learnt on his three-and-a-half-year-old daughter. Encouraged by her improvement, Dr Dabas created a programme for para swimming. He approached an NGO, Amar Jyoti Sansthan, caring for polio-affected children. He started with four children from this NGO and that number soon grew to 90 as news of the benefits of aqua therapy spread. In 2000, he organized the first national-level para swimming championship. Now, he was training me.

Attending this camp was crucial—it was the first time that I was going to put to test all that I had learnt at the ISIC about living an active wheelchair life. I needed help getting in and out of my wheelchair, but once I was in the lying position, I could take care of myself. I had made pouches with all my essentials: underwear, medicines, diapers, sanitizer, urine bag, Dettol, clothes. I would ask Sandeep to lay the pouches out for me on the bed. This allowed me to reach for what I needed without anyone having to handle my personal items, soiled clothing or used diapers.

We were flying out of Bangalore for the FESPIC Games. I arrived in the city and stayed in an army guest room arranged by a classmate of mine who was posted there.

Before we left, we were given a grand send-off at the Vidhan Soudha, the seat of the Karnataka government. We were asked to pose for a photo-op in front of the grand building, dressed in our official Team India tracksuits. I had carried my tracksuit; now there was the matter of finding a place to change into it. A nearby gym seemed like my best bet.

As I wheeled myself into the gym to change, a voice stopped me. 'Women are not allowed here,' the man said.

If looks could kill, he would have dropped from the stare I gave him. 'Keep quiet. Don't mess with me,' I shot back.

'Who are you?' he asked me, taken aback by my assertiveness.

'I'm in the India team. Who are you?' I countered. Before he could reply, I continued, 'I'll come there and set you right if you don't stop hassling me.'

With that exchange, I got ready and left. He had no idea that I was once again the super-confident Deepa of Sophia College, bubbling with energy and pride to be going abroad for the first time, carrying the faith of the nation, representing my country.

Later I learnt that the stout strongman I had tangled with was Farman Basha, India's para powerlifting champion. Affected by polio as a one-year-old, he needed calipers and a wheelchair for mobility. He had recently made headlines by winning a gold medal in an event for able-bodied powerlifters. This feat had left the able-bodied federation red-faced, and they had then proceeded to change the rules and barred disabled powerlifters from competing in such events.

At the airport, I was faced with a challenge I had not foreseen. I had foolishly assumed that all of us para athletes would get attendants or volunteers to help us navigate the practical hurdles of travel and adjust to the challenges of moving around in a new city. This did not end up being the case.

As I sat in my wheelchair at the airport entrance, surrounded by other members of my contingent, the reality of our situation struck me. I looked around, trying to catch the eye of any contingent officials to ask them to wheel me and my luggage into the airport. But no one glanced my way. Everyone was busy looking out for themselves.

My gaze settled on a young man, six feet tall, clad in our team tracksuit, looking as lost as I felt. With him were his parents, who had come with him all the way from Pilibhit in Uttar Pradesh to see him off before his first international competition.

Their anxiety was palpable; they were uncertain about letting their visually impaired son, who had not yet mastered the use of a cane, go alone. I wheeled myself towards them and offered to help him if he helped me.

They readily agreed, grateful that their son would be in the care of an English-speaking woman, even though I was in a wheelchair.

The young man was Hitesh Sachdeva. A tragic road accident, when he was just a teenager, had robbed him of his sight. He had collided with a truck while riding a motorbike, and though he had emerged otherwise fairly unscathed, he suffered irreversible damage to his eyes and lost his vision completely.

What a sight we must have been that day at the Bangalore airport. It was still a few years before everyone had smartphones with cameras; otherwise, we definitely would have gone viral. There I was in my wheelchair, pushing the luggage trolley loaded with our bags, while he was behind me, pushing my wheelchair. I directed Hitesh, telling him when to go straight or turn left or right.

He acted as my legs and I his eyes. And that's how we reached Kuala Lumpur.

☙

On the swim team with me were Kanchanmala Pande, who was visually impaired, and Rajni Jha, affected by polio. We were assigned to share a room.

Kanchanmala was a lovely young girl, blind from birth and untrained in the use of a cane. Despite her visual impairment, she had sharpened her other senses to such an extent that she navigated spaces with the confidence of someone with perfect vision.

She entered the room we were to share before us. '*Ruko, pehle mujhe kamra dekhne do*' (Stop, let me first *see* the room),' she said.

She walked in, counted how many steps it took to get to the bathroom and to her bed, and mapped the room by feeling the walls to figure out the layout. Once she had familiarized herself with the space, she gave us the green signal to enter. She had her systems in place. Her clothes had a thread knot sewn on to the labels, so she could pick out her tracksuit from a pile of similar clothes.

Rajni Jha was average height. She came from a humble background. I remember, she had a very cheerful smile and was a positive person. I can never forget her smile. She wore her long hair in plaits.

Now, she's moved from swimming to canoeing and has a government job. She won the highest state sport award from MP.

They were both the same age as my daughters, and we soon formed a close bond.

The first day of the Games was for getting our medical categories verified by the Games officials. In para sports, these categories are complicated but crucial. Miscommunication about the degree of disability or inadequate medical documentation can lead to an athlete being placed in the wrong category, which could dramatically affect their chances of competing fairly. For instance, an athlete with a more significant disability might be disadvantaged if placed in a category with athletes who have less significant disabilities. Conversely, an athlete with a lesser disability could unfairly benefit from being placed in a category meant for those with more severe disabilities. To prevent this kind of uneven playing field, the process of medical classification is rigorous.

As we waited for the categories to be announced, one member of our contingent broke down. Sukanta Das of Tripura had been medically disqualified—his disability was deemed 'not serious enough' for him to participate in the Games. He had put in so much effort to train and raise the money for the travel to Kuala Lumpur— all for nothing. His distress, his heartbreak, affected us all.

We were all fighting our own battles at the FESPIC Games. I struggled with mobility. I had no one to wheel me around and my wheelchair was too heavy for me to manoeuvre it on my own.

Hitesh had been a great help till we arrived in Kuala Lumpur. But his coach did not deem it appropriate for him to be my wheelchair pusher, arguing that pushing my chair would fatigue the muscles he needed for his own field event. All the athletes had to look out for themselves, he said, delivering a spiel about a boy who had lost his chance at a medal at a previous international meet in Rio because he had tired himself out by pushing someone else.

My mental strength had lasted a long time, but now, I had reached breaking point. I felt so totally alone and helpless. In tears, I had a showdown with my coach and accused him of not taking care of me or helping me.

Word of our exchange spread among the Indian contingent. During one dinner, I had met Sukhbir Masterji from Bhiwani. We had connected as my cousin was married to the niece of former Haryana Chief Minister Bansi Lal. This Haryana connection was enough for Masterji to come to my rescue. He rallied the other Haryana para athletes, urging them to protect me.

Rajesh Lathia, who was from a village close to my husband's in the district of Sonipat, stepped forward to address the issue. He came to 'talk' to my coach along with three other boys and told him in no uncertain terms that I was to be treated with care. 'She is our bhabhi,' he said. 'Think carefully before you make her cry again. Any further problems and you will have to answer to us.'

He later reassured me. 'Beta, bhai, devar—you can call me anything you like. But just know that I am there for you.'

Suddenly, I was no longer the outsider, no longer the privileged English-speaking madam. I was one of them. I belonged. From that day forward, I always had one of the Haryana boys by my side.

The day of my competition arrived soon—the 50 m backstroke. My particular disability category is so rare that I had no direct competitors. In para sports, if such a situation arises, then two or more categories are merged. This was to my disadvantage as I, with chest-below paralysis, was competing with swimmers with less severe disabilities.

Despite the odds, I came second.

Unfortunately, there was another rule that went against me. In events with only a few participants, medals are awarded only to first place. Second and third place are given certificates. Despite deserving a silver medal, I received just a certificate.

My spirits were dampened. I had so wanted a medal as proof of my achievement. There had been so many people back home who had doubted me, who had tried to hold me back, who had sniggered at me. My medal was meant to justify everything: my time away from home, the strenuous training camp, flying to a foreign country, leaving my daughters behind.

To distract myself, I began spending more time with the Haryana boys who had been helping me. I began to understand and enjoy their events—shot put, javelin and discus throw.

One day, I heard a loud and cheerful 'Good evening, ma'am' in the lobby of the hotel we were staying at. I turned to see a young man marching briskly towards me. I recognized him as one of the officers who had frequented Dee's Place. He was a Sri Lankan officer who had attended the Young Officers course in Ahmednagar. Bikram had been his instructor. An amputee with a prosthetic leg, he was here to compete in archery. As we caught up, he fondly remembered the special pains I would take for him while he was homesick for Sri Lankan food. He recalled the fish I would cook specially for him—full of spices, coconut and curry leaves, instead of the ubiquitous coriander, which was as close as he could get to home cooking. It was now his turn to repay my good deed for him. As an officer, the

Sri Lankan embassy had given him a car for the duration of the Games. He offered me full use of the car. Since my event was over, I began playing the role of intrepid tourist from the very next day. I went to the theme park Genting Highlands and enjoyed every ride, including the roller coaster. I roamed the flea markets of Kuala Lumpur, shopping for myself and my girls: skirts, tops, lacy gloves, hair accessories—things I thought they would like.

When we touched down in Delhi, it was Rajesh who pushed my wheelchair this time. We had grown quite close over the course of the Games. The silver medal he'd won in his category proudly hung around his neck. He was going to go home to Sonipat by road, and I had planned to take a flight to Jaipur to meet Devika, who was studying there, before returning to Ahmednagar.

As we said our goodbyes, my tears spilled over. I could control them no longer. Rajesh reassured me, telling me that he was my brother and that whenever I needed him, all I had to do was call. His words only made me cry harder.

I don't know what came over him, but without giving it a second thought, he took off his silver medal and put it around my neck. 'You have put in so much hard work, so much effort. You cannot go back without a medal. You deserve it. You won it.'

That was how my brother from Haryana gave me a send-off I can never forget.

I was waiting for my flight to Jaipur, when a young woman in the striking red Kingfisher Airlines uniform approached me with a clipboard in hand. 'Are you taking the Kingfisher flight to Jaipur?' she asked.

'Yes,' I confirmed.

'Ma'am, could you please sign this form?' she asked, proffering the clipboard and holding out a pen.

I had a look. It was a standard indemnity form. But there was a term in it that made me see red: 'wheelchair patient'.

'I will not sign this. I'm not a wheelchair patient. I'm a sportsperson who has just represented India internationally. I'm wearing the Team India tracksuit. I have a medal around my neck. And you are denigrating my achievement by labelling me a patient. I refuse to sign any such form,' I said.

The young woman was totally flustered. Nothing in her training had prepared her for this kind of situation. After staring at me for a moment, mouth agape, she said, 'Ma'am, if you don't sign this form, we will be unable to allow you to board.'

At this, I completely lost my cool. The cumulative stress of the FESPIC Games, where I had acutely felt my disability at every juncture—having to beg for assistance, being unfairly categorized, losing a rightful medal—boiled over.

'If you dare deny me boarding, I'll call the media right now. Then we'll see how Kingfisher—"the king of good times"—gets out of being in the headlines for off-loading an international athlete,' I replied, ready for the fight.

It was crucial to me that she, and everyone else, realized that not all wheelchair users are patients. A wheelchair is an assistive device, an aid for an active lifestyle for people post-recovery from medical setbacks. It is a symbol of activity, not of restriction. Just as everyone who wears spectacles is not blind, everyone who is in a wheelchair is not a patient.

Clearly overwhelmed, the young woman kept trying to cajole me, but I dug my heels in. 'If you want me to sign this form as a patient, then get every passenger on the flight to also sign this form stating their medical conditions, whether it's a heart condition or high blood pressure or anything that might affect their health during air travel,' I countered.

I now insisted that the manager be called, but instead of a face-to-face conversation, I got a phone call. 'Ma'am, please sign the form. It's a Directorate General of Civil Aviation requirement. We cannot allow you on board unless you sign it,' he said.

'And *you* cannot treat people with disabilities like this. I strongly object to the use of the word "patient",' I told him.

After a lot of back and forth, he agreed to replace the word 'patient' with 'passenger', and I took the flight.

But that was not the end of it. While onboard, I opened my laptop and drafted a complaint detailing how insensitive it is to label wheelchair users as patients. As soon as I landed, I sent the email to Kingfisher's customer care and all the top brass of the company.

This email of mine would have a great impact for all future wheelchair flyers, as well as for me personally.

I returned to Ahmednagar feeling like a victorious warrior back from a conquest. And I was welcomed as such. My achievement was acknowledged by everyone, starting with the Army Wives Welfare Association (AWWA). The commandant of the Armoured Corps Centre and School at the time was Maj. Gen. J.P. Singh. His wife, Rita, invited me to share my experiences with the families of our officers and troops posted there.

I spent considerable time preparing, making a PowerPoint presentation with lots of images.

Given that my audience comprised women, many of whom were mothers, I tailored my talk to resonate with them.

The first set of slides showed me with my girls before my surgery and after my paralysis. It was titled 'A Mother Then, a Mother Now'.

The next lot was named 'A Wife Then, a Wife Now', and continued with 'A Homemaker Then, a Homemaker Now' and 'A Sportswoman Then, a Sportswoman Now'.

My core message was that the paralysis and use of a wheelchair had in no way made me any less of a woman. It was a story of overcoming the challenges life had thrown my way, not a sob story but one of courage. It was a story of how I had a beautiful life as an army wife before my surgery and how I had refused to let my paralysis snatch that away from me, how I had reclaimed it, bit by bit.

But it was the last slide that was most important to me. It showed me on a bike and was titled 'A Biker Then ...', followed by a blank slide. I ended on a hopeful note, promising to one day fill that blank slide, the day I reclaimed that particular role in my life.

I had got into para sports as a way of finding a life outside Ahmednagar, but my dream was to become a biker again.

Rita Singh presented me with a cheque of Rs 21,000 in recognition of my achievement. That cheque provided the means for my first holiday post-paralysis.

The last holiday our family had enjoyed together had been after I won the pageant at Staff College in Wellington. The prize was an all-expenses-paid vacation to the beaches and backwaters of Kerala. This time, I chose Goa. Rajnish, a schoolmate now stationed in Goa with the army, and his wife, Shalini, planned the trip for us. We booked a cab from Ahmednagar to Mumbai, picked up my young friend Sushant and headed to the sun and sand of Goa. I spent the vacation on a recliner, sometimes on the beach and sometimes in the water. We basked in the sun and indulged in whatever we wanted to eat. It was a well-deserved break after almost a decade.

Social media connects people through a web of friendships, much like real life, where knowing one person leads to introductions to others. And so it was with Rajnish, whom I reconnected with on social media through another classmate, Raj Mohanty, the maths whiz topper of our class. Raj was now in Delhi, working as the regional head for Clear Channel Communications, a leading OOH company, and offered to help realize my bike dream by connecting me with corporations that could support my dream through their corporate social responsibility (CSR) initiatives.

I tweaked the presentation I had made in Ahmednagar for the army wives and shared it with him.

The first person Raj introduced me to was Adille Sumariwala. Adille was not only a sportsman who had represented India at the Moscow Olympics but also a sports administrator and entrepreneur involved in media and communications. I met him when he was associated with Clear Channel and the paper *Mid-Day*, at his office in Mumbai's Lower Parel. After a long conversation with me, he connected me with Hemal Ashar, a journalist at *Mid-Day*.

I had been written about earlier in the local media in Ahmednagar, but this article by Hemal created a stir. She had headlined my story 'Not Just That Lady in the Chair'. She detailed my life's journey, highlighting the challenges I had overcome to reach the international sports arena and talked about my dream of reclaiming my life as a biker.

By the time the article was published, I had already left Mumbai. While I was enroute to Ahmednagar, I got a call from renowned director Rakesh Roshan's office—his wife wanted to meet me. I suggested connecting on my next trip to Mumbai. We never did meet, but it was the next call that brought significant prospects. It was from the 'king of good times' himself, Vijay Mallya. The tycoon, who ended up in a sea of trouble, was riding the wave of success at that time. 'I read your complaint,' he began in his characteristic tone, referring to the email I had written on my flight to Jaipur.

'We are changing the language of the indemnity form,' he continued. 'We'll now be calling all wheelchair-using passengers "wheelchair guests".'

I was thrilled. This was the first change I had been able to effect that would have an impact on the dignity of wheelchair-users in the entire country. It might seem minor to most people, but for someone in a wheelchair, this shift in language was a big step towards being treated with dignity.

He invited me to attend the airlines' anniversary party in Mumbai. What a party it was, filled with celebrities, and I found myself completely enchanted. Vijay introduced me to the top brass of his group of companies, and I shared my dream with them. 'I love wheels. But don't judge me by the wheels I sit on now—these aren't the ones I chose for myself. I want my bike back. I want my dream of riding a bike again to come true.'

'Give this girl her dream,' Vijay declared.

With his encouragement, it was time for me to take things to the next level. My contacts at Clear Channel committed to following up with Vijay's marketing team. Raj Mohanty and his team chased this further and finally got me an appointment with the United Breweries (UB) team, who handled the group's sports initiatives. They in turn sent me to Bangalore to meet the Royal Challenge team, known for their sports sponsorships.

I garnered more media attention when the news channel Times Now featured me on their talk show *Life's Like That*, alongside a panel of people who had fought against the odds. They included Ambika Pillai, Terence Lewis, Kunal Kapoor and Surgeon Lt Commander Wahida Prism Khan. The Times Now crew also visited Ahmednagar and shot extensively at Dee's Place.

Dee's Place began attracting celebrity visitors. Jaideep Sen, from Rakesh Roshan's team, stopped by with the crew of *Krrish* en route to Shirdi. They invited all of us to Lonavala, where the film *Krazzy 4* was being shot. I went along with my Dee's Place boys and met Arshad Warsi, Irrfan Khan and Juhi Chawla.

I began maintaining meticulous records of all the people I met. Politicians, media persons, Bollywood celebrities, corporate leaders—I noted their contact details in my diary using my own system of shorthand to keep track of where we had met and the networking possibilities they offered.

I arrived in Bangalore for the National Para Swimming Championships. I combined that with my visit to the UB office to discuss my bike sponsorship.

I looked around in awe as I sat in their plush office, waiting for my appointment. A Formula 1 race car with a chequered flag was placed in one corner and a model Kingfisher aircraft was suspended from the ceiling—the thrill it gave me to be in an environment that celebrated my passion for wheels was indescribable. I thought about how my passion for biking had brought me to this office, and how my journey in competitive swimming was fuelled by that same passion. Everything was interconnected and everything was unfolding because I was manifesting my dreams. The power of manifestation was at work, shaping my future. And just a kilometre away from the UB office was Kanteerava Stadium, where I would soon shift from swimming to athletics. This shift would eventually lead to my crowning glory—a silver medal at the Rio Paralympics.

My reverie was cut short when I was called into my meeting. The discussion was brief: UB agreed to sponsor me. All they wanted was an invoice.

'Invoice for what?' I asked.

'For the product,' they replied.

'What product?'

'The bike—you get the bike, and we'll pay for it.'

The ball was now firmly in my court. I had to get the bike.

It was with all these thoughts running through my mind that I headed for the swimming championship. I performed well and ended up winning three gold medals—my first—and bettered all my previous timings.

I was ecstatic. Everything seemed to be moving in a positive direction. My athletic performance had improved, earning me my first golds, and my biking dream seemed to be on the way to becoming a reality. On top of that I had got so much media coverage that I was becoming a bit of a celebrity. Eager to share my happiness with Bikram, I decided to surprise him in Ahmedabad, where he was enrolled in the executive MBA programme at the Indian Institute of Management.

My dear friend Mezbeen, who had been my go-to person in Ahmednagar, once again came to my rescue. She was from Ahmedabad, and as soon as she learnt of my plan, she took charge of the arrangements. I booked my flight from Bangalore to Ahmedabad, and Janak, Mezbeen's neighbour in Ahmedabad, picked me up at the airport. It was only when I reached the gates of IIM that I finally called Bikram.

'Where are you?' I asked him.

'In my room,' he replied.

'Come to the gate. I'm here.'

That meeting brought back memories of how Bikram had landed up at the gates of the Sophia College hostel all those years ago. This time, I was the one who had surprised him.

I spent the day with him and met all his classmates. It was interesting to see a new side to Bikram. He was the student now, working on assignments, hanging out with his much younger classmates, going for movie outings. He seemed to be in a good place, but I left Ahmedabad with mixed feelings because of our precarious financial situation; he had still not started receiving his pension.

Back in Ahmednagar, I realized that to truly pursue my biking dream, I needed to be in Delhi. UB's sponsorship was promising, but I had to find a bike first. With high hopes, I arrived at the Hero Honda office in Manesar, inspired by their tagline 'the power of dreams'. It felt like fate had led me to the right place.

I presented my vision to their marketing team, requesting a custom modification of a bike.

My enthusiasm and passion, however, were met with a wall of realism and caution. They were noncommittal, and I sensed that they were not going to help me realize this dream. They were bound by intellectual property rules that prevented them from making any modifications to the original design of their bikes.

Disappointed but not disheartened, I immediately began to look for alternatives. I found out about KRP, Kaulson Racing Products, a family-run outfit specializing in bike modifications and motorsport equipment. I found their address and promptly visited their workshop in West Delhi. It was run by the Kaul family, specifically three brothers and their father.

The brothers heard me out but responded with a vague, 'We'll see what we can do.'

I was unwilling to let go—there was no way I was leaving without a firm deal. I didn't move my wheelchair.

The brothers would come and speak to me sporadically, each taking turns between their regular work. They were clearly swamped. Meanwhile, another visitor was waiting to speak to them. Bunny Punia, a journalist specializing in cars and bikes, was documenting the intricate paintwork being applied to Latin American Vespa scooters at the workshop. As he took pictures, I struck up a conversation with him, and I shared my folder of news clippings and certificates.

The wait for a commitment from the Kaul brothers stretched on, but I refused to budge. Even when my urine began to leak, I did not move. I just asked for some old newspapers and placed them under my chair.

I sat there for ten hours.

Finally, a breakthrough occurred. An older man, bearing a striking resemblance to the brothers, emerged from the back of the workshop. This was clearly the father of the 'Kaulsons'. Seeing them I was reminded of the Raj Kapoor movie *Kal, Aaj aur Kal*. The senior Kaul scolded his sons for having kept me waiting for so long.

'What can I do for you?' he asked.

'I want to be a biker again, and I've even got sponsors to back me. I need to get a modified bike so that I can ride it despite my chest-below paralysis,' I explained.

He offered me an ATV.

I refused. 'I don't want something like a jeep! I want a bike—with gears. It needs to have a backrest for support when I am strapped in. I want big headlights. I want the works.'

With this brief, Kaul and his sons agreed to start work on modifying a bike for me.

Meeting Bunny Punia opened another door for me. He wrote about my quest for wheels of my choice for the magazine *Bike India*. This article caught the eye of Cyrus Broacha from MTV. He connected me to Raghu Ram, who was handling the show *MTV Roadies*.

'I may not be a biker in the conventional sense, but I'm a biker in my soul,' I told him. 'All my life I have fought to ride. I got married to my husband because he gave me his bike to ride the very first time we met. Now, despite my chest-below paralysis, I want to get back into the driving seat. I want to use my bike to connect with the youth and change mindsets. The youngsters I can connect with will become architects and engineers—they will build an inclusive world for us.'

He promised me that the day I got my bike, he would put me on *MTV Roadies*.

Meanwhile, alongside my biking journey, my para sports journey gained momentum. While I continued swimming, I also ventured into athletics, and began practising for the javelin throw event. The International Wheelchair and Amputee Sports Games (IWAS) were coming up in Taiwan, and a two-month pre-game camp was to be held in Delhi.

I decided to shift to Delhi for these two months. I saw sports as a stepping stone to biking. I could use this opportunity to push for my bike to be made. I also wanted to get away from Ahmednagar because I realized that if I wanted to live the rest of my life, I needed to be in a place big enough for my dreams. Devika had already moved out of Ahmednagar to complete her education. If I stayed back, my life would end. With a heavy heart, I took the tough decision to leave Ambika with her grandparents and joined the camp.

I now needed a place to stay for two months. As luck would have it, the general who had recognized my commitment to the families of our troops in Jhansi during Op Parakram was now a lieutenant general and posted in Delhi as the director general of mechanized forces or DGMF. Lt Gen. D.S. Shekhawat graciously granted me permission to stay at the Sabre Mess in Delhi Cantonment for the duration of the camp.

Now that accommodation was sorted, I needed transport to take me to the camp and back every day. Here, the Kaul brothers came to my rescue. They introduced me to the family that owned Ayur Herbals, who provided me with a car and driver.

The camp itself felt like a return to my college days. Plus, being in Delhi, I reconnected with my gang from the Indian Spinal Injuries Centre. The physiotherapist who had helped me so much, Virendra Vikram Singh, was among the first people I got in touch with. Rajesh Lathia was also at the camp, and together with others on the athletics team, we practised javelin throw under Coach Naval Singh's guidance. Despite being the oldest participant, we all connected. The camp provided not just training but a much-needed sense of social integration, which had been missing in my life.

Just like Aamir Khan and his friends in *3 Idiots*, I would, in my own way, gatecrash weddings at the Sabre Mess. Whenever a wedding would take place in the lawns there, I would invite my friends over and tip the waiters to sneak some of the goodies to my room. Nobody came to know and we were able to party for next to nothing—money was tight!

Post-camp every day, I would return to my room and freshen up, then head to the Kaulson workshop to check on the progress of my bike.

My debut in the international athletics arena wasn't great. I ended up in fourth place in Taiwan. The good thing about the experience was that my medical category was fixed for international competitions at F53. I also learnt that my technique—throwing the javelin while seated on a stool—was flawed compared to the other athletes, who used a throwing frame. There had been a lack of scientific rigour in my training; I had been throwing based purely on what felt right. There were techniques that I needed to learn if I was going to do this seriously, and a two-month pre-games camp was not enough.

But what I lost on the medal board, I gained in relationships. I made a lot of friends. I interacted with officials from the international para sports bodies. I learnt about the fine print in the rule books. I networked.

But biking was still top of mind for me, so I picked up a gift for myself in Taiwan. It was a world-class helmet with ventilation systems, wide visibility and a chin guard. And I also bought a gadget used to make cars clutch-free because amid all this, I had realized the need to be more mobile and wanted to get a car modified for my use.

With the device I got from Taiwan, I decided to get a car modified in Chakan, Pune. The first step was getting a car at a concessional rate through the Canteen Stores Department, which required the car to be registered in Bikram's name. For a person with disabilities to drive a modified car, it must be registered in their name to obtain the necessary permissions. Despite this, I bought a Wagon R and sent it to the workshop for modifications.

I now needed a special licence to drive. For this, I had to submit a medical certificate indicating my fitness to drive before applying. I first got a learner's licence.

Once my car was ready, I needed to learn how to drive it. Yet again, my friends came to my aid. Rupa Gosain, a school friend, was living in Pune as her husband was posted there. I stayed with them, and Rupa's husband offered me an open ground at his location so that I could get the hang of driving with my hands. For supervision, I called Sushant. He came down from Mumbai to be my co-driver.

Happily, we came back to Ahmednagar and headed to the regional transport office (RTO) to register my modified car. While the systems have become more user-friendly now, I had to struggle for nineteen months to navigate the bureaucratic hurdles and get my car registered.

The Ahmednagar RTO said they had no category for registering vehicles modified for people with disabilities.

After having put in so much money and effort to get my car, I now faced a wall of red tape. I wrote to the head office in Mumbai and connected with Satish Sahasrabudhe to inquire about registering my vehicle.

Over a period of nineteen months, I had several meetings with Mr Sahasrabudhe. After one such meeting, I was returning to Ahmednagar in a cab, when the driver jumped a red light. Sure enough, a traffic cop stopped us. He walked to the driver's side and, without any warning, reached in and pulled out the key. He took the driver's licence and instructed him to report to the police station to pay his fine and collect the key and licence.

From the passenger seat, I pleaded with the officer, explaining that I couldn't walk and that he needed to come to my side and speak to me. But the traffic cop paid no heed and simply walked off.

I faced a predicament: my wheelchair was in the boot of the car, which needed the key to be opened. The key, however, was in the pocket of the police officer. There I was, stranded on the side of a busy Pune road, in a car with a driver who had no clue of how to transfer me and couldn't access my wheelchair.

I had got into the cab prepared for the routine two-hour journey to Ahmednagar. I was wearing a diaper and could not afford to be stuck for too long. Once again, one insensitive person had reinforced the limitations my disability forced me to live with. Once again, I had to fight a system that was challenging me at every step.

Full of rage and frustration, I dialled 100 for the second time in my life. I ranted to the operator, threatening to sue the Pune police for rendering me helpless without my wheelchair. I even threatened to call the media. The operator gave me the number of a senior police officer, Vikram Deshmane. After listening patiently, he acted promptly. The traffic cop who had taken away the key came back to return it, offering his apologies to me.

This incident stayed with me. It brought home the harsh reality of high-handed officialdom that the average Indian faces every day. These hardships multiply manifold when the person at the receiving end happens to have special needs. The need for increased awareness and sensitivity among public service officials cannot be highlighted enough.

I was now actively competing in para swimming and para athletics, specifically javelin and shot put. My performance was good across six events, consistently earning me gold medals.

In 2008, I was selected to represent India at the World Open Swimming Championships in Berlin with the para swim team.

Before the games, we had to attend a preparatory camp at the LNIPE in Gwalior. Dr V.K. Dabas was the main coach, but we had another coach, Rajesh Nishad from Allahabad, also training us. He was from the local Mallah community of boatmen, who are naturally strong swimmers.

For the duration of the camp, I stayed in army accommodation and would drive myself around in my modified car.

Here I got the opportunity to speak to some very bright young women at the Scindia Kanya Vidyalaya. The administrator there

was the father of one of our regimental officers, and he invited me
to talk to the girls. I addressed the students, sharing insights from
my own school and college days and from my athletic experiences.
I emphasized how sports had helped me navigate through life's
darkest moments.

While I received a great deal of respect at the camp, there was also
an incident that reflected a certain tone-deaf attitude people have
towards those with disabilities. A local politician paid us a visit and
distributed one apple, one banana and one packet of biscuits to each
para swimmer. I felt demeaned, like I had asked for alms. While
other countries were investing in advanced equipment for their
athletes, like a sharkskin swimsuit for Rs 25,000, our own support
felt patronizingly minimal.

Amidst our training, a crisis was brewing. The government was
paying for our tickets, but the visa fee we had to pay for ourselves.
This was coming to Rs 56,000 for the entire contingent. This group
consisted of Bhola, an autorickshaw driver with one leg, Binod
Kumar, who had no arms, and three minors, none of whom were in
a position to shoulder this expense.

In the evening, we all sat with the coaches to discuss the matter
and devise a strategy.

I suggested reaching out to the local media to spread our
story and raise funds. Dr Dabas was sceptical about whether the
media would help and also uncomfortable 'taking charity', but the
consensus among the rest of us was clear: it could be a long shot, but
it was our only shot.

I contacted the local FM radio station and connected with one of
their most popular RJs, RJ Amit, whose tagline was 'Deewana bana
doonga' (I will blow your mind). He understood the compelling

nature of our situation and interviewed me, making me the celebrity of the week for his show '*Zindagi—Vo Bhi Khoobsurat*' (Life—And That Too Beautiful).

Through the interview, we were portrayed as tenacious heroes poised for the world championships, yet tragically constrained by a lack of a few thousand rupees. The campaign unfolded over a week, with daily features of me interacting with people at popular locales. One day, I went to a local college hangout. Next, I went to an international Ramlila festival, where artistes from around the world were performing their version of the Ramayana. I met Manjula Patankar of the Roshni Ramakrishna Ashrama, who was doing phenomenal work with children with disabilities. She ended up being my guide when I set up my NGO, Wheeling Happiness.

Simultaneously, I connected with the local Rotary chapter. They became instrumental in raising the funds we needed for the visa.

Now began the race against time to get to Delhi and the German embassy because we were late. Outside the embassy, we pleaded with the guards to let us meet the person in charge. Noticing our situation, a staff member who had been working inside invited me in, heard me out and, despite the tight timeline, expedited our applications.

Berlin felt special, perhaps because getting there had been so tough. Here I was exposed to how accessible a country can be. All public transport was wheelchair-friendly. The swimming pools were heated. Everything was geared to make our lives easier, smoother, more comfortable.

My performance, however, was not up to par. I was competing with para athletes who, despite their challenges—whether due to polio or as amputees—still had the use of their lower limbs. Standing at 5'9" with weak shoulders, my body below my chest felt like a dead weight. It was at these games that I realized the need to set smart goals for myself. Rather than waste my energy in swimming, where I was fighting against my own body, I needed to focus on athletics.

Dr Dabas, who had studied in Berlin, introduced us to his classmates. On the last day of the games, we dined at an Indian restaurant. C. Raghu, the team manager from the Paralympic Committee of India, asked, 'Who performed the best at the games?'

Names like Prasanta Karmakar, Kanchanmala Pande and Binod were suggested.

Mr Raghu shook his head. 'No, it was Deepa.'

Everyone was surprised. I had only placed tenth in my event.

'Every one of you either matched or fell short of your previous times in India. Deepa is the only one to have improved her time by twenty-two seconds,' he explained.

That is how much of a difference good infrastructure can make. My time had improved purely because the swimming pools were heated.

After returning to India, I needed to stop in Gwalior to collect my car before heading to Ahmednagar. I was disappointed about going home without a medal and wanted to do something about it.

Rajesh Nishad, my coach in Gwalior, had once trained a five-year-old girl to swim in an open river. I told him that I wanted to create a Limca Record. He suggested that if I could swim in a tank without touching the sides for thirty minutes, he would be able to help me attempt a record for being the first woman to swim against the river's current.

Though Dr Dabas was not in favour of me trying this due to safety concerns, I was determined. We reached out to the Limca

Book of Records office to understand the technical requirements for creating a record.

While all the other participants of the Berlin games returned to their homes, I stayed on in Gwalior to train in earnest. Gradually, I increased the duration I could spend in the water without needing to touch the sides.

Coach Rajesh set a target: I needed to be able to swim for at least 120 minutes at a stretch. I would train in the morning, rest during the day and then go back for another round of training in the evening. This went on for forty-five days before Coach Rajesh said I was ready. I would be the first woman with chest-below paralysis to swim in the Yamuna for 1 km.

This swim would get me into the Limca Book of Records, but it was far more complex than it might appear. Swimming in open water is not the same as swimming in a pool. Plus, I had to swim upriver to qualify for the record because swimming with the current is easier—all you need to do is keep afloat and the water does all the hard work. In my case, all the weight of my 5'9" frame was on my shoulders and arms. In typical swimming, the legs assist by paddling. I had to use only my upper-body strength to pull along my entire weight.

Since Coach Rajesh was from Allahabad, it was decided that I would attempt my record in the stretch of the river there. We set the date—15 June 2008. But I planned to arrive earlier so that I could practise.

During this planning phase, I remembered the officer who had been Bikram's boss in Gurez. He had been the one who had loved my cooking and had pushed me to get my foot drag checked. He was now the deputy general officer commanding or deputy GOC in Allahabad.

He was thrilled when I called him and was eager to help but had to depart suddenly as his father had had a fall. Since he was in a rush, he handed the phone to a colonel in his formation, promising that I had their support.

I began to introduce myself to the officer but was cut short. 'Oy! I know you!' came the booming voice.

This was another instance of how life keeps coming full circle. This officer, now a colonel, was none other than the young NDA cadet to whom I had sent a card while in Kolkata—the card that had been intercepted by my brother and sent to my father, which sent me to the village right after my exams.

I had once again found friends in the unlikeliest of places. I often feel that because God has sent me so many challenges in life, he has also ensured that I find support at every tough juncture.

The colonel told me to just get myself to Allahabad and leave everything else to him. He coordinated with Coach Rajesh. When I reached the city, his wife and an officer from his unit, a young woman, came to receive me. This officer accompanied me for my practice swims in the swimming pool and was there to assist whenever I needed anything.

On my first visit to the river, I was struck by its vastness—it seemed to stretch endlessly. As my starting point, we chose Gau Ghat near the Sangam, the confluence of the Ganga, Yamuna and the mythic Saraswati rivers.

Instead of starting from the banks, I was to be lowered into the river from a point farther inside and swim 1 km upstream from there. The first plunge into the river was terrifying: the water was vast, deep and unpredictable. It was a stark contrast to the controlled environment of a swimming pool. But with Coach Rajesh's guidance, I soon adapted to these conditions. We practised every day, and then finally 15 June dawned.

Everything was in place. I had covered the expenses for the observers from the Limca Book of Records to come and stay in Allahabad. The record attempt required thorough documentation, so we had a camera team from Zee TV to cover the event, along with a local videographer. Safety measures were vital, so we had a boat within 20 metres of my swim path to ensure help if I needed it.

Then, at the very last minute, we hit a snag—I was told I also needed a doctor on standby. Getting a doctor at such short notice seemed impossible. But here, Coach Rajesh showed his resourcefulness. After a flurry of calls, we had a doctor. The catch— he was a veterinarian!

But as I commenced my attempt, another hurdle emerged. The safety boat stirred the water, creating ripples that made it difficult for me to swim. We were forced to stop my attempt.

Coach Rajesh was not fazed and came up with a brilliant plan. Being a member of the Mallah community, he had boatmen ready to rally for us. After he made some calls, a flotilla of all kinds of rowboats gathered at our location. I soon had a stationary boat positioned every 20 m along the entire 1 km I was to swim.

Everything that could have gone wrong, did. We had one more test in store, though, this time from the weather gods. The skies opened, unleashing the season's first rain—and it was a downpour.

As we deliberated whether to postpone the swim, I felt a surge of determination. I entered the water.

'Deepa, even if you touch a dead body, don't stop your hands. Keep swimming,' said Coach Rajesh. 'If you find yourself being sucked into a whirlpool, give me a signal and I'll save you.'

Now I had two more things to worry about: bodies floating in the river and whirlpools. I told myself that I wouldn't stop moving my arms even if I accidentally touched a cadaver, but the idea of the whirlpools at this confluence were harder to reckon with. If I was caught in one, my paralysed lower body would be unable to do anything to save me. I would just get sucked in.

Under these challenging conditions, I began my swim, cutting through the river diagonally against the flow of the water. When I reached the last of the boats that were marking my path, I knew that my swim was done.

But before we could celebrate, we had to wait for confirmation from the official observers.

The minute they gave us the thumbs up, the celebrations started.

On that day, 15 June 2008, I created a new record—I was the first woman in the world with chest-below paralysis to swim 1 km upstream in the Yamuna, clocking a time of thirty-five minutes and thirty-six seconds.

Now, finally, I could go home a winner.

12

Wheels of My Choice

THE SHOOT DAY OF *MTV ROADIES* DAWNED, AND MY bike was still not ready.

The idea was to feature me on the show as someone who embodied the never-say-die spirit of a true roadie. Raghu Ram, the anchor and producer, had given me the choice to select the city for my episode. They were holding auditions for the new season in all the major metros. For me, they agreed to bring the auditions to Jaipur. In fact, that was the only season they held auditions there.

I picked Jaipur not just because my parents were there but because this was the city where my passion for biking had first been ignited. It was where my cousins and I would gather to watch all the biking fanatics perform stunts. I wanted to revisit those memories.

With my bike unfinished, the Kaul brothers provided an alternative. They equipped an ATV with a customized backrest and seat belts for my use.

The episode featuring me was split into two segments: one where I rode my bike in Delhi and another where I was interviewed in Jaipur. I carefully considered my look for both events.

For the shoot on the bike, I decided on camouflage shorts, a deliberate choice to show my legs. It was a reaction to all the mainstream media representations of people in wheelchairs with a green shawl thrown over their laps. I wanted the world to see the legs of a person with paralysis.

For the on-stage interview in Jaipur, I chose black corduroy trousers paired with a coffee-coloured T-shirt adorned with gold stars. Over the years I had collected various brooches, badges and pins, which I fastened to my trousers. I also wore a black bandana and army-style dog tags to add to my biker chic look.

This was a huge moment for me, and sharing it with my parents and Devika made it that much more special. Devika was so proud of me—she invited all her friends to come and see her mom in action. My young friend Sushant also came down from Mumbai for the shoot. His words thrilled me: 'Aunty, you are a diva. You're going to rock it.'

The shoot began. The ATV was totally new to me. I had not had a chance to practise sitting on it or driving it. But once I took off, I was in my element. What a feeling it was! In that one moment, I was the sum of so many Deepas: the little kid who stood in front of her father as he drove his Lambretta, the young girl who loved stunting on the sly and who paid the price for her passion by being banished to the village, the in-love woman who fell for the first man who did not try to stop her from being in the driver's seat.

We then made our way to Jaipur, where we were greeted by a huge queue—these were the enthusiastic youngsters eager to audition for the show. As I was led to the entrance, I heard a catcall. 'Madam, *humein bhi le jao*' (Madam, take us with you). I turned and spoke to the young man who had called out to me. The crowd looked on in confusion, unsure what a woman in a wheelchair was doing at the auditions for a show renowned for its gruelling physical challenges.

I made my way into the hall and met Raghu and Rannvijay Singha. They asked me about my passion for biking. My answer was simple: being a biker was not about having the use of my legs or not;

it had nothing to do with the fact that I was paralysed below my chest; it was not about being physically tough. It was about being mentally tough. My message to the audience was not to judge me or anyone by their physical condition. God may have decided to give me a chair with wheels, but I would exchange those wheels for ones of my choice. 'My dream has always been to be a biker, and I have made that dream come true,' I said. 'So what if I need someone to lift me and put me on the bike? I'm still in the driver's seat.'

As I narrated my story, I could sense its impact on the audience. One young man stood up and said, 'Ma'am, I want to touch your feet. I came here today to become a Roadie, but now I realize it doesn't matter if I'm selected or not. Hearing your story alone has made my journey successful.'

It was the same young man who had stopped me outside, asking me to take him along. He was Ashutosh, who was not only selected but also went on to win the season. He later told me that the only reason he got the opportunity to join the show was because the organizers had held an audition in Jaipur for me. He had earlier appeared in the Delhi auditions and failed to make it. The Jaipur auditions proved lucky for him. His television success didn't stop at *Roadies*; he later won another reality show, *Bigg Boss*.

I found Rannvijay true to his on-screen personality of being a gentleman and Raghu Ram, who comes across as so rough on screen, to be the complete opposite off-screen—extremely sensitive and chivalrous to me throughout the shoot.

The shoot ended and it was time to return to real life. The episode was yet to air, so what I experienced on the drive back to Delhi wasn't something I expected at all. While digging into parathas at a dhaba named Mid-Way on the Delhi-Jaipur highway, I was mobbed by a group of youngsters. They had been at the Jaipur auditions. Their love and adulation overwhelmed me.

In that moment, I truly became a Roadie.

When my episode was finally telecast, the biggest kick I got was seeing the title sponsor of the show: Hero Honda. Hero Honda had been unable to make a bike for me, and yet, there I was, on a bike in a show sponsored by them.

Being on the show opened the biking universe to me. I discovered so many groups of hardcore biking and motorsport enthusiasts. I connected with them on social media. And the traffic was two-way—so many people connected with me on social media. I had fans!

Soon these connections proved invaluable to me. I was to take the train from the New Delhi railway station, but was stuck in a terrible traffic jam on the way there. We were not too far from the station, but because of the gridlock I couldn't even open the car door to get out.

A bus had broken down near Kashmere Gate, sparking the jam. People were abandoning their cabs and autos and walking down to the station, lugging their luggage. I was perilously close to missing my train.

Here, a group of biker fans, who had come along to see me off, came to my rescue. They literally pulled me out of the window of the car. They carried me on their shoulders and formed a chain to pass me along, and I crowd-surfed like a rock star to the station. Someone carried my wheelchair and someone else carried my luggage. Random strangers helped me.

But reaching the station revealed another challenge—it was all dug up for re-tiling, completely unsuitable for my wheelchair. Once again, strangers came to my help. Due to my paralysis, I require careful handling to prevent injury. Two people took my luggage, one handled my wheelchair and three more supported me. Someone knelt so I could rest my back safely, another supported my armpits and a third held my legs. In this fashion, we moved forward slowly for me to enter the train and reach my seat.

As I was carried through the crowd, I overheard a passenger's comment: '*Kitni sundar hai, par bechari ko kaise zinda laash ki tarah le ja rahe hain*' (She looks so pretty, but poor thing has to be carried like a living corpse).

I responded, '*Maharani ki palki ko bhi to chaar log uthate hain*' (Even a queen travels in a palanquin carried by four people).

By the time I returned to Ahmednagar, my long-awaited bike had arrived. The first time I went for a proper ride on a proper bike, albeit a modified one, had to be special! And what a spectacular ride it was—it was like the entire city came out to celebrate with me.

Pawan Gandhi and Gautam Munot, pillars of the local community and known for their social work, took the lead in organizing my inaugural ride, transforming it into a rally of sorts. Their involvement energized the youth wings of the local political parties, and all manner of bikes were ready to escort me as I went on my victory lap around the city. Narendra Firodia, from the family behind Force Motors, joined in his jeep. Some young officers from the Armoured Corps Centre and School also came along on their bikes. Our first stop was Ahmednagar College. There were so many bikes! I could not count the number, so I would love to say there were hundreds of us gathered there that day. Everyone who loved wheels was out there—even little children on their toy bikes and old-timers in their vintage cars.

That day, I felt like my dream was finally coming true. I had achieved recognition for my para sports, I had created a Limca record, I had been featured on *MTV Roadies*, and now I had led a bike rally.

But the fire in my belly was still going strong. I now wanted to create a biking record. This was fuelled by a decade-old memory of Shakti Bajaj, the car rallyist I had met in the Army Hospital Research and Referral. When I'd asked him if I could become a car rallyist, he'd said, 'In our next life, we'll do it together.'

One day, I got a call from Jignesh Desai, a youngster from Mumbai. He had been following my progress since *MTV Roadies* and had got my number through Bunny Punia.

'Ma'am, we organize an annual Ride for Safety in Mumbai to promote road safety. We'd be honoured if you could join us,' he said.

'I'll come only if I can drive alongside John Abraham and Akshay Kumar,' I replied, half in jest.

But as it turned out, there was a good chance that these stars would actually endorse the event. Light-heartedness aside, I was genuinely thrilled to be invited to be a part of this initiative.

I also saw it as an opportunity to attempt another record for the Limca Book of Records. I spoke to them and proposed to set a record as the first woman with chest-below paralysis to ride a modified bike over a specified distance. The condition, however, was that my ride had to be marshalled, meaning I had to contact the Federation of Motor Sports Clubs of India (FMSCI) and get a registered marshal from them to certify my ride. They pointed me in the direction of another Limca record holder, Shrikant Karani, who holds the record for conducting the maximum number of motorsport events in India. He agreed to marshal my attempt.

With funding secured through UB's brand Royal Challenge, all that remained was organizing the event.

To create a media buzz, I reached out to my classmate Richa Goyal, who was working for a media house and was well-versed in managing media campaigns. Her husband was in the Indian Navy, and she lived in Mumbai's Colaba. For Rs 25,000, I was able to hire the services of her company to organize the press conferences and ensure media coverage. I had already spoken with Raj Mohanty, who had put me in touch with Jaideep Sen at Clear Channel. Clear Channel, with their specialization in out-of-home advertising, would help with publicity.

In such situations, my mind operates like an octopus—each tentacle tackling a different task with precision. I am in my element when I'm coordinating, planning and multitasking. One of my biggest skills is networking; I can reach into the recesses of my brain and fish out details of friends, friends of friends and acquaintances to reach out to for help. I have also found that most people are always willing to help—it's just our own inhibitions that hold us back from asking.

Within a short time, everything fell into place: Jignesh organized the bikers and designed the event posters. Richa drummed up publicity. Raj took charge of the hoardings. Shrikant Karani was going to marshal. Royal Challenge T-shirts came in. The date was set—30 November 2008.

All we now needed was a celebrity to flag off the ride. We managed to get an appointment for 26 November with Bollywood sweetheart Juhi Chawla.

I arrived in Mumbai a few days early and stayed with 2 Grenadiers, my father's regiment. Col. Arun Sharma, a second-generation officer, was commanding the unit. Arun and I had known each other since childhood. Arun's father, Lt Gen. Y.N. Sharma, PVSM, AVSM, VSM, was a war hero who had lost one leg in the 1971 Bangladesh war. My father had been with him when he was injured and had saved his life. As a child, I had seen Yogi Uncle, as I called him, cycling with his prosthetic leg.

As we neared Juhi Chawla's home in Malabar Hill, I was taken back to my college days. Her debut movie, *Qayamat Se Qayamat Tak*, had just been released back then, sparking a frenzy among all of us girls in the hostel. We swooned over Aamir Khan and envied Juhi for her role as the love of his life. One viewing wasn't enough—we had to watch the movie again and again. We even had a competition going: every time we went for it, we had to pin our ticket to the hostel notice board to track who had watched it the most. For one of the multiple times that I bunked college to go see *QSQT*, I had 'borrowed' a day scholar's cycle. I was reported, and my father was summoned to meet the principal.

Now, meeting Juhi in person was thrilling. She was as charming in real life as she appears on screen, and welcomed us into her beautiful home, where she served us the most delicious Gujarati lunch. She happily agreed to support our initiative and flag off our ride.

While we sat chatting with her, my phone rang. It was the police.

'Madam, you need to come to the police station. What is this "ride" you are doing? Have you taken permission? Where is the money coming from? What is this liquor you're selling?' The questions came at me like a hail of arrows. But keeping my wits about me, I responded calmly, careful not to let Juhi sense the brewing crisis. We took our leave with the promise of seeing her at the flag-off on 30 November.

My first call was to Arun. He told me that he would send an officer from the Corps of Military Police (CMP) to meet me at the police station.

When we entered the station, the officer who had called me was taken aback to see me in my wheelchair and even more overwhelmed to see the smartly turned out, red-beret-sporting CMP officer with me. It was his turn to be on the back foot now.

Slowly, I was able to piece together the entire story. It turned out that Jignesh had been organizing the Ride for Safety for the past few years with another biker, Vijay D. Jain, known as Wheelie Boy. This ride was also supported by the Mumbai Traffic Police. But this year, the poster graphics that Jignesh had prepared had left out Wheelie Boy and the Mumbai Traffic Police from the creatives. Plus, the poster mentioned my sponsor Royal Challenge, a liquor brand, which was my sponsor. Piqued at being left out, Wheelie Boy had complained to the police, citing concerns about the involvement of a liquor brand, a sensitive issue under Indian advertising regulations.

There was also the matter of the funding. I was able to explain the money trail, accounting for expenses to the tune of Rs 3.5 lakh without issue. But then the police officer threw a googly at me. 'Where did the Rs 80 lakh for the hoardings come from?'

I was speechless—80 lakhs! I had not even seen that much money in my life. I called my Clear Channel friends. They had put up my posters on hoardings 180x40 ft and 30x20 ft in size. I had not even realized it, but my face had been beaming down at Mumbaikars from huge billboards at prime locations like Nariman Point and Juhu. Clear Channel had done it as a part of their CSR commitment, and anyway, the 2008 recession had forced most companies to cut their advertising budgets—their hoarding spaces had been lying unused.

While we were able to sort out the question of funding, we still had to resolve the issue between Wheelie Boy and Jignesh. The police said they had no problem with the ride as long as we removed the Royal Challenge branding from the hoardings and convinced Wheelie Boy to withdraw his complaint. Bunny Punia came to the rescue for that. In true Mumbai style, we had to get a mandwali (settlement) done between two motorbiking factions by seeking the intervention of the biggest name in the biking community. Sundeep Gajjar, aka MotoGrapher, was the founder of the largest online biker community in India, xBhp. I called him.

'You've created this community to promote the spirit of true biking. But here your boys are going against the very philosophy that bikers follow—looking out for each other and supporting fellow riders. Here I am, a woman in a wheelchair, paralysed below my chest. I have come so far to fulfil my dream of creating a biking record. But today, instead of supporting me, instead of showering me with the camaraderie that is the hallmark of all true bikers, your boys have chopped off my legs.'

Sundeep had a few words with Wheelie Boy and, after we agreed to add his logo to our publicity material, he withdrew his complaint.

With the matter resolved, we headed out to celebrate, deciding to figure out the Royal Challenge issue later. I offered to treat everyone at the famous Colaba restaurant Leopold Cafe.

However, Jignesh suggested a more economical option: grabbing some snacks at the army mess I was staying at. We reached Colaba, stopped at Sassoon Dock to get the car refuelled and reached the mess. Just as we entered, a series of sharp sounds filled the air.

'Deepa Ma'am, the celebrations for your next Limca record have already started. See, people are welcoming you by bursting crackers,' said Jignesh.

But having grown up around the army, I knew that the sounds we had heard were not firecrackers—they were gunshots.

It was on this fateful day, 26 November 2008, that Mumbai faced an unprecedented attack. Armed militants sailed into the jetty at the Gateway of India and launched an indiscriminate assault on civilians. The Taj Mahal Palace and Towers hotel, Leopold Cafe— where we had been planning to go, Chhatrapati Shivaji Terminus, the Oberoi Trident hotel, Cama Hospital, Nariman House, the lane behind *The Times of India* office—no place was safe from their violence.

All these locations were in the same vicinity as the army mess in Colaba. Soon after our arrival, we saw the gates being closed. For the next three days, we were not allowed to step outside. Phone calls from family members and friends kept coming. We spent all our time glued to the television set, following every update on the events unfolding around us. I got a call from Rannvijay Singha. His friend Ashish Chaudhary's sister was in the Trident, and they were desperate for any information about her safety. The constant sight of soldiers coming and going added to our tension. Amidst our earlier concerns about explaining to our sponsors why their logo had to be removed from the publicity material, we now faced the graver reality of our nation under siege.

One particularly striking moment on the news came when a reporter covered the standoff at Girgaum Chowpatty, where ASI Tukaram Omble heroically intercepted the terrorist Ajmal Kasab. In the background of this chaotic scene, a hoarding announcing my upcoming ride was visible, a surreal juxtaposition in the midst of this tragedy.

On 28 November, I remember meeting some officers from the National Security Guard (NSG) in the mess. Among them was a smart young major: Maj. Sandeep Unnikrishnan. I remember exchanging greetings with him, little knowing that he would never return. That was the day he fell in the line of duty, sacrificing his life in the battle with the terrorists.

We were allowed to leave the area on 30 November, and I returned home to Ahmednagar, relieved that our soldiers had contained all the terrorists.

While still grappling with the aftermath of the Mumbai attacks, an unexpected call shifted my focus. Sundeep Gajjar, aka MotoGrapher, invited me to be a judge at the prestigious Castrol Biker of the Year awards. I was happy to accept, but when he told me who else was going to judge alongside me, I was ecstatic. Film star and biker John Abraham would be there as the brand ambassador for Castrol.

I was finally going to have my fangirl moment.

This is the power of manifestation that I firmly believe in. It was a playful wish I had expressed to Jignesh when he had asked me to join his Ride for Safety. And here the universe had heard me and granted me my wish.

While at the event, I also made some new friends. Among them was Ashish Bahl. He was a mechanical engineer who was passionate about wheels. He had started a company called Adventure Wheels in Gurgaon, India's first ATV and motorsport hobby store. It was a delight to connect with someone equally passionate about wheels.

The next piece of good news came from Shrikant Karani: everything was set for my record attempt. The T-shirts were ready, my logo stickers were in place, and the marshals had been arranged, as had the venue and media.

In the wake of the 26/11 attacks, Mumbai was no longer an option. Shrikant suggested Nashik. I would ride from Nashik to the Trimbakeshwar temples and back, journeying almost 60 km—perfect to create another record for the Limca Book of Records.

On 4 January 2009, I sat on my bike and started from Nashik, drove to Trimbakeshwar and returned. I covered a total distance of 55.25 km in 1 hour and 45 minutes.

I had created a record for being the first woman with chest-below paralysis to perform this feat.

Fresh off this achievement, I headed for the National Para Sports Championships in Faridabad. I had now moved from swimming to athletics and was competing in the javelin category.

During the games, I stayed with Col. Yagpal Nagar, a regimental officer, and his wife, Priya. Performing well was crucial—these were the qualifiers for the International Wheelchair and Amputee Sports (IWAS) Games that were to be held in Bangalore later in the year.

I had also secured a no objection certificate from Maharashtra and switched my allegiance to Haryana for these games because my husband's family belonged to Sonipat. The previous year, I had been invited to Madhuban in Karnal for a para sports event. Karnal is my mother-in-law's hometown, and since Bikram had also accompanied me for these games, we met some of our relatives, one of whom was a sessions judge. He was the chief guest on the day of my event and, as luck would have it, I won gold. It was here that the media asked me why I was not representing Haryana, leading to my decision to change the state I was representing.

I now represented Haryana in athletics. My training in javelin throw took place at the familiar space of Dee's Place, with a spear that cost me Rs 500.

With that level of preparation, I qualified for athletics for the IWAS Games.

But this trip to Faridabad was about more than one kind of sport—I came to know about the Suzuki Desert Storm motor car rally that was going to be flagged off.

I reached out to Ashish Bahl, whose brother-in-law owned the hotel The Connaught in Delhi. I secured a room there, giving me a base while I tried to figure out how to attend the Desert Storm flag-off.

I was mesmerized at the flag-off—jeeps, Gypsys, sedans, SUVs, each adorned with a collage of stickers more elaborate than the last. Although I was a stranger to most, I recognized some of the marshals from the FMSCI whom I had met during my Limca Book of Records ride.

Vehicle scrutiny was underway, a critical process where compliance with every rule is confirmed. Crucial details like the stickers displaying the names and blood groups of the driver and navigator are mandatory, serving a vital role in case of an accident. The requirements for a fully equipped toolbox are important in case of breakdowns. Tow-chains and jump cables are essentials for any rallyist, as are a shovel and mat.

As the marshals inspected the vehicles, I looked around for those with a Maharashtra registration, hoping to form local connections so that I could prepare myself better. I approached a Pune-registered vehicle and introduced myself to the Pune Millennium team— veteran rallyist Sanjay Takale and Pawan Kumar. They were a bit bemused to see this woman in a wheelchair asking them all sorts of questions about rallying. I showed them my file of clippings, which I always carried with me. It was my portfolio. 'I want to go for a car rally too,' I said. 'Will you guide me?'

'Sure!' they replied enthusiastically. 'We have chai and bun maska at this Parsi cafe near Fergusson College every Saturday at 5 p.m. We'll catch you there the week after next, once we return from this rally,' they said.

We exchanged numbers, and I returned to Ahmednagar, excited to see yet another dream of mine beginning to come true. Devika was studying at Fergusson College, so getting to the Parsi cafe was no problem.

On the appointed Saturday, after spending some quality time with Devika, I arrived at the cafe at 5 p.m. and settled in to wait. And wait. And wait. 5 p.m. became 5.30. I kept my eyes on the road and an ear cocked for the sound of their distinctive Gypsy. But no one came. Finally, after waiting for forty-five minutes, I called Sanjay Takale. He picked up after a few rings.

'Mr Takale, you are not a man of your word,' I said without preamble.

It took him a moment to recognize my voice. As he mumbled a tentative greeting, I continued, 'You had given me your word that you would meet me at this Parsi cafe at 5 p.m. today. I have been waiting and you are not here,' I said.

My words had the desired impact. Within thirty minutes, Sanjay and Pawan reached the cafe. We spoke for a bit before agreeing to meet again the next morning. It was now clear to them that this woman in the wheelchair was serious about rallying. They gave me the low-down on the Raid De Himalaya, scheduled for October.

The Raid De Himalaya is renowned as the world's highest raid, and in 2009, it was to be conducted over six legs from Shimla to Srinagar. It is India's toughest motorsport event. Sanjay and Pawan explained the process of registration, the preparation required and their own experiences from the past. There are different categories, including one that follows the time, speed, distance (TSD) formula. Participants are given a road book with tulip maps, and the navigator has the tough job of interpreting the instructions while also calculating the speed at which the team has to drive.

Armed with this information, I thanked them and left, my mind buzzing with plans and possibilities.

While I was trying to find a way of entering the Raid De Himalaya, Ashish called me with an exciting proposition. Polaris, a global giant in ATV manufacturing, was organizing an ATV challenge in Jaipur. He asked if I was game to participate. He didn't have to ask me twice. The prospect of this adventure was not only thrilling, the event was also being held in Jaipur, my hometown, at Hotel Clarks, where I had learnt the ropes of biking.

Surrounded by bikers at the venue was like going back in time. I was on an ATV sponsored by Ashish's Adventure Wheels. With my protective gear on, I looked like a gladiator and felt certain that I could conquer the world. I was flagged off with the other bikers and off we went.

Driving an ATV on even terrain was manageable for me. But this ride included all kinds of off-roading. Typically, ATV riders use their knees for grip and often stand to minimize the impact of the ups and downs. Without the use of my legs and with a weak torso, this was beyond me. I could not complete the ride and had to step down after 40 km.

I had not conquered the rough terrain, but this ride was important because it marked a watershed moment in my relationship with my father.

He had come to the event, and when he saw me in my element, he did something I had not expected him to—he apologized.

'Deepa, I am so sorry we tried to curb your spirit for adventure. I can see that it is this passion for bikes that has kept you alive after your paralysis. Without this passion to reclaim, you would not have survived. I'm so sorry for not understanding your dream and for trying to stop you. I'm glad you found Bikram to support you. And I'm so proud of you.'

That day, we began rebuilding our relationship, which had been strained since Kolkata, when he had packed me off to the village as punishment. Through my biking, I won back his respect, his unstinting support and his love.

From then on, he was there for nearly every ride I was a part of.

I had thought that taking part in Raid De Himalaya would be a piece of cake once I got the organizers on board. All I had to do was fill up a form, pay the fee, find a car, find a team and show up to drive. Of course, it was not that simple.

The biggest roadblocks for me were the legalities, starting with insurance. Even if I were to navigate instead of drive, I needed high-risk life insurance because of the nature of the sport. No insurance company was willing to give me that kind of insurance. But somehow, after a lot of badgering, follow-ups and 'persuasion' I managed to get the insurance cover.

The next challenge was convincing the governing bodies of the sport to accept my participation. As the first woman in a wheelchair to apply, they did not know how to respond to me. After all, this was a long, arduous drive in extreme weather conditions at high altitudes, with low oxygen levels and sub-zero temperatures. They seldom had women participants, let alone a woman in a wheelchair who had had her spine cut open three times.

The Himalayan Motorsports Association (HMA) and the FMSCI had a lot of questions. The first positive response I got was from Vijay Parmar, the founder of Raid De Himalaya and a true champion of the spirit of adventure. He reserved an early bird spot for me and my team. Sceptics tried to keep me out of the race by citing potential dangers unique to my situation—like not being able to escape a burning vehicle should there be an accident. To respond to this, I got help from the marshal community, who told me about instances where even able-bodied rallyists had been unable to walk out of a flaming vehicle.

I was also told that the organizers would not be able to evacuate me if required. I would have to make arrangements for that eventuality. For this, I approached the Indian Army, who agreed to undertake my evacuation if required. In fact, they said, they would be there to evacuate any of the other rallyists as well, should the need arise.

With the backing of Vijay Parmar and rally officials like Rajan Sayal, Sudev Brar and Hari Singh, I was finally given the go-ahead to get my team together.

I reached out to Rajasthan-based Rakesh Diwan. He was an experienced rallyist, but more importantly, I was able to find a personal connection with him. He was from Ganganagar, where my father's mentor, Ramesh Tauji, lived. Tauji's son was running a nursing home in the city and knew Rakesh's family. When I spoke to him about my dream, he quickly agreed to be my teammate. He said I would need to arrange for the car and Rs 50,000 and to leave the rest to him. True to his word, he got the sleeping bags, the snow chains and clothing for the cold. Alongside Rakesh and me, Bikram was the third member of the team, acting as my attendant.

We were all set.

Or so I thought.

Nothing in life comes easy to me. During my swimming record attempt, I faced a torrential downpour. Before my biking record attempt, the 26/11 terrorist attacks unfolded. Now, before I could take off to fulfil my dream of being a rallyist, we got the heartbreaking news of the passing of Rakesh's brother. To make matters more ominous, he had died in a road accident. There was no way Rakesh could join the rally now. He told us that we could take the car, which he had made rally-worthy. We went to his home to attend the prayer meeting and pick up the car. As we were leaving, his father stopped us and turned to Rakesh.

'You have made a commitment to help your sister, who is divyang, fulfil her dream. You must keep your word.' With his blessings, he sent us off.

At the Shimla flag-off, most people assumed I was there to see someone off or that I was there as a spectator. But when I affixed the sticker bearing my name to the car and draped my participant ID card around my neck, everyone looked at me with respect. Just the look on their faces was enough for me—I had been able to prove once again that disability is just a state of mind, not of the body.

Just before flagging off, I spotted a familiar figure: Shakti Bajaj.

'Hey, Shakti,' I called out to him. 'Not in my next life. In this life.'

He was stunned, watching in silence as our car was flagged off. His salute to me was the last thing I saw in the side view mirror before we sped off into the distance.

We began our eight-day odyssey along with 118 other teams in different categories. Though our routes were the same, our pace and format were different. We had to travel from Shimla to Srinagar in eight days via Manali, Kunzum La, Rangdum, Patseo, Leh and Kargil. The route spanned more than 2,000 km and we had to drive an average of 300 km per day on some of the narrowest mountain roads in the country.

Everything went well till we were halfway through the rally. The high altitude and low oxygen levels proved exhausting, but the adrenaline surged through me, keeping my spirits high.

A vehicle ahead of us had stopped for a time check and the vehicles in the Xtreme category were overtaking us on the right.

We were moving at a slow pace when suddenly, the vehicle in front of us braked. The icy roads compromised our ability to stop in time, resulting in a collision. There was no apparent damage, so we continued, only to discover that we had cracked the radiator of the car. We attempted a stop-gap repair, but the extreme cold prevented the patch from holding, causing the radiator to continue leaking. We had to stop at every water spring we came across to fill the radiator. Vijay Parmar, monitoring the rally from the sweep car, followed us till we reached Patseo. Here we tried to get the radiator fixed at a workshop, but the damage proved irreparable. We were in third place in our category at that point, but we had no choice but to withdraw and get a tow back from Patseo.

Though we couldn't complete the rally, I had had my moment. A decade after my surgery, I was doing something that even able-bodied people find tough. I went back without winning, but I was undefeated.

My participation in this rigorous rally marked a significant milestone. Manjeev Bhalla of the HMA declared that the rally would now be open to people with disabilities. I had shattered the glass ceiling in this arena for so many people like me. I went home with the True Grit Trophy, awarded for my extraordinary courage and tenacity.

Well and truly bitten by the rally bug, my next challenge was to participate in Desert Storm—this time as a driver. I spoke with Raj Kapoor, one of the co-founders, and asked for a seat in the 2010 rally that was to wind through Rajasthan and end in the Rann of Kutch. He agreed to let me participate at the early bird entry fee of Rs 25,000.

I successfully obtained a rally licence from the FMSCI, becoming the first paralysed person to do so. Himanshu Chitnis, of AUTO-mate, who had modified my second car, a Ritz, offered to be my co-driver. But when we went back to Raj Kapoor to register, he unexpectedly told us that the fee now was Rs 1.25 lakh.

Just when the dunes of Desert Storm seemed within reach, I was suddenly confronted with this huge obstacle. There was no way I could come up with that much money at such short notice.

We were ready to give up when I got a call.

'Hi, this is Hardy,' boomed the voice on the other end. It was Sanjay Sharma, head of motorsports at JK Tyres, also known as the father of car rallying in India. He had heard of my performance at the Raid De Himalaya the previous year and had been impressed by my bravery and grit.

News of how the organizers were trying to keep me out of Desert Storm had reached him. 'Lady, you are going to do this rally,' he said to me.

'But I don't have the money for the registration,' I said.

'Your registration fee has been paid,' came his response.

And just like that, once again, I was given a hand, almost as if by divine intervention. Moments like this have helped me retain my faith in the basic goodness of humans.

Hardy was there for the flag-off, so I was able to thank him in person.

The rally was fraught with challenges. Competing in the Xplore category and following the TSD formula, we started strong. But soon we encountered trouble when sand and dirt clogged our fuel tank, causing our car to stall and forcing us to miss an entire leg of the rally. Though we stood no chance of winning, I decided to finish the rally. Having had to withdraw early from the Raid De Himalaya, I was resolute not to let the same happen again.

As we carried on at a comfortable pace, I suddenly noticed that our fuel gauge read empty. We were stranded in the middle of the desert, with no sign of civilization, let alone a petrol pump, for miles.

We stopped and decided to take stock. We had just topped up that morning, so there had to be a leak somewhere. Himanshu examined the undercarriage and discovered a freak event: the fuel tank had probably hit something on the road and was bent upwards right in the centre. Effectively, the tank was now divided into two compartments. The side with the absorption pump now had a capacity of only 10 litres.

While we puzzled over what to do, an unexpected form of help appeared: a camel cart. We brought out our tow chain and hitched a ride to the nearest petrol pump. We had to be the only car in Desert Storm to employ not horsepower but camel power.

We finished the rally and arrived in Gujarat for a glamorous prize distribution ceremony. Flushed with a sense of achievement, I was all set to share my experience. But while the emcee of the evening interviewed almost all the participants, I was totally ignored.

Once again, Hardy stepped in. He put the might of the JK Tyres PR team behind me and organized a press conference in Ahmedabad specifically for me.

Life was accelerating for me. I was gaining momentum in para sports and becoming well-known in the biking and rallying circuits.

I had fought hard against societal biases and had broken a lot of new ground. Thanks to my efforts, people with disabilities were now getting rally licences, registering modified vehicles and getting insurance companies to provide them with high-risk policies for participating in adventure sports.

Life in a wheelchair can be so constricting that many people resign themselves to these limitations. Before my own paralysis, I hadn't noticed the absence of people in wheelchairs in everyday settings. My passion for wheels drove me to engage in adventure sports, but my bigger goal was to create awareness and show other people with disabilities that their lives need not be defined by their physical restrictions.

I was now also going to awareness rallies for social causes. One notable event was a Ride for Safety sponsored by Durex condoms, where we visited a red-light district to promote safe sex.

Another rally, this time for orphans, saw me partnering with Wheelie Boy—the same Wheelie Boy who had earlier filed a police complaint against me! I met leading biker groups like India Thumpers, Road Shakers and BOB MC (Brotherhood of Bulleteers Motorcycling Consortium). I even went on to host Road Shakers at Dee's Place in Ahmednagar.

Among them was Baljeet Kochhar, who specialized in modifying vehicles. I had my heart set on a bright orange jeep and he offered to customize one for me. We went down to Aurangabad, where the Airport Authority of India was auctioning off old jeeps. One of these was modified for me and painted the bright orange I had pictured.

While all these new avenues were opening for me, destiny also gave me a nudge to move forward and not go back. The terror attack at German Bakery in Pune had led to heightened security measures in nearby Ahmednagar as well. Dee's Place, which had been running on autopilot in my absence, was experiencing a decline in clientele. The signs were there: it was time to close the Ahmednagar chapter of my life and see what else was in store for me.

13

Torchbearer

———◦•◦———

I WANTED TO PINCH MYSELF. I COULD NOT BELIEVE THAT it was not a dream—because this was something I had dreamt of since I was a child. Ever since I had seen the opening ceremony of the Asian Games in New Delhi in 1982, I had often dreamt of being among the athletes waving to the crowds as they took a lap around the stadium.

This dream became a reality in 2009, and the reality was one step ahead of the dream. At the opening ceremony of the International Wheelchair and Amputee Sports (IWAS) Games in Bangalore, I wasn't just among the athletes—I was the torchbearer.

The honour of carrying the sacred flame for the games was bestowed upon me by R. Satyanarayana, a former runner turned sports administrator. Though I was still relatively new to para sports, he decided that I should carry the flame—much to the chagrin of several seasoned para athletes—because he had seen something in me.

'There is a fire in her eyes. I can see that she has potential. She will go places. I can recognize talent when I see it,' he had said to members of the organizing committee when they questioned him as to why he picked me to be the torch bearer.

His faith in me was immense, pushing me to introspect and dedicate myself even more. I felt a profound sense of achievement.

Those Games proved to be transformative. At the 2007 IWAS Games in Taiwan, I had competed in the javelin throw in the F54 category and did the same at this event. I threw well, but my result was not announced. I waited for some time and then, uncertain, approached the technical committee to get to the bottom of the matter.

'You have been medically disqualified,' came the shocking revelation.

The observers believed I was in the wrong medical category; they felt that F54 was the wrong category for me. I felt waves of devastation wash over me. But I stood my ground and showed them all my medical papers. After they were reviewed, I was reclassified into the F53 category.

I was in tears, but Satyanarayana was upbeat. He assured me that F53 was a more suitable category for me. At the moment, his words felt like a consolation, and I was too upset to appreciate them. I wanted to appeal.

The javelin event was over. I had been disqualified and there was nothing more for me to do at these Games. But Satyanarayana told me to take part in the shot put event scheduled for the next day.

Without any practice or preparation, I showed up for the shot put event. And got a podium finish.

I won a bronze.

It was then that I understood the benefit of the reclassification. The medical categorization reflects the athlete's functional capacity and the extent of their impairment. My impairment was more severe than that of para athletes in the F54 category. My disability had paralysed more groups of muscles than those of the para athletes against whom I had been competing. My movements were more restricted, and I had less torso stability. Competitors in the F54 category were more powerful and had greater mobility and better balance than I did, putting me at a distinct disadvantage.

With the change in my category, I was competing with para athletes who had a similar extent of movement. This levelled the playing field.

While participating in the 2010 Desert Storm car rally, I got the news that based on my shot put bronze at the IWAS Games, I had been selected for the Commonwealth Games to be held in Delhi in October.

The Commonwealth Games are among the first international sporting events to be inclusive. Earlier, para games were held alongside able-bodied games, but in 2002 in Manchester, the Commonwealth Games became fully inclusive. Para athletes competed with able-bodied athletes in the same arena and at the same time, and their medals were added to the total tally of each participating contingent.

Only seven para athletes had made the cut from India for 2010, and I was one of them.

I was also authorized a competition partner. Devika, who was hemiplegic, was in her final year of college and became the natural choice to be mine.

Immediately after Desert Storm, which ended in Gujarat, I headed to the practice camp in Gandhinagar.

Arriving a few days late because of the rally, I was already in the headlines, thanks to a press conference Hardy had organized for me in Ahmedabad. When I arrived at the camp, I was preceded by newspaper and television coverage of my Desert Storm achievement.

I was on a high from Desert Storm but quickly came back to earth when I saw the accommodation at the camp.

The camp was being held at the SAI campus. Construction work was still on at the new building, so I had been allotted a room on the ground floor in the old girls' hostel. The good news was that the room had an attached bathroom. The bad news was that there were two steps to enter. There was no ramp. The stop-gap arrangement that had been made was a broken door, which had been placed across the steps to serve as a ramp. My room was damp and mouldy due to seepage. Despite these conditions, I focused on the convenience of having an attached bathroom.

There were only three girls in the entire camp for para sports: Manjula, also in para athletics, and Pragya, a para table tennis player. Pragya and I had first met at the Indian Spinal Injuries Centre, where she used to take yoga classes.

In addition to the para athletes, the camp hosted other able-bodied teams, including basketball, netball and kabaddi.

We began our training in earnest. One of the coaches, R.D. Singh, was from the area of Hanumangarh in Rajasthan, near my village. Satyapal, the other coach, was several years younger than I was.

We would train in the morning and evening while resting in the afternoon. Getting up early was second nature to me, after years of doing it to get vegetables for Dee's Place.

The training itself, however, posed certain challenges. The coaches, being younger and less experienced with para athletes, as they were used to training able-bodied competitors, did not really know how to handle us. They were wary of pushing us too much and treated us with kid gloves. I overheard someone talking about me, saying, '*Maum ban gayee hain haddiyan*' (Her bones have become soft like wax).

Most of the training I did was by instinct and without much scientific underpinning.

The physical activity would leave me with sore muscles. I consulted Virendra Vikram Singh, my trusted physiotherapist from the ISIC. He suggested hydrotherapy as the best way of relaxing my spine and muscles after training. The camp's pool had staggered timings for various teams. I picked the afternoon time, when the pool was free, and requested three youngsters to help me get in and out of the pool. This irked the coach, who did not appreciate the benefits of cross training.

Despite these issues, camp life was amazing, reminiscent of being back in college. I was the oldest athlete there, and I was met with great respect. The younger athletes often sought my blessings by touching my feet and came to me for advice and even help with practical matters like checking train schedules and booking tickets. My laptop proved invaluable, not just for these logistical tasks but also to show them their rankings on the Paralympics Committee of India website.

Mealtimes were a highlight. We had a rich diet with dry fruits and high-protein foods. We could have eggs to order, as many as we wanted. We got the freshest juice—so fresh because we had a dedicated juicewala, a young man with a manual juicer ready to press the juice of our choice right after training sessions.

I was unable to go to the TV room, which was on the first floor, so most evenings, I would attend the evening arti at the campus temple. My assistant, Maya, Draupadi's sister, would keep me company. I found a lot of peace while attending the prayers and would use that time to introspect and plan for the next day.

The nights were tough. Positioned near the kitchen, my room was adjacent to the area where the kitchen staff discarded the food waste. This attracted a pack of stray dogs each night, whose skirmishes for the tastiest scraps provided an unwanted soundtrack right outside my window. I had ringside seats to their doggie concert. Over time, I became so accustomed to their barking, snarling and growling that I could assign each bark a character trait. One night, the absence of a familiar bark troubled me, and I discovered the next day that the dog in question had been killed in the canine war.

At practice, I needed someone to lift me and put me in the throw frame. For this, I took the help of a young athlete who was also training with us. His father was from the army and had served with Bikram. We coordinated our practice times so that he could assist me. This led to some light-hearted banter and pairing off, which no one took seriously. The camaraderie signalled their acceptance of me as one of their own.

We had been at the camp for almost four months when the Shahrukh Khan hit *Chak De! India* was released. One Sunday, we girls decided to watch it. Ratti Bhaiyya, married to one of the kitchen cooks, drove an auto. Actually, not just an auto, but what we called the disco auto—a rickshaw decked out with a boom box and jazzy lights to match. Whenever any of us needed to go anywhere, we could call him. He was happy to take us to the movie. The problem, however, was that I needed two people to lift me into the auto. As luck would have it, the able-bodied runners of our camp were around. They had just returned from a shoot for the movie *Paan Singh Tomar*, based on the life of the athlete turned outlaw. I requested them to help.

Just as we were set to leave, we were stopped in our tracks by the coach.

'Where do you think you're going?' he boomed.

We explained our plans to watch a film, but he would have none of it and told us to return. While the younger girls meekly gave in, I stood firm. Disregarding him, I went for the movie and joined up with some of our other camp members who lived locally and not in the hostel. Watching the movie was great fun, but this incident marked the beginning of a tussle between me and the coach.

He had already been put off by my forthright personality and my media presence even before the camp had started. Now, I was giving him fuel to drive the rift deeper between us.

Our next altercation occurred over a party. I was invited to dinner by the local army general, who had served with my father-in-law during their early days in the army. I informed the supervisor training centre and even submitted a written application for permission to return late. An officer came to pick me up in a staff car along with a pilot vehicle, and off I went in style. The problem arose when we returned at around 11.30 p.m. The hostel's practice was to lock the iron gate at 9 p.m. That night, it was firmly locked. We called the guard, a retired army soldier, and asked him to open the gate. He said that the coach had ordered that 'whoever is outside after curfew can stay outside'. I lost my cool. As I ranted, the officer who was escorting me promptly summoned the retired honorary captain who was the head of security to unlock the gate.

Though I won that night's battle, the repercussions of these skirmishes between me and the coach would come soon. He sent reports to the higher-ups that I was a troublemaker who had returned drunk from an unauthorized outing and created a ruckus.

I needed a break from the camp's tension, and an opportunity came via Janak, my friend Mezbeen's neighbour in Ahmedabad who had picked me up at the airport when I had come to surprise Bikram. He came to meet me at the camp one day with his friend Sameer Kakkar. Sameer had a polio-related disability, and after learning of how I had got my car modified, he had done the same. He also wanted to take part in a car rally.

I had been invited to take part in the upcoming Royal Rajasthan Rally, but the coach refused me permission, citing the government's insurance for my training—any incident would leave them liable. I gave my rally slot to Sameer but took a few days off from camp and went to Jaipur for the flag-off.

On my return I was greeted with the devastating news that Dee's Place had closed down. It was as if I had lost a child. For two days, I wept. I developed a high fever. I couldn't understand why this had happened, especially since Bikram had been looking after it full-time.

He visited for our anniversary, bringing Devika and Ambika along. After he left, the girls stayed on with me for another ten days. We had a wonderful time together—a young mother with her girls in a youthful environment. They loved watching me practise, and after my training we'd enjoy our meals together in the canteen. Something must have clicked with Devika when she saw me in my element because she also developed an interest in para sports. She began to research categories, classifications and rules. By the time her twentieth birthday came a round, Devika had found her category and was ready to take the plunge into para sports.

Before the Commonwealth Games, we had the chance to participate in an international meet in Nottingham, England. In September 2010, we went to compete in the CP Sports event there, which was crucial as our performance there would help us qualify for the Asian Para Games in December.

I participated in all the para athletics field events: javelin, shot put and discus. Fresh from the training camp, I was at my best and got gold in both shot put and discus. These Games worked on the principle of minus one: they awarded one fewer medal than the number of participants. If three athletes competed, only two medals would be given, and if there was only one contestant, no medal would be given.

In javelin, I was the only contestant. For it to qualify as a medal event, at least one more para athlete needed to participate. Otherwise, I would get only a participation certificate. This certification was still vital, as it would officially record my participation on the International Paralympic Committee website.

I was eager for a medal and approached Manjula, who had participated in the shot put event, to consider taking part in the javelin throw. Unfortunately, she declined as she had injured her hand.

The result was that though Manjula participated in the Commonwealth Games in shot put, she could not go for the Asian Para Games. Had she participated in the javelin throw at the CP Games, she could have gone for the Asian Para Games.

I came home with two golds and one ranking certificate, securing my place at the Asian Para Games.

Soon after our return to India, I joined a practice camp in Patiala at the Netaji Subhas National Institute of Sports campus to stay in form. While in Patiala, I needed a medical check-up, so I went to Chandigarh's Silver Oaks Hospital. There, I reunited with the doctor who had performed my surgery in 1999. It had been eleven years. It was an emotional moment: he said that he had never seen a person with the extent of my disability be so positive. Meeting him gave me another shot of josh and reinforced my resolve.

Janak, my rally friend from Ahmedabad, was also in Chandigarh. He was preparing for an adventure trip to Ladakh. They requested me to flag them off, saying that I was the one who had inspired them to do this. We also got a lot of media coverage for this ride.

I was discovering a new Deepa. I was getting more comfortable staying on my own, away from home. And I was making friends—friends who were connecting with me for myself, not out of obligation. I was inspiring people, and they were joining my community.

I was no longer just coping with my disability—I was transcending it, removing the 'dis' from my ability.

The excitement was palpable when I reached Delhi for the Commonwealth Games.

This was to be my first time at such a big event. It was going to be a gathering of 4,352 athletes from 71 Commonwealth countries and dependencies. I was a part of the Indian contingent of 495 athletes.

All the para athletes would be staying at the Commonwealth Games Village, including myself, with Devika joining me as my competition partner. However, our accommodation hadn't been assigned yet, adding a layer of anticipation to our arrival.

Before Delhi, I had become reacquainted with a young man from our extended family who had contacted me on my social media, moved by my journey and challenges. Prateek Gahlaut was also a biker but had met with an accident that resulted in a crushed leg and permanently mangled foot, necessitating a rod insertion and a corrective brace. The accident had drastically altered his walk and plunged him into a deep depression. His family had shown him news clippings and social media posts about how I had been living an adventure-filled life despite my paralysis. Our shared experiences fostered a bond. Aware of my upcoming participation in the Commonwealth Games, he offered to help me in any way that he could.

In those days, the Paralympic Committee of India (PCI) was still in the process of establishing itself as an organization dedicated to addressing the comprehensive needs of para athletes, not just organizing the Games. This meant that when I landed in Delhi, I had to carry all my paraphernalia with me: my throw frame, my luggage, my wheelchair. Devika was with me, but I needed more help. Prateek stepped up and came to the airport to pick us up with two vehicles.

Since we could not go to the Games Village right away, Prateek's father, a retired Central Reserve Police Force (CRPF) officer, arranged for our stay at the CRPF guest house. Here, the entire Gahlaut family came to meet me.

When we moved to the Games Village, I was struck by its enormity: 14 apartment blocks, 34 towers, 1,168 apartments and more than 4,000 rooms. All the athletes received welcome kits with their uniforms for the opening ceremony. Interestingly, we were given sarees, but no petticoats! The room I got did not have a special bath stool to suit my requirements. Prateek immediately offered to get me everything I needed. To facilitate his easy movement in and out of the Village, I got him a guest pass. He ensured that my room was kitted out: bath stool, toilet paper, bedpan (mine had broken in transit), urine bags—he even brought a tailor who took measurements for my petticoat. Eventually, that tailor ended up stitching the petticoats for many of the other athletes before the opening ceremony.

Life in the Games Village was like nothing I had experienced before. It was divided into different zones: residential, international and operational. There were multiple dining areas with all kinds of cuisine, open round the clock and offering everything free of charge. Huge refrigerators stocked with refreshing beverages were accessible for us to help ourselves. The training area had everything any athlete needed: synthetic tracks, powerlifting equipment, training equipment, even an Olympic-size swimming pool. To navigate the expansive campus there was a bus service and customized carts. There was a polyclinic and a media centre as well, even a beauty parlour, where Devika enjoyed a birthday treat with a haircut and a mani-pedi.

But the most fascinating were the public spaces. Every evening, we had a concert of some kind: one day it was Mohit Chauhan, another day it was Palash with the band Euphoria. Athletes from different countries would break into street dances, fully immersed in enjoying the moment.

The streets of the Village bustled with international sporting celebrities. I had my fangirl moments and took pictures with hockey legend Sandeep Singh and boxing star Vijender Singh.

I remember the entire hockey team preparing to leave for their match, when I overheard them talking about their Olympic hopes. 'When we get to London, we will all get a tattoo of the Olympic rings,' I overheard one player say. This stayed with me. Despite my fear of needles, I was inspired. In fact, overcoming my fear of needles became another goal for me.

The Village was a vibrant tapestry of national flags waving, athletes in their country's tracksuits walking around and live performances energizing the atmosphere. It was an experience I wanted my family to enjoy. Devika was already with me, but I convinced my parents and Ambika to visit. Spending time together like this was something our little family needed.

Devika had already begun researching for her own para athletics journey. She realized the seriousness of the opportunity that had come to us. We grew closer during our time at the Village. Both of us in the same uniform, with our accreditation cards on lanyards around our necks, the twenty-one-year age gap between us vanishing. We were not just mother and daughter—we were teammates representing India.

The only sour note came from an encounter in the international zone. On seeing us, a journalist mockingly commented, 'The Games have not even started yet and already our athletes are injured and in wheelchairs. What will they do on the sports field?'

'Madam, you may not be aware, but she is a para athlete,' Devika retorted sharply.

'What para—will she use a parachute and paradrop into the stadium?' she said with a laugh.

Unable to take this level of ignorance, I said, 'Madam, if you move away from reporting about broken bridges, you will realize what para athletes are and what para sports is all about.'

For me the Commonwealth Games were as much about parenting as they were about sports. I had largely been away from Ahmednagar since my sporting journey had started. After I attended the six-week workshop at the ISIC, I had focused on myself. In just four years I had established a presence at national and international sports meets, attended several practice camps, created two records for the Limca Book of Records, been on *MTV Roadies*, participated in the toughest car rallies—the Raid De Himalaya and Desert Storm, and now, here I was at the Commonwealth Games.

The period may have been only four years, but these were crucial developmental years for my daughters. In 2006, Devika was sixteen and Ambika eleven. By the time I reached the Commonwealth Games, Devika was twenty and Ambika fifteen. While Devika had moved out of Ahmednagar for school and college, Ambika was still there with her grandparents. In between all my commitments, I had tried to snatch moments with my girls. It had been tough, and I could see that I needed to work hard to reclaim my relationship with them.

Having them with me at the Commonwealth Games was my way of showing them all that I had achieved. I was able to show them that the sacrifice I had made by being away from them had not been for nothing. While Devika had found her direction, I needed to now focus on Ambika and open the world for her too.

The Opening Ceremony of the Commonwealth Games brought back a strong sense of déjà vu. As Devika wheeled me alongside the Indian contingent at Jawaharlal Nehru Stadium, I recalled sitting in the stands with my father during the 1982 Asian Games. The dream I had cherished since then had come true.

Dressed in the official saree of the Indian contingent, with one daughter wheeling my chair and the other cheering from the audience, I felt a cycle of my life completing.

I was at the head of the contingent alongside the other para athletes, like Rajinder Singh Rahelu, Pragya Ghildial and Bhavina Patel. Leading us, waving the tricolour, was India's Golden Boy, Abhinav Bindra.

Though I placed sixth in my category in the Games and did not win a medal, I got so much more from participating. It deepened my commitment to my sport and made me recognize the immense opportunity para sports offered me. The onus was now on me to capitalize on it. I now had something to prove at the Asian Para Games, and it was with this spirit that I headed to Guangzhou, China.

Devika was unable to accompany me to Guangzhou as she needed to catch up on college work after her time at the Commonwealth Games. Bikram had just started a new job and would not be able to take leave. Once again, Prateek stepped up—he volunteered to accompany me. His involvement with me and other para athletes at the Commonwealth Games had helped him overcome his own challenges, boosting his self-esteem. He was now keen to give back by volunteering.

Our families had grown close over bike rides together, picnics at Jim Corbett National Park and trips for rallies. Prateek, towering at 6'4", was particularly adept at assisting me with my wheelchair. Thus it was decided: Prateek would be my attendant for the Asian Para Games.

I returned to Ahmednagar for the first time since the closure of Dee's Place. Many unresolved issues needed to be discussed. Neither Bikram nor his parents had come to see me at the Commonwealth Games. When my husband should have been there to share my success, he was not there. Instead of coming, he had sent Ambika alone to Delhi. She had been put on a bus from Ahmednagar to Pune with one of the boys from Dee's Place, and she had taken the flight from there on her own.

Frustrated with how the conversation was unfolding, I announced that I was going to Delhi to prepare for the upcoming

Asian Para Games. I said that I would manage everything on my own steam and, putting my bag in my Ritz along with my wheelchair, I drove off. Enroute, I picked up Devika and met with the same police officer who had helped me when the traffic cops had taken the keys from my cab driver. He arranged the night's stay for us in Mumbai and also helped us get a driver for our onward journey to Ahmedabad. In Ahmedabad, Janak and Sameer joined us. They drove us to Jaipur, where Prateek came to pick us up.

In Delhi, thanks to Ashish Bahl's connections, his brother-in-law provided a comfortable, accessible room at the Connaught Hotel. My stay was made even more gracious as they waived the charges for our meals.

I met officials at the Sports Authority of India office every day. With the PCI suspended and no official governing body for para sports, I found myself in a precarious position. As a medal hopeful for the Asian Para Games, I explained my situation to them while requesting a place to stay. They allocated me a room at Hotel Atithi in East of Kailash, making Room No. 3 in the hotel my temporary address. Devika had to go back but the staff at Atithi were extremely supportive. One of the partners of the hotel was Tilak Madan, whose partner's son had been in one of the car rallies I had participated in. Now that I had a safe and comfortable place to stay, I could focus on my training.

I had my car with me but driving in Delhi was extremely difficult. Managing the clutch, brake and accelerator with my hands was complicated, especially in the middle of slow-moving traffic. The situation became even more fraught with tension when it came to flyovers. It would take me time to change gears and often I would begin to roll back or roll forward on the slopes. In the middle of bumper-to-bumper traffic, driving like this was a source of considerable stress for me. However, as I acclimatized to Delhi's roads, I began navigating from Atithi to Jawaharlal Nehru Stadium independently.

Coach Naval Singh trained me, but once again, I sensed that the training was instinctive rather than scientific. Most of the coaches, accustomed to the body structure and needs of able-bodied athletes, had yet to fully grasp the science of training para athletes. I soon formed a group with the other para athletes and we trained together.

The status of para sports in India at this time was still like that of orphaned children, with the PCI working in an ad hoc manner. Before our departure for the Para Asian Games in China, the chef de mission and other administrators had already left. We were left to go to China on our own. Though we had been given tickets, we were expected to fend for ourselves for the visas. It was a repeat of what had happened before Berlin.

At the Chinese embassy, we were given a bill of Rs 1,37,000 as a group visa fee to be submitted up front. We begged and pleaded to be allowed to pay individually, but the embassy officials did not budge.

Officials from the PCI were with us but unable to do anything. One of the para athletes, driven to frustration, grabbed the collar of the PCI president and demanded that they do something to get him a visa. Every one of us had reached this far after endless struggles. I had also fought with everyone and left home for these Games. There was no way I was going back empty-handed. I led the charge and asked everyone to contribute whatever they could. I put up Rs 80,000, someone added Rs 20,000 and another managed Rs 30,000. Scrounging for rupees, we finally managed to reach the magic sum of Rs 1,37,000 and finally got our group visa.

Victorious, we headed to the airport and boarded our aircraft to the sound of cheers and jubilation. We celebrated with laddoos brought by one of the para athletes. But soon we realized our celebration may have been premature. As we settled in with our seatbelts on, we waited for the customary departure announcement. It never came. Instead, after making us wait on the tarmac for four and a half hours, we were told that the flight was being cancelled due to technical issues.

Our celebration turned into tears. The delay meant that several of the athletes would arrive too late to make it to the medical classification for the Games. They would not be able to participate. I saw dreams shatter on that plane—heartbreak that could have been easily avoided had the administrators done their job in a competent manner.

We were put up in a hotel for the night before finally leaving the next day, arriving in Guangzhou twenty-four hours behind schedule.

We reached to find the team members who had reached earlier waiting in the holding area, suffering from further administrative neglect: the entrance fee for the contingent had not been paid and so their accreditation was incomplete. Without accreditation, they had not got access to their accommodation and had spent the night in the waiting area.

Despite these setbacks, we finally made it to the Asian Games Village and settled in.

Since we had missed the medical classification, many athletes were unable to compete. Fortunately for me, having participated in the shot put event at the Commonwealth Games, my medical classification was up to date.

The day of my event dawned and what a day it was. The temperature had plummeted to -2° Celsius and it was raining. Moreover, I was placed in a combined category. Despite the odds stacked against me, I made my throws.

When the results were announced, there was jubilation in the India camp. I had won a bronze, making me the first Indian woman para athlete to win a medal at the Asian Games. Tears of joy streamed down my face as I draped the tricolour around my shoulders, accepting my medal with pride.

After the ceremony, I collected my certificate from the chef de mission, who offered his congratulations. 'Deepa, you are the first Indian woman to win a para Asian event. Congratulations.'

With this bronze medal, my series of firsts continued.

Along with my certificate, he handed me a card—a special privilege from the local organizing committee in Guangzhou, awarded to each medal winner. It granted the use of a personal car for the remainder of the Games. With my event over, I was free to explore the beautiful city of Guangzhou.

I had the luxury of a six-seater car at my disposal, and I chose to take the front passenger seat. Over the years, I had developed strong bonds with many para athletes, often acting as interpreter during international events. They relied on me for various tasks: interacting with airline staff, filling out immigration forms, assisting with event registrations. At mealtimes, I helped them decipher the ingredients in unfamiliar dishes, since a lot of them had dietary restrictions and preferences. I looked up information about selections and rankings on the internet. Being the oldest among them and because I made a concerted efforts to get to know them, they responded with love and respect. I never let my age, my financial status or my education become barriers in my interactions with the rest of the contingent.

Now, in Guangzhou, I invited the other para athletes to join me as I ventured out.

Guangzhou, among the three largest cities in China, straddles the Pearl River and boasts a rich history dating back more than 2,000 years. This major port city is a fascinating blend of tradition and modernity, where ancient temples and sleek skyscrapers coexist harmoniously.

I returned from China richer by a bronze medal and memories of a visit to a beautiful city.

I hadn't expected a hero's welcome, akin to what cricketers receive when they come back after a victorious international tour. But I had also not expected total silence in the media. I had returned to India as the first woman from our country to get a medal in para athletics at the Asian level. Our para team of 102 para athletes had returned home with fourteen medals, including a gold.

Yet, the media spotlight remained fixed on the results of the able-bodied games.

I was still trying to reconcile with this disregard, when I learnt that the PCI had been declared defunct by the government due to compliance issues. This created a new challenge: I had been selected to participate in the International Paralympic Committee (IPC) Athletics World Championships scheduled to take place in New Zealand in January 2011. With no PCI to take care of the paperwork for my participation, there was now a big question mark on whether I would be able to go. The five of us who had qualified for the championships were now left in limbo.

While grappling with how to get to New Zealand, I received an invitation from the Haryana government to attend a felicitation event in Chandigarh, where Chief Minister Bhupinder Singh Hooda would present cash awards to sportspersons.

I was already in Chandigarh when, at 6 a.m., I received a frantic phone call from the head of the Paralympic Committee for Haryana. He was on the train to Chandigarh and had just received some disturbing news. After the Commonwealth Games, the Haryana government had awarded money to athletes from the state: Rs 15 lakh to the gold medallists, Rs 10 lakh to the silver medallists and Rs 5 lakh to the bronze medallists. They were also given cars, mobile phones and large tins of ghee. All participants who hadn't medalled were given Rs 2 lakh each. It had been announced that similar awards would be given to the Asian Games winners. However, it now turned out that para athletes, previously awarded equally after the Commonwealth Games, would now receive only one-tenth of the announced amount for the Asian Games. He urged me to meet the chief minister to address this disparity.

Amar Chacha, my father-in-law's brother who had been at my side during my surgery in 1999, was a former classmate of the chief minister. I called him to help fix an appointment for me.

When I arrived at his official residence, the chief minister was playing tennis. As soon as he finished his game, he came over to me.

'*Beti, kya ho gaya?*' he asked me, placing his hands on my head in a sign of affection.

'Please give me your blessings,' I began. 'You have been promoting sports in a big way and we are all grateful to you for that. But I want to ask you, is the tricolour that was flying high when I won my medal in Guangzhou only 10 per cent of the flag that flew for the other athletes? The medal I have brought home is not 10 per cent of any other medal. And I have brought it back for all 130 crore Indians, not for only 10 per cent of us. So today, at the felicitation function, I will not be able to accept a cheque that is 10 per cent of what the able-bodied athletes are getting. That would be an insult to my medal. When the playing field was the same, the game was the same, the place was the same, the city was the same, the competition ground was the same, why is the reward money not the same? I will not accept the cheque. The media will be present at the event and my refusal will cause an uproar and embarrassment. I do not want to disrespect you in front of everyone. So I'm going back to Delhi after this meeting.'

He immediately called for his cordless phone and made some calls. After concluding his conversations, he told me that I must attend the function and that I would not be disappointed.

Later that day, at the award ceremony, I was handed an envelope containing not one but two cheques—one for Rs 1 lakh and the other for Rs 9 lakh. The other two para athletes who had medalled at the Asian Games got the same.

This victory was significant. It wasn't just a personal triumph but a major win for para athletes, ensuring equal recognition and rewards from state governments. But I now realized that this was a battle I would also have to take to the central government.

After the function we returned to Delhi, and Amar Chacha suggested that I visit the chief minister at his Delhi home to thank him for what he had done.

As we approached his residence in Lutyens' Delhi, I realized that I had been here earlier. This grand house had once been allotted to Kumbha Ram Arya, my bua's father-in-law. This was the house we had stayed in when we had come to Delhi to attend the Asian Games in 1982. Memories came flooding back as we entered and were greeted by the chief minister himself.

Beneath the very tree I had played under as a child, he graciously hung my medal around my neck once again. This garden had been the stadium for our medal ceremonies, where my cousins and I had used biscuit tins as podiums and crafted medals from bangles.

Today, in the same garden and under the same tree, I was being felicitated in another medal ceremony—only this one was real. Though seated in my wheelchair, I felt taller than ever before.

Another episode in my life came full circle that day. Dreams, no matter how deeply buried, have a way of coming true if they are fervent enough.

Overwhelmed, I broke down, unable to control my sobs. When I shared the reason for my emotion, the chief minister's eyes filled with tears. His wife led me inside, curious about my memories of the house and how much it had changed since 1982.

With the cash award from the Haryana government, some amount of financial uncertainty faded from my life. But the more immediate problem that had to be tackled was twofold: I had to find a way of going to New Zealand and a way to extend my stay at Hotel Atithi. My agreement with the hotel covered only the duration of the Asian Games. Now that the Games were over, I was expected to vacate the room.

Amidst this stress, one of the coaches suggested a bold move, instead of wasting my time pleading with the sports ministry officials. 'Why not knock on the door of Sonia Gandhi [then chairperson of the United Progressive Alliance, MP, Congress leader]?'

I found a contact number on the Congress Party's website, but despite several tries, I received no answer. One day, I decided on a more direct approach. I got into my car, parked it near her house and wheeled myself up to the gate, right in the line of the security cameras. I sat there in the cold, shivering in my Team India tracksuit. After about two hours, a security guard approached me to invite me inside. I was soon speaking to a senior officer. When I told him I was a sportsperson, he suggested speaking to Rahul Gandhi, who was dealing with matters related to youth affairs and sports.

The next day I went to Rahul Gandhi's house. He met and spoke with me, and after seeing my medal and hearing about my predicament with accommodation, he called Ajay Maken, minister for sports and youth affairs. On his directions, I was given permission to stay at Atithi till the 2012 London Olympics.

As I continued training for the IPC Athletics World Championships to be held in Christchurch, New Zealand, I also petitioned the government to guide us as to the procedures to be followed in the absence of the PCI.

In discussions with the IPC, they advised me to go through the SAI. This meant cutting through considerable red tape.

My days would begin with my training sessions at JLN Stadium. Then I'd be off to the SAI office to knock on the doors of the sports administrators. After my training, I would need to change my diaper. But going back to Atithi, changing and going all the way back would waste too much time. So I devised a way of changing my diaper at the stadium. Since I needed to lie flat to change, I carried two yoga mats with me. After practice, I would ask my fellow athletes or even the security guards to take me to the washroom, place the yoga mats on the floor and place me flat on them. After changing, I would call out to them to once again to pick me up and put me in my wheelchair.

After much perseverance, when the authorities were finally convinced, the SAI agreed to send the five of us to New Zealand. Prateek Gahlaut stepped up once again, volunteering as our team manager. Our six-member squad was ready.

New Zealand was incredible. Everything was so well organized and wheelchair-friendly in Christchurch. Our accommodations were in a picturesque college, complete with charming wooden buildings and a grassy central courtyard. From my room I could see a majestic tree, its leaves yellow because of the time of year. A stream flowed by, and brown ducks waddled around, followed by their bright yellow ducklings.

The opening ceremony was a beautifully conducted event held in the Cathedral Square and all the participants—about 1,000—paraded through the streets greeted by cheering crowds. The parade concluded at the square where we were given a traditional Maori welcome.

Surrounded by the stunning scenery of Christchurch, we took the shuttle to the venue for the Games. The organization was impeccable—there was no confusion, no chaos. The Games were held at Queen Elizabeth II Park stadium, which, tragically, was destroyed in a devastating earthquake just three weeks later.

This made the Games the last international event the stadium would ever host. I participated in the javelin throw and shot put. My javelin performance fell short, but in the shot put event I won a silver.

Thrilled with my first international silver medal, I now turned my attention to exploring Christchurch. The accreditation card that all the participants had been given doubled as a pass for free public transport and entry to many attractions. I found the public transport system remarkably accessible. The buses had low floors with ramps, allowing easy wheelchair access, and featured a unique ability: they could kneel! Their hydraulic systems enabled them to lower to curb level, so wheelchairs could simply roll on.

I noticed that most of the vehicles were non-polluting e-vehicles. Everything was so clean, and the people so friendly. Many of those serving in public spaces were senior citizens, extremely courteous, efficient and dedicated.

During a gondola ride, I met a young man whose story stayed with me. A finance student at the university, he worked part-time as a boatman. He had a unique take on his work. 'Why should I pay for a gym membership to stay fit when I can get paid to work out here, while also enjoying the beautiful outdoors?' He was right. Every stroke of his oar was a full-body workout, making each ride with tourists a fitness session.

'The next time we meet, I may be the CEO of a company,' he told us as we left.

When it was time for us to return to India, my thoughts were consumed by finding financial stability, especially now that Dee's Place had closed. I had to find a way to ensure a steady income for the years ahead.

I returned to India with a silver medal—the first Indian woman para athlete to do so—but also with uncertainty about my financial situation.

As I was battling these concerns, I got a call that once again reinforced my belief in the Almighty. He had given me so many challenges in life, but for every challenge, he showed me the path to overcoming it.

'Hello, Deepa, this is Partho,' came a deep voice. 'From Kendriya Vidyalaya, Kolkata.'

'Partho, the boy who made all those drawings?' I asked.

Partho Sengupta had been a classmate back in Kolkata. Every day, without fail, he would draw a caricature of me on the blackboard, always accentuating my legs.

'You remember the drawings, but do you remember the guy?' he asked playfully.

Of course I remembered. Back in school, I had been known for my long legs. When I competed in the long jump, the boys would line up next to the pit just to watch me land. Partho had got my number from another classmate, Sukanya, who was working for IBM in Bangalore and had connected with me after the Commonwealth Games. Partho was working with the advertising agency Hakuhodo Percept and, coincidentally, lived in my neighbourhood.

We chatted about old times and made plans to meet. When Partho visited me in my modest room at Atithi, he was moved. He later told me that despite seeing me in my wheelchair, he couldn't get the image of me flying over hurdles during school athletics out of his mind. He returned to his office, still trying to wrap his head around this new version of his school friend Deepa. At work, he found his young colleagues complaining about things like deadlines, cabs and the weather. Their issues seemed so trivial and insipid to him compared to what I had gone through. To him, the transformation was stark yet inspiring: from the beautiful, long-legged girl who had all the boys swooning to a woman living in one room in her wheelchair but still fiercely tackling life's uphill tasks, driving herself from training sessions to the SAI office and navigating bureaucracy with a smile. In his eyes, I was no less than Superwoman.

Partho discussed my story with his partner at the agency, leading to an invitation to speak to their team. Speaking from the heart, I shared my life's journey—from my dreams before paralysis to the relentless pursuit of those dreams despite my disability. I told them about my problems and the resilience they instilled in me, driving me into problem-solving mode for every hurdle.

There was not a single dry eye in the audience that day. Partho told me that my story had moved his team so much that there was little else they talked about for a week after.

Moved by the effect of my talk, Partho's wife, Julia, an educator at Delhi's Shri Ram School, invited me to address the students. Speaking to a packed auditorium of 500 students, I emphasized inclusivity, sensitivity and the importance of seizing opportunities.

Partho's son, Iman, who was about eleven years old then, spent a day with me, learning to push my chair, help me into my car and assist with small tasks. Seeing me so in control and so 'able' to go about life just like anyone else created what Partho calls 'a visual of the impossible' for Iman. Partho still says that he doesn't see me as a person with disabilities unless he notices my wheelchair. On my fiftieth birthday, he gifted me a painting he had made of me—I was the same long-legged Deepa from school, leaping over hurdles. That is how he sees me, as a champion who can overcome anything.

While we rekindled our friendship, Partho also opened new avenues for me. Through his connections, he got me an invitation from Deutsche Bank to conduct three motivational workshops for them. This was my first paid motivational speaking gig. I was flown to Mumbai in business class—my first time not taking economy. A Mercedes car was sent to the airport to pick me up. I stayed in a suite at the Grand Hyatt. My three talks went well. Before I boarded my flight back to Delhi, I was presented with an envelope. I opened it on the plane and found a cheque for Rs 15,000. I was thrilled, but my middle-class mind did some mental maths and wished that instead of treating me to so much luxury, they had flown me economy, ferried me in a regular car, put me up in a smaller hotel and paid me the difference! I was that much in need of hard cash at the time.

This talk opened more doors for me. My next motivational talk earned me a cheque of Rs 75,000, and the one after that got me Rs 1.5 lakh. Today, a large part of my income is from these speaking engagements.

Ambika had just completed her tenth-standard board exams and was awaiting her results. This was the perfect time to reconnect and strengthen our relationship. We had been apart for several crucial years. Though her grandparents cared for her, she had missed the maternal support only I could offer.

And there were enough people in Ahmednagar to point this out to her. Teachers kept needling her about my absence, classmates made cruel comments about why her parents lived apart and even the maid complained about extra duties like packing her tiffin box. In her young mind, a lot of these comments must have resonated. Unable to comprehend the layers and complexities of adult relationships, she must have perceived me as the mother who abandoned her children, the wife who left her husband, all for sports. This teenage angst manifested in troubling behaviour, like using her compass to gouge holes in her bedroom wall. To mend our bond and give her a stable environment, I brought her to Atithi. The plan was for her to complete her last two years of schooling at the Maharani Gayatri Devi Girls' School (MGD) in Jaipur, the school Devika had graduated from.

But for now, it was time for me to create as many positive mother-daughter moments as I could. It was not easy—from her perspective I could sense the feelings of abandonment and resentment she must have harboured, believing I had 'chosen' something else over her. She must have felt betrayed.

Earlier, despite my wheelchair, I had been present. We had our time together, playing games at Dee's Place, swimming and working on projects. To have all this taken away must have been tough for her to process and understand. Now at Atithi, the Ambika that came to live with me was not the sweet eleven-year-old I had left behind. She was a teenager, full of so many emotions, so many grievances against her mother, so much anger. When she had been younger, I had introduced her to go-karting and she had loved it, showing a lot of potential for motor racing—after all, she had Bikram's and my genes. But I had not been able to nurture that interest due to the prohibitive costs involved.

Day by day, we began repairing our relationship. Ashley Lobo, the famous dancer and choreographer, unintentionally played a key role in this healing process. His Danceworx workshops were being conducted at a school near Atithi, and I enrolled Ambika in these classes. It was a joy to see her blossom there. She loved it, and her enthusiasm was evident. At the end of the workshop, the group staged a performance at the Talkatora Stadium, for which Ambika landed the coveted role of Michael Jackson. Watching her perform the pop icon's signature moves made me feel as though my feet had grown wings. I wept as I watched my previously conflicted daughter channel her emotions into dance, shedding her anger and resentment onstage.

Meanwhile, Devika secured an internship at Fortis Hospital and joined us at Atithi. Now our gang of girls was complete.

I took them to Rishikesh, where we went on the zip line. The team at Jumpin Heights adapted their set-up to accommodate us, equipping us with special harnesses. Although I hesitated initially, unsure of the logistics involved in navigating the zip line with my paralysis, their team went above and beyond. They assisted me with the ascent to the launch ramp while I was in my chair, and after the zip line, they pushed me uphill.

Seeing me navigate life so actively had an impact on Ambika. While I was still a way off from winning her trust completely, that summer marked a new beginning.

Before Ambika went back to school, I had another big adventure planned for her. I was still smarting from having had to be the navigator in the Raid De Himalayas. I was now craving adrenaline-pumping adventure from behind the wheel. After a lot of brainstorming, I connected with the Limca Book of Records with a proposal for my third record with them.

I aimed to be the first woman with chest-below paralysis to drive across nine of the highest motorable passes in India. Prateek, who had done this drive multiple times on his bike before his accident, agreed to be my co-driver. And Ambika would accompany us on this journey.

The next task was to find a suitable vehicle.

I came to learn that Tata was auctioning vehicles previously used to transport athletes and officials during the Commonwealth Games. I connected with Tata Motors, and they directed me towards their dealer Sandeep Bansal.

Sandeep, a vintage car collector, was so impressed with my grit that he immediately agreed to help us get a good vehicle. From him I was able to get an almost new Tata Safari at a highly concessional rate.

We decided to drive across nine high-altitude passes in nine days—routes that rank among the highest motorable roads in the country. No other woman with chest-below paralysis had ever done this. To officially validate my attempt, I needed to document each major milestone I crossed with photographs and videos, get a certificate signed by a gazetted officer at every night halt and keep every fuel receipt as proof that I had driven in the same vehicle throughout the journey.

The next task was finalizing the route. Our planned route was from Delhi to Ambala, then on to Udhampur, Srinagar, Kargil and finally Leh. The overnight halts were arranged after coordinating with the army authorities and requesting them for accommodation. The officer in charge would also certify my presence for the Limca Book of Records.

The drive was excruciating. The rugged terrain and high altitude pose a challenge to anyone, but for me it was compounded by the fact that I only have the use of half my lungs. Driving was tough, but soon breathing became difficult too. The altitude was giving me terrible headaches. To remain hydrated, I had to drink at night—I avoided drinking during the day to minimize the need to empty my urine bag. But drinking water that was cold at night resulted in a throat infection. I was driving when we were crossing the Chang La Pass. The last thing I remember is my chin dropping to my chest while I repeatedly mumbled, 'I must be mad.' I realized that I had collapsed only when I heard Ambika scream, '*Mummy behosh ho gayee*' (Mummy is unconscious). My head was slumped against the dashboard. Prateek, seated behind me, quickly pulled me up by the back of my hoodie and managed to stop the car using the hand controls. I was revived with oxygen, which became a nightly necessity at each stop thereafter.

We covered the nine highest passes: Zoji La, Changlang La, Khardung La, Tanglang La, Lachung La, Nakee La, Baralacha La, Rohtang La and Fotu La. We had travelled 3,000 km in ten days and driven at heights over 15,000 feet.

My dream to complete a raid in the Himalayas had come true.

By the time we returned from our record-making trip in Ladakh, Ambika's board results were out and it was time to get her admission at MGD in Jaipur. My father was able to get her the school admission, but the hostel admission was proving difficult, particularly since the principal was not meeting any parents or guardians.

Determined, I rushed to Jaipur and landed up at the school. I steamrolled my way into the principal's office and along with Ambika's application for hostel accommodation, I also placed all my medals on her table. Before I could say anything, the principal said she knew me. We had never met, but before she had come to MGD, she had been at the Scindia School in Gwalior. There, she had sent her students to meet me, and I had spoken to them. Once again, another old connection proved invaluable. She understood the necessity of giving Ambika hostel accommodation to give me the peace of mind I needed to focus on my competitions.

The year had begun on a high note, with me winning silver at the IPC Athletics World Championships in New Zealand—a first for India. It ended on another high. At the IWAS Games in Sharjah, I clinched two bronze medals and created two new Asian records.

The following April, in Malaysia—the country where I had started my para sports journey—I created a new Asian javelin record in my F53 category at the first Malaysian Open Athletics Championships.

I was at my peak. My regular training had made me stronger and I was focused on para sports. Like Arjuna with his unwavering gaze fixed on the eye of the fish, I was singularly focused on one thing: the London Paralympics.

14

Road to Rio

———◦•◦———

I SCANNED THE LIST OF ATHLETES FOR THE LONDON Paralympics, searching for my name. It wasn't there. 'Disappointed' is too small a word to describe what I felt. India had got a quota for ten para athletes to go to London and chose an all-male squad to represent the country.

Missing the Paralympics was gut-wrenching. For any athlete, the Olympics and Paralympics represent the pinnacle of achievement. While every medal has its value, the holy grail is the Paralympic medal. Representing India on the world's grandest stage was a dream that would have made everything I had endured so far worthwhile.

And what rankled most was knowing I could have made it, if not for a series of setbacks. To secure my spot in London, I needed a registered javelin throw of at least 9 metres. While training, I was consistently exceeding this mark. However, at the international meet in Malaysia, my distance was 8.87 metres, a new Asian record and one that got me a gold medal. But I still needed to attend an international meet before the London Paralympics and register a throw of 9 metres or more. Given my level of training and results in the practice throws, I was confident of making it and now needed to attend the Grand Prix scheduled to take place in Paris before the Paralympics.

After my record-setting performances in Sharjah and Malaysia, my coach became highly sought after by other para athletes. Attempts were made to create a rift between us. I remained fully committed to my training, but unlike other athletes who went out for drinks with their coaches, I was not able to socialize with him.

Misunderstandings fuelled by vested interests began to surface. My status as an educated woman, familiar with the rules and capable of communicating with the authorities, became an issue. The coach's attention shifted, and he began to offer me only perfunctory training sessions, devoting more time to the others.

My peers continued to rely on me to advocate on behalf of all the para athletes with the SAI. They asked me to get official sanction for a camp in Delhi. We got the camp, but not at JLN Stadium. It was at R.K. Khanna Tennis Stadium.

Here, I faced further challenges because the parking was some distance from the tracks. At JLN, I could park close to the tracks and someone would assist me into my wheelchair. Now, I often found myself waiting in the parking lot for the coach to send someone for me, but the coach would delay this. Unlike other para athletes who were from nearby towns and had the support of family members acting as assistants, I had no one.

My attempts to connect with the coach for training were futile. I would be told to come to the field only to find him at the gym; when I would go to the gym, he would be in the sauna. I was given a proper runaround. The message was clear: the coach did not want to train me.

Amidst these struggles, the newly reconstituted Paralympic Committee of India was handling my application for the Paris Grand Prix. One and a half months before the games, I submitted my passport to the PCI for visa applications and other formalities.

However, I was shocked to see my passport come back to me with the visa application rejected. The reason? The visa had been applied for 'post the competition date'.

Without the Paris validation as a qualifier, I was out of the running for London.

Missing the Paralympics led to a host of related problems. My stay at Atithi, which the SAI funded as part of my preparation for London, came under threat. The immediate fallout of missing London was an order to vacate my room at Atithi.

My dream had crashed and now I was out on the street.

I spoke with the manager at Atithi, who agreed to let me stay on for another month, but at a cost of Rs 75,000. It was a big amount, but I had no other option.

I was in a seemingly hopeless situation—the coach had been manipulated to ignore me, I was soon going to be homeless and I had no one to turn to.

Had Bikram still been in the army, I might have had access to military accommodation. Without financial resources and needing wheelchair-accessible accommodation, my options were limited, as ground-floor residences were more expensive.

I also knocked on the door of the Olympic Gold Quest, an NGO dedicated to supporting sportspersons on their journey to winning gold at the Olympics. I made my case to them, seeking help with funding, but was turned away. They were focusing on able-bodied sportspersons with Olympic gold dreams and Olympic gold potential. The Paralympics were not on their agenda.

(However, I am happy to share that since my tenure as president of the PCI, the Olympic Gold Quest has begun working closely with para sports bodies and supporting para athletes across various categories.)

But every cloud had a silver lining. While my international sporting records, adventure sport and motoring records and media coverage sparked envy within the para sports community, they also garnered substantial support for me from the rest of the world.

Even as I was dealing with internal politics, I was appointed to the working group for the formulation of the Twelfth Five-Year Plan (2012–17) on sports and physical education. This significant nomination came from the Planning Commission's HRD division on behalf of the sports ministry. I was now in a position to make a difference at the policy level. I had the opportunity to address the challenges I had faced: visa facilitation to attend international events, provision of attendants for camps and meets, better facilities at camps, more scientific training, better systems for selections. I could no longer go from event to event with a begging bowl asking for camps, asking for participation, asking for accommodation. I needed to be in Delhi now more than ever.

Alongside this prestigious appointment, I received exhilarating news: I was to be honoured with the Arjuna Award for outstanding performance in sports and games. The Arjuna Award is a highly esteemed recognition of sporting talent in India.

I received the award from the President of India, Pranab Mukherjee, in August. Ironically, this coincided with the opening ceremony of the London Paralympic Games. While I was thrilled to be at Rashtrapati Bhavan, receiving the award in the presence of my entire family, I couldn't deny that part of me yearned to be in London, competing in the Paralympics.

Most of the women awardees wore a saree and a blazer, but I had to opt for the male uniform. A saree isn't practical with multiple transfers—moving from wheelchair to cab, cab to wheelchair and back again. That day, the need for adaptive transport also hit home, as finding cabs that were wheelchair-friendly was challenging.

Most cabs have CNG cylinders in their boot, leaving no space for a wheelchair.

Receiving the Arjuna Award alongside cricketer Yuvraj Singh, I felt a deep sense of equality in our achievements within our respective sports. That day I, Deepa, sat with two young Deepikas—Pallikal and Kumari—and our collective glory lit up the hall. Of course, I was forty-two years old, and they were practically teenagers, yet we were all receiving the same award. Though I was the oldest athlete to receive the award, I knew this was not my swansong.

As I wheeled towards the President to receive my award, the applause in the grand Durbar Hall was thunderous, resonating more for me than for any other awardees, I was later told. This hall, where defence awards are presented, held a special significance that day. Applauding me were the four army men in my life—my father, my father-in-law, my brother and my husband. While we were getting ready for the ceremony, my father and father-in-law had diligently polished their ceremonial medals to match their side caps so that they would look their best as they saw me receive one of the biggest sporting awards of the country from their supreme commander. After the function, the three aides-de-camp of the President, one each from the Indian Army, Navy and Air Force, sought me out and saluted me together, a mark of respect for a sportswoman from their fraternity.

My sense of achievement was immense. Receiving this award combined with having my entire family stay with me at the Ashok Hotel in Delhi filled me with pride.

The euphoria of receiving this honour had me over the moon. But as the evening dimmed and dawn broke on a new day, I was back where I had been—on the verge of being evicted. Isolated from my team. Abandoned by my coach. Everyone was telling me that it was now time for me to retire. After all, with the Arjuna Award, I could easily hang up my javelin and go back to Ahmednagar with my head held high, having vindicated myself against all who doubted me.

Everyone assumed that the Arjuna Award should have been enough for me.

Everyone said I was so lucky.

'So lucky, you got the Arjuna Award.'

'So lucky, you got your picture with the President.'

'So lucky, you got your name in the Limca Book of Records.'

'So lucky, you've travelled abroad.'

'So lucky, you've won so many national and international awards.'

'So lucky, your husband didn't leave you.'

I wanted to shout back at everyone who called me 'lucky'—luck had nothing to do with it. It was all down to my hard work. I had worked so hard to ensure my life was not limited to a bed in one small room, a common fate for many with paralysis. I had worked so hard to devise methods of taking care of my bladder and bowel movements so that I could be mobile. I swam against the flow in the Yamuna in pouring rain—a tough task for even able-bodied swimmers. I drove through the highest motorable passes in India— having only half my lung capacity. I sacrificed my time with my daughters—something so many mothers couldn't do.

Luck had nothing to do with my Arjuna Award.

And I was not ready to go back. So what if I could not go to London? I would go to Rio instead. The 2016 Paralympics became my new goal.

As I struggled to find a place to stay and for money to sustain myself, once again, Haryana extended a lifeline.

Shortly after the Olympic Games, the Haryana government held a felicitation ceremony for its numerous medallists, and I was also invited for having received the Arjuna Award. At this event, a monthly allowance of Rs 5,000 was announced for all Arjuna Awardees. This was a blessing—it would take care of my fuel bill.

At the ceremony, I reunited with Vijender Singh, Sandeep Singh and Sardar Singh once again. I recalled our conversation about tattoos at the Commonwealth Games. They had planned to get the Olympic rings tattooed once they participated in the Games. Now, they proudly showed me their tattoos. This reinforced my resolve to give my 100 per cent to go to Rio. I, too, wanted my tattoo.

I found a place to stay in the Lal Dora (urban village) area of Shahpur Jat, nestled in the heart of upscale South Delhi. Though it was a congested, unplanned area, the location was crucial—it was close to everywhere I needed to be: JLN Stadium, Siri Fort Sports Complex, R.K. Khanna Tennis Stadium and the Sports Authority of India office.

It was modest—a single-room flat that ended almost as soon as it began. There was a small kitchen, a storeroom and a bathroom. The plus was that it was on the ground floor and even better was the rent: Rs 8,000.

But even that small flat felt like a palace because it was my own. Transforming it into a home became a personal project. I got a bed and bedside tables from the nearby Amar Colony furniture market. My biker friends proved invaluable. One of them, Ashish, specialized in modifying flats. He offered to do up my place. The most important modifications were replacing the Indian-style commode with a Western toilet, installing a geyser, widening the doorways to accommodate my wheelchair and constructing a ramp.

The housewarming was a chance to host old friends and new, and I was happy to have Bikram there. My old friend Diya, who had helped me create media attention for Dee's Place in Ahmednagar, cooked and brought over a delicious Bengali feast. I had set up my kitchen with a fridge and a microwave, a small gas cylinder and lots of colourful utensils from a big hypermarket. Diya gifted me the kadai (wok) she had brought the food in. Casual dinners, where I would also cook, became my thing whenever I would have friends over.

Devika moved in with me as she was now doing her master's at Delhi University. I tried my best to make our house feel like a home. One of the walls was adorned with a special image that captured one of my happiest moments. During a biking event, I had met a young biker who was also a graphic designer. He had modified a picture of me on a bike. In the photo, I have taken off my helmet and have a broad smile on my face. He had added a sunrise behind me. This picture was up on my wall, serving as a daily source of positivity and strength, much like a modern-day mood board.

To help around the house, I hired two maids—a mother-in-law and daughter-in-law duo. Interestingly, they preferred not to work at the same time due to their strained relationship. This suited me as I had help at home for a longer time.

Shahpur Jat was bustling with fashion designers, their workshops often doubling as retail spaces, creating a constant flurry of activity. It was always difficult to find parking. I frequently found my car hemmed in by others, despite my 'handicapped vehicle' sticker. Fortunately, one of my neighbours, with whom I had developed a friendship, allowed me to park in his area, and I never had to be boxed in again.

My days started early here. To reach the stadium for morning practice at 6 a.m., I had to get up at 4 a.m. Devika would help me make my transfer from the bed to the bathroom. She would lay out all the essentials for me to bathe myself. Then she would help me dress and transfer me to my wheelchair again. She would take me to my car, help me into the driver's seat and stow my wheelchair in the boot. I would then drive to practice.

After training, I would rush back so she could leave for college. The morning maid would assist me into bed. It would now be time for me to change my diaper. The maid would place my bedpan, sanitizer, absorbent sheets, talcum powder, a hair dryer and two buckets next to my bed. One bucket with Dettol water for cleaning and one with scented water for me to empty the bedpan into. The absorbent sheets took care of any leaks or if I spilled urine on the bed. But in case I wet the bed, I would sprinkle talcum powder on the urine stain and use the hair dryer to dry it.

I also had my laptop, my cell phone and the TV remote within my reach. The maid would give me my breakfast, clean up and leave, locking the door from outside. I'd spend the midday hours alone until the other maid arrived to give me lunch and attend to the remaining chores. She would empty out the buckets near my bed and refill them.

Devika would return by 4 p.m., and then it was time for my evening training. This schedule bound Devika closely to my routine, and I often felt guilty that my needs curtailed her ability to fully enjoy her college life in Delhi. Her social life was further impacted by my intense fear for her safety. That was the year the Nirbhaya case occurred, where a young girl was brutally gang-raped in a moving bus and later succumbed to her injuries. This incident filled me with so much fear that I did not let Devika explore Delhi as other normal college students would. She was in the prime of her youth, strikingly beautiful—a fact highlighted when a *Delhi Times* photographer took a picture of her on her first day of college, which was published on the front page the next day. She should have been out partying with her friends but here I was, keeping her in. She listened to me out of love and compassion, and she understood my fears, but I still feel the guilt of limiting her experiences and encroaching on her time.

I was completely focused on my training, committed to double shifts: strength training on my own and skill training with the coach.

In the past, whenever I threw, I would hold back, not using my full strength. This was because of my physical condition. Having no control over my bladder and bowel movements meant that I was constantly in danger of soiling myself. Simple triggers like the mechanical whirr of the treadmill in the gym or the loud rock music played during training could cause leaks. Every exertion risked a leak, leaving my diaper soaked by the end of training. To mitigate this, I was drinking less water—a decision that contravened basic athletic training principles, which emphasize the importance of hydration before, during and after exercise. Drinking less water caused muscle cramps and exacerbated my spasticity. I needed post-training physiotherapy to help with the spasticity, but I couldn't afford it.

Frequently, I would return from practice and find my diaper soiled. One day at JLN Stadium, I pushed myself harder than usual during a throw and my worst nightmare came true. I soiled myself so badly that even my track pants were ruined. I was mortified, overcome with embarrassment. I sat on my throw chair, unable to say a word or make eye contact with anyone. Eventually, I regained some composure and called Devika for help. My child came rushing to the stadium. With the help of some other athletes, she moved me to my wheelchair and took me to the washroom. To my dismay, due to ongoing renovations, there was no water or toilet paper, only some discarded cardboard boxes. Lying on the bathroom floor on my yoga mats, I wiped myself with those pieces of cardboard. I put on a fresh diaper, but my pants were soiled beyond use. I had to throw them away. Now, I had nothing to cover myself with. Devika went to the parking lot and fetched the car cover, which she draped around me.

That day, I went home wrapped up in my car cover.

Determined never to be caught unprepared again, I established a new routine. Every day now began with an enema to ensure that my bowels were empty. I assembled emergency kits with everything I might need: Dettol, wet wipes, towels, toilet paper, bedpan, sanitizer, diapers and a change of clothes. I placed one in my car and kept the others handy to carry whenever I left the house in another vehicle.

Sometime after this, another unsettling situation unfolded, making me realize my vulnerability when alone and locked inside my home, yet also reminding me of the big community I was part of.

Devika had left for college, and I had settled into bed. The maid, who had been cooking, suddenly burst into my room. Breathlessly, she explained that she needed to leave immediately because she'd got word that her son had been in an accident. She left, locking the front door from the outside as she always did. But in her hurry, she had forgotten to turn off the stove. The pan was on, and slowly, I could hear the water evaporate and the pan start to sizzle. The smell of burnt food filled the house.

I picked up my phone but discovered that it was dead and the charger out of reach. I lay there in bed, staring up at the ceiling, wondering what I could do. For a moment I thought this was how things were going to end—because of a kitchen fire.

Suddenly, I had a brainwave. So what if I did not have my phone—my laptop was within reach. I quickly opened Facebook and posted a status asking if any friends nearby could direct message me, as I was home alone and in an emergency situation.

Immediately, notifications came flooding in. Once again, my biker friends came to my help. I shared my address and soon enough, around fifteen bikers arrived. They broke the lock, entered the house and switched off the gas, averting a potential disaster.

That day, I realized the power of social media.

Once again, I felt the financial pinch of trying to manage everything on my own. My only source of income was the award money I was getting. After competing in Malaysia, I went to the German Open Athletics Championships in Berlin. This was the qualifying event for the IPC Athletics World Championship games in Lyon. I was the only woman from the Indian team to qualify. At Lyon, I got the diploma position.

My training was progressing well. My fitness levels were up. My strength training had paid off, and I could sit up for longer. But my coach had other athletes to train. His focus was on the younger para athletes, as he saw them as Paralympic hopefuls. Just as every para athlete has Paralympic dreams, so does every coach.

But with my tenacity, I trained like Eklavya. I turned my car into a mobile gym. The boot had my medicine ball, resistance bands and a bucket full of rocks—to practise my throw for discus, the coach would make us throw river rocks at a net.

Our training was relentless. When access to the stadium was restricted due to other events, we went to a park to train. But getting into a public park in Delhi was impossible—every entrance had a turnstile. There was no way for me to make it through on my own. Somehow, with a lot of help from others, I was able to get inside and then my wheelchair followed. Bracing my wheelchair against the trunk of a tree, to prevent it from toppling over from the force of my throw, I trained in the park. At the stadium we used a throw frame for training, which is stable and firmly anchored because of its weight, and consists of a seat and a support arm, using which most paralysed para athletes make their throws for javelin, discus and shot put.

The Right to Information (RTI) is a powerful tool that empowers citizens to hold the government and bureaucracy accountable. However, like any formidable instrument, it is also prone to misuse.

An anonymous RTI enquiry was filed with the Haryana government targeting me, questioning my eligibility to represent the state when my family was living in Maharashtra.

While the aim of the query was to throw me off my game, it actually turned into a boon. In the process of proving my credentials, I connected with my family in Haryana and formed a strong bond with them.

In my response, I presented my family's extensive history in Haryana, with documents dating back to 1929. My mother-in-law, from a well-established Karnal family, counts three MLAs, session and high court judges, several lawyers and champion shooters among her uncles and cousins. My husband's ancestral village is Bhainswal Kalan in Sonipat. My grandfather-in-law was an ex-army man and former sarpanch of the village.

Though I had never visited the village before, when I did go there to get proof of my family's long-standing Haryanvi roots, the love and affection I received filled my heart.

Needless to say, the RTI query fell flat and was consigned to the dustbin.

When I received the Arjuna Award, my Bhainswal Kalan family invited me there to honour me. I was taken around the village in an open jeep, greeted enthusiastically by the residents, including the local MLA. True to Jat traditions, elders showed their affection by gifting me some money.

This visibility led to further recognition. I became that rare sportsperson to first get a national award and then get a state award—the Haryana government presented me the Bhim Award, the state's highest award for sportspersons of national and international repute, which comes with a cash prize of Rs 5 lakh.

I met some extremely committed sports administrators, like O.P. Singh, who was the director of sports in Haryana. As the author of the book *Say Yes to Sports*, he invited me to interview him at the book launch. His book details how Haryana developed a sports culture, which has yielded results in the form of rich medal hauls at international events. It explores initiatives like the Play for India scheme and the SPAT sports scholarship, which link grassroots sports programmes to performance metrics.

So whoever filed the RTI ended up doing me a good turn.

In my fight for inclusion, I was once again helped by *MTV Roadies*. I was invited back on the show, this time as a challenger in the 'money task' segment. Contestants have to perform certain tasks to earn cash for their team. It was thrilling to share this platform with another sportsperson, two-time Olympic wrestler Sushil Kumar. We were the challengers the contestants had to defeat. While the men had to survive a round of kushti with Sushil, the women faced me in the swimming pool. To level the playing field, they swam with their legs bound—they were given life jackets, of course. I had to swim

100 m and the women, in teams of two, had to match me in 50 m relays. None of them could beat me.

The bigger message that went out pushed my At Par agenda, where I was fighting for equal monetary benefits and facilities for para athletes as able-bodied athletes received. Putting me and Sushil Kumar on the same show broadcast a powerful message of inclusivity.

My decision to stay in Delhi had been my own. I had moved from a beautiful farmhouse in Ahmednagar to a one-room flat in Delhi. After the Arjuna Award, Bikram had told me to return, but I still had many miles to go. And I was doing it all on my own steam. I chose not to take any financial support from him and was managing with my prize money and savings. However, the financial strain was mounting with obligations like Ambika's school fees.

It was at this time that I was honoured with the Amazing Indian award by the news channel Times Now, which had earlier featured me on its show *Life's Like That*. Now, Arnab Goswami told me to seize the opportunity at the awards function to tell the world about my journey and to advocate for para sports. He said that the chief guest was the vice president of India, who would speak for three minutes; he as editor-in-chief of the channel would speak for two minutes; but I, as the recipient of the award, would have fifteen minutes to speak. 'You are my showstopper. Speak your heart out,' he said.

My audience that evening included thirty ministers, ambassadors from several countries, captains of industry and other influential figures. Holding their attention for fifteen minutes required a speech that was not only well-researched but also deeply impactful. When the lights dimmed and the stage was all mine, under the glaring spotlights, I began: 'I want to play for my country.'

I listed the hurdles in my way. I talked about money. I talked about the lack of policy. I talked about the ad hoc-ism of training. I talked about the fate of para athletes. The audience listened in rapt attention as I told them that I needed three javelins for training, each costing Rs 1 lakh—a sum I couldn't afford. The room fell silent when I revealed that I often trained in pain and with injuries because I limited my water intake to avoid leaks. I confessed that I held back in my throws for fear of soiling myself, yet I frequently ended my training with a soiled diaper. There was not a single dry eye in the hall.

'I need to play for India. With the right support from you and access to the right equipment, I, and other para athletes, can bring laurels for India. Can you help me?' I concluded before leaving the stage.

I remember meeting two MPs after the event—Piyush Goyal, who later became a cabinet minister, and Naveen Jindal, who was himself a sportsperson and industrialist. Piyush Goyal spoke to me and encouraged me as he himself was closely associated with an NGO working with the disabled. Naveen Jindal came to me with his phone in his hand and took my number. I found it so refreshing—usually, people give you their number and ask you to contact them. He said that he would get in touch.

Sure enough, two days later, I got a call from his human resources head, Rajeev Bhadauria. We set up a meeting and he came to my flat in Shahpur Jat. I sat in my wheelchair while he took one chair and Devika took the other, beside him.

I didn't hold back in our discussion. I laid out the stark realities of para sports in India, which lacked the government support it needed. There were no policies in place: no annual training calendars, no

camp schedules, extreme opacity when it came to selections and
no fixed remuneration for the coaches. This inconsistency was due
to their pay being tied to completing 280 days at government-
sponsored camps, which themselves were sporadically scheduled—
sometimes for thirty days, sometimes sixty.

I shared my personal struggles, too. Despite being the daughter-
in-law of a general and the wife of a colonel, here I was, living
in one room. I told him that I was determined to be financially
independent, not taking any money from home. My expenses were
growing, from my daughter's school fees to the cost of training,
which required a personal attendant. I had been relying on the
kindness of strangers to help transfer me from my car to my chair,
to place me in my throw frame, to retrieve my javelin, discus and
shot put after my throws. I needed a trained attendant at home to
take care of my enema and hygiene—I could no longer depend on
my daughter for this. With my training becoming more intensive,
I was suffering from cramps and increased spasticity, and needed a
physiotherapist after every session.

My only source of income since the closure of Dee's Place was
the reward money I would get for winning medals at state, national
and international competitions. I occasionally earned speaker fees
from motivational talks, but this income was sporadic. As a result, I
found myself dipping into my fast-depleting savings.

Rajiv Bhadauria promised to get back to me with a plan. In
the meantime, Rotary Club of Delhi MidTown pitched in and
sponsored two new javelins for me. I had also reached out to ONGC
for help, who provided some financial support to help me manage
my immediate expenses.

A few days later I got a call from Naveen Jindal's team, inviting
me to meet him at his office in Bhikaji Cama Place. While waiting
in the lobby, I noticed a motorized wheelchair. I wondered if he was
going to gift it to me! But later I learnt that this was for his niece

Sminu Jindal, who had become paralysed after an accident at the age of eleven.

Inside Naveen Jindal's expansive office, he made a simple request. 'I heard you speak at the Amazing Indian event. Just speak like that to our people. Four days a month is all I ask. Seeing you and hearing from you will inspire and motivate them.'

He assured me that my speaking engagements would be scheduled around my sports commitments. I was to visit various locations where the Jindals had their factories, townships and offices. I would speak to their workers, at their schools and to the spouses of their employees.

For this role, I would be paid Rs 70,000 per month.

Before I left, he added one more assurance—that Ambika's education would be fully sponsored by them.

I have no words to describe how that conversation made me feel. As an army wife, I often felt destined for something greater, yearning for my own career and identity. When Bikram had been posted to Hisar, I would look at the other army wives who were working at the Vidya Devi Jindal School there and envy them their sense of purpose and salary. Now, for the first time, I would be earning a salary. I had a job. I felt more empowered that day than I had ever felt before.

The money that came in transformed our lives. I could now hire a trained woman attendant, which eased the pressure on Devika. Now there was no need for her to rush home by 4 p.m. I had a physiotherapist coming home regularly, which greatly improved my athletic performance. And we began to enjoy the simpler pleasures of life—now that we had a bit more money, we could indulge in an occasional visit to one of the quaint cafes in our neighbourhood or splurge on a new dress for Devika and Ambika.

But the benefits extended beyond financial relief. The four days a month that I spent speaking at different Jindal locations renewed a sense of purpose—I had a mission, I was raising awareness about inclusivity and I was passing on my can-do spirit, positivity and grit.

The Jindals treated me with such kindness, a level of pampering I had never experienced before. A luxury car would come to pick me up, driving with great difficulty through the narrow, overcrowded streets of my neighbourhood. At the airport, I waited for my flights in the VVIP lounge, generally reserved for heads of state and other dignitaries.

When it was time to fly, I would travel to the aircraft in style, directly to the flight in a chauffeured car. Inside the private aircraft, it was typically just me, my attendant and a couple of staff members facilitating my visit. Mid-flight we would have some small bites from an icebox. I felt no less than a queen.

I got to travel to places I might never have otherwise visited: Angul and Barbil in Odisha, Patratu in Jharkhand, Raipur in Chhattisgarh. At some destinations we used commercial airports, while at others, we landed on private airstrips. For particularly remote locations, where even the twelve-seater private aircraft could not land, we had to transfer to a smaller Cessna. I still remember looking down from the plane before landing in one such place—we could see a polo ground with horses running wild, surrounded by jungles.

My sessions were always well-received. I tailored my content to my different audiences—delivering a message of positivity to floor workers, parenting tips to their families and engaging stories to school children. For management teams my talks were crafted to offer them valuable takeaways. I couldn't just hop on a plane and speak; it required a lot of preparation to ensure my content was relevant and impactful.

I must have been doing something right because I soon began to get invitations from other corporations to speak at their events.

One such invitation came from Sathyabama Institute of Science and Technology in Chennai for a Women's Day event. The call came from Mariazeena Johnson, the daughter of the university's founder, Dr Jeppiaar. Both father and daughter are passionate educationists and firmly believe in inclusivity. Our interactions began in 2013, and by 2022, they had transformed their entire campus into a fully inclusive and accessible environment.

I spoke to their students, many of whom were studying aeronautical and automobile engineering. I presented them with a challenge: design a car for people like me. While sensitizing them towards inclusivity, I asked them to use their skills to create solutions that cater to those with disabilities.

I shared a personal challenge to illustrate my point. In Shahpur Jat, where I lived, the overhead water tanks would leak constantly, creating slush outside my door that hindered my wheelchair's mobility. When I had tried to divert the direction of the overflow, it had created an ugly scene with local residents, who charged at me, accusing me of encroaching on public land. I had put this problem to the students of IIT Delhi, where I had gone for a panel discussion. Within a week, they came back to me with a solution: an auto cut-off sensor for the water tank that was set to stop the water when it reached a certain weight. Problem solved.

'Now it's your turn,' I said to my audience at Sathyabama. 'I want to drive. I *can* drive. But there are not enough vehicles for people like me. If you can design one for me, I'll come back and drive it.'

It hadn't even been a month when I got another call from Mariazeena. Her students had made a car for people without the use of their legs—amputees and those with paralysis. This new vehicle, a modified Renault Duster, had been sponsored by Renault itself.

I called it my WOW Drive—Will on Wheels. We planned my test drive to coincide with my birthday on 30 September. I would drive from Chennai to Delhi, covering eight cities in eight days.

To make this happen, I quickly assembled a team. Hardy secured a co-driver sponsorship from JK Tyres. The All India Banks Association, offering guest rooms in each city we were halting in, became our hospitality partners. Renault organized media interactions in their showrooms at every stop. Cardekho.com not only sponsored a media car but also had their team accompany me, blogging about my drive with multiple updates every day. The story about my journey got the most hits on their website. Later, the journalist also got an award for the best reported story.

The journey began with a warm reception in Chennai, where I was welcomed by the Madras Bulls bikers. More than 150 bikers escorted me to the car, celebrated the flag-off and accompanied me till we reached the city limits. This enthusiastic escort of my biker friends was present in every city we drove through. When we reached Jaipur, I received the greatest honour of all: my father joined the biker gang to escort me into the city. He rode in the sidecar of a vintage motorbike, driven by another seventy-year-old biker. I still remember Papa's proud smile.

After reaching Delhi, we headed to Gurgaon's Lemon Tree Hotel, where their vice president, Aradhana Lal, had organized a grand reception-cum-media interaction-cum-birthday celebration for me. Lemon Tree Hotels are committed to inclusivity, employing a significant number of individuals who are hearing impaired, non-verbal and with physical disabilities.

That was a special birthday for me because I had also created yet another record for the Limca Book of Records, this time for the longest drive across India by a paraplegic woman. I had covered a distance of 3,278 km. And I received the best gift imaginable: Sathyabama presented the Duster to me.

The impact of the Chennai-Delhi drive was immense. I now had women in wheelchairs reaching out to me. They had retreated to their homes after becoming wheelchair users and now wanted to learn how to navigate life with more ease, particularly about bladder and bowel management, critical yet often overlooked aspects of being a wheelchair user.

In March 2014, during the bustling run-up to the general elections, I met Mr Narendra Modi for the first time. As part of his extensive outreach, Modi ji was engaging with different constituencies through a series of Ask Me Anything conversations around the country. I was invited to his 'Chai pe Charcha' held on Women's Day, where I was among a panel of empowered women including sportswomen, entrepreneurs and social workers.

When it was my turn to speak, I raised concerns about the sporadic support for para sports and the lack of policies. I emphasized that I would vote for Modi ji if he promised to do something to end the ad hoc-ism that prevailed. We needed a structured policy that would prevent us from having to scramble for training camps and funding for travel for international events. Para sports needed to be treated with the same importance as able-bodied sports.

Modi ji, who had been the chief minister of Gujarat for a record twelve and a half years, told me about the Khel Mahakumbh of Gujarat and the para sports events started by Manu Bhai and Kanti Bhai. He mentioned a programme for inclusivity in sports called the Dream Project. A presentation about the project had been made centrally to all state governments and he had implemented it in Gujarat.

I also highlighted the need for more respectful terminology to describe people like me, criticizing the Hindi terms apang and apahij. 'In English we may be called people with disabilities, but in Hindi we remain "apang",' I said.

Later, in 2015, when Modi ji had become the prime minister, he introduced the term 'divyang' to replace the regressive terms 'apang' and 'apahij'.

Ambika had finished school, and now the tussle over her college choice began. She wanted to go to Aurangabad to study hotel management, but I couldn't bear the thought of her being so far from me again. I had just got her back and wasn't ready to let go. She fought me on this, but I was able to bulldoze my way through and secured her a place at O.P. Jindal Global University in Sonipat to study management. The argument that won her over was that with this course she could keep her options open and not be restricted to a career in the hospitality industry alone. She gave in.

It took her a while to settle in, and I had to help her find tuition classes for maths. While she worked hard in college during the week, it was the weekends we both looked forward to. She would take the metro back home, often accompanied by friends from college, and all of us would do the fun things that all mothers and daughters do—cooking together, going for the movies at the nearby hall and just enjoying our time together.

The world of para athletics was slowly evolving. More women para athletes began to emerge. One such para athlete was Karamjyoti Dalal, a former kabaddi player who, after a fall that impaired her motor functions, transitioned to para athletics as a discus thrower. My old coach took her under his wing.

In those days, para sports had just started to get recognition, though the environment was still disorganized. Para athletes were beginning to get on par reward money, so more people with disabilities wanted to join. But instead of rejoicing in the increase in the talent pool and promoting para athletes to compete against the world, the environment created a vicious atmosphere of infighting. The message that went out was: 'Deepa is now too old; the new girls will finish her.' The narrative fostered was one of unhealthy rivalry.

I witnessed this first-hand when my coach abandoned me for fresh talent. The infighting between the different camps within para sports affected not just me but also Devika.

Both Devika and I had gone to China for the IPC Second China Open Athletics Championships. Devika and Karamjyoti needed to play here to receive their medical classifications. In India, every wheelchair-bound para athlete was automatically placed in my category: F53. This is a tough category for para athletes with limited mobility and more muscle groups paralysed. Consequently, athletes with a lesser degree of paralysis classified under this category could perform disproportionately well. But in China, Karamjyoti was assigned to the F55 category after her medical examination. Remarkably, even this was seen as something I had 'managed'.

Devika was classified in the T37 category for her event, the long jump. Though she had started out as a sprinter, she now had to change to long jump in preparation for the Commonwealth Games in Glasgow. She was very new to long jump, and all six of her tries were red flagged for false starts. Despite this, she qualified for the Glasgow Games because the aim of combining para sports with the able-bodied games was inclusivity and the promotion of sports.

On our return from China, Devika began to train seriously. By the time the World Para Athletics Grand Prix in Tunisia came, she was in peak form. She clocked 2.61 m in her long jump and won a silver medal while creating a national record that was unbroken till 2024. With this silver, she was even more confident that nothing could stop her from going to the Commonwealth Games in Glasgow.

She left her job in Delhi as a corporate trainer and shifted to Sonipat. Here, she trained with my friend Rajesh Lathia, whom I had first met at the FESPIC Games in Kuala Lumpur. She trained with intense diligence. Her routine was: train, eat, sleep, repeat. She lived in one room with a bed and a cooler, ate good home-cooked food and continuously improved her performance.

As the date for the Commonwealth Games approached, she came back to Delhi to complete the paperwork. She began writing to the PCI for her team tracksuit, her accreditation, asking about the passport and visa formalities. But her long chain of twenty-odd emails drew unsatisfactory responses.

We went to the office of the International Olympic Committee (IOC) president in India to resolve the issue, since the Commonwealth Games fell under their purview. On seeing her medal from Tunisia and her correspondence, the president asked his assistant to activate her accreditation. She came back after a few minutes and said that the accreditation could not be processed because the deadline had already passed.

Despite setting a national record in the qualifiers, Devika was not going to the Commonwealth Games.

We later learnt that her name had never been submitted by the PCI to the IOC because the PCI president had only been made aware of results in China, not her triumph in Tunisia.

Just as I had missed the London Paralympics, she missed the Commonwealth Games in Glasgow.

This experience left her disheartened and disillusioned. Maybe it was because of her background in psychology, but she was able to process her own grief. However, she became aware of the need to look after the mental health of para athletes, prompting her to consider research in this field.

As we both grappled with our respective challenges, for the first time, I felt like I truly needed help. One day, while I was on my way to the stadium for practice, I found myself stuck in traffic on a flyover. My car at that time had manual controls. I was controlling the steering wheel with one hand and the brake and accelerator with the other. The problem arose when I had to change gears in tricky situations like this, stuck on an incline in the middle of bumper-to-bumper traffic. My car stalled. With no way out, I once again resorted to dialling 100, the third time in my life I was calling the police helpline. I quickly explained my situation and soon enough a Police Control Room van arrived, and the Delhi Police constables helped me out.

This situation starkly highlighted my vulnerability, compelling me to seek help, something I had always resisted.

I turned to my father for assistance. He understood that I needed a reliable, trustworthy attendant who could manage everything. He introduced me to Taj Bhaiyya. Taj had wanted to become a soldier but was unable to meet the height requirement. He was working at the office of a security agency run by a retired junior commissioned officer from my father's regiment. Taj Bhaiyya soon became an indispensable part of my life.

Together, we would go to the stadium for practice. He was by my side when I was being given the runaround by the coach. He helped me carry my equipment, retrieve my javelin, and aid with my transfers. In the absence of the coach, he even stepped into that role, advising me on the angle of my throws and recording videos for me to review.

And on those days when I felt too tired to wake up for another round, he would patiently sit outside my flat and call out to me.

Frustrated with how the coach was ignoring me and passing on my training to other players, I decided to do it alone. For strength training I went to Siri Fort. From my Shahpur Jat flat there was a short cut to the Siri Fort Sports Complex from inside the colony through the Asiad Village. I could get there on my wheelchair—this became my warm-up. I focused on my strength training there and would then move to a nearby park for my skill training. I got my throw frame from JLN and chained it to a tree. I would practise my throws with Taj Bhaiyya providing feedback. Virendra Vikram would stop by sometimes to offer advice on the exercises I needed.

This was the regimen I followed to prepare for the 2014 Asian Para Games in Incheon, South Korea.

When the contingent for Incheon was announced, I found my name on the list, but Dharam Singh, a para athlete with visual impairment, was not included. It was heart-wrenching to see this young man, wearing a pagri—a symbol of honour bestowed by village elders— learn at the very last minute that he had been dropped. Struggling to accept this news, he repeatedly said that he would kill himself, that he could not face returning empty-handed to his village after the honour of receiving the pagri and such a ceremonious farewell. He pleaded for an alternative, suggesting that if he were just sent to Incheon, he could at least take some pictures with the team to show everyone back home.

His pain was too much for me. It brought back memories of how I missed London and how Devika was dropped from Glasgow. I spoke to Dharam Singh and got him a ticket to Incheon. He was grateful to be able to save face.

This incident came to the attention of Satyanarayana, who had made me the torchbearer in Bangalore so many year ago and was ascending the ranks in para sports administration. He had also heard of how I had helped another athlete, Shahbad, in a similar situation earlier.

He asked me why I had helped them when their names weren't on the list and they weren't likely to win any medals.

'I saw my daughter cry when she was left out of the Commonwealth contingent,' I told him. Due to the opacity of our selection policies, para athletes were often left at the mercy of the whims of the selectors.

If the processes became transparent, the heartbreak of last-minute drops could be prevented. The current system, which toyed with the emotions of para athletes by having them put their lives on hold for intense training only to drop them like this, was wreaking havoc on their mental health. There was a precedent for concern: the whole world had witnessed how para athletes were treated in India when a national-level meet in Ghaziabad had ended as one of the worst fiascos in para sports history. The organizers had been totally unprepared for the number of para athletes who showed up on their own to take part in the games. This mismanagement led to the PCI drawing scrutiny from the International Paralympic Committee. The government also wanted to know why the meet had been mismanaged when the ministry had given Rs 401.84 lakh to the PCI for 2014–15 to ensure proper conduct of such events, camps and training. This was just one example of infighting and groupism plaguing para sports administration.

'*Deepaji, ye jo aap kar rahe hain, Satyanarayana yaad rakhega. Jo aapka dil athletes ke liye feel karta hai, main yaad rakhega*' (Deepaji, I will remember what you are doing for athletes, how you care for their well-being), he said to me.

Incheon holds a special place in my heart because here I proved what I could have done had I gone to London. The chef de mission was an army officer, Col. Tarsem, a polo player from the Armoured Corps. The coaches who had sidelined me tried to manipulate him into giving me a raw deal. But when they saw him greet me with the customary respect shared among army officers, they were sorely disappointed.

I had been kept out of London because I had not been able to register my qualifying throw at an international meet before the games. But here, my throw crossed the 9 m mark, creating a new Asian record. I won silver. My performance was the biggest comeback to throw in the face of all my detractors.

We returned to India with a rich haul. Eighty-seven para athletes had competed, and together we bagged thirty-three medals: three gold, fourteen silver and sixteen bronze. All the Haryana para athletes were looking forward to a well-deserved cash prize from the state government.

But elections had just taken place, and the government had changed. Everything was in a state of flux: would the new government continue with the policy of cash awards for para medal winners? Unlike previous occasions, our return this time was met without the usual fanfare, tempering our expectations.

We were told that a new sports policy was in the offing and were advised to wait.

Soon enough, the Target Olympic Podium Scheme (TOPS) was announced by the Ministry of Youth Affairs and Sports. This flagship programme was to support athletes with Olympic aspirations. Processes had been streamlined, project officers had been appointed and some semblance of order was created.

But there was more good news in store: our award money had been increased. Gold medal winners got Rs 3 crore, silver got Rs 1.5 crore and bronze Rs 75 lakh.

I had never received so much money in my life. It was a princely sum, exactly what I needed to break away from all the negativity that had crept into para sports and to do something to give back to the community. I used that money to move out of Shahpur Jat and into a nice apartment in Silver Oaks in Gurgaon.

For the first time in a long time, I had a home with a proper dining room and dining table, and I enjoyed the luxury of more than one room.

Along with the money, I also got an ex-cadre post as assistant coach with the Haryana government.

By this time, Devika had decided to leverage her training in psychology to assist para athletes. She had seen me help other athletes with tickets and visa fees. She saw these as sporadic, albeit necessary, gestures. Determined to extend this support on a larger scale, she proposed a more structured approach.

Together we decided to establish an NGO, aiming to extend broader support to more para athletes in a systematic way.

This desire to give back was a natural progression for me. I had been doing that in Ahmednagar as well, when I had taught the children of labourers in my home, when I had helped my Dee's Place boys with vocational training and placements, when I had stood up for a wrongly detained young man.

We found a lawyer and registered our NGO: Will on Wheels. But this was not a simple process. We had to go to court to register the NGO. But when we arrived at the courthouse, we discovered that it was not wheelchair-accessible. This meant our lawyer had to shuttle between court and me, managing documents that needed my signature and then rushing back to get them countersigned. In this tedious process, an oversight occurred: the lawyer inserted a clause appointing himself a signing authority in our NGO, without our knowledge. Before this led to any misuse of funds or embezzlement, we were faced with another crisis. The name Will on Wheels, it turned out, was already taken. This discovery allowed us to invalidate the initial registration under the pretext of needing to rename the NGO. This thwarted the lawyer's attempt to pull a fast one on us.

We registered our NGO under its new name, Wheeling Happiness, this time without the overreaching lawyer. Wheeling Happiness has since thrived, making a difference at both the individual level and the policy level.

By now I was thoroughly disillusioned with the constant infighting and petty politics in the world of para sports. Having proved myself at Incheon, I began contemplating giving up on my Paralympics dream and retiring on a high note. My main event, javelin throw, had also been taken off the Paralympic list. Perhaps I could focus on national and Asian competitions, where I continued to hold records across all my events, and balance this with my job.

I had already stopped going to train at JLN before Incheon, training on my own instead. As rumours of my fallout with my coach circulated, I began to receive phone calls from people wanting to take his place. One particularly persistent caller was a coach with a defence background. To quell his relentless attempts, I finally agreed to meet him.

I drove myself to the meeting. After he saw me transfer from the car to my wheelchair and then after our talk back to the driving seat, he said something that got me thinking.

When I transfer to and from my wheelchair, I bear all my body weight on my hands. It requires a great amount of strength in the arms and shoulders to be able to take the full weight of my 5'9" frame. He said that although javelin was no longer an option, this much strength made me an ideal candidate for the shot put event. In the F53 category for women in the Paralympics, the weight of the shot put is 3 kg. This reignited my Paralympic dream.

I decided to give it my best shot and began training with the new coach. But even before my training started, we began running into disagreements.

He wanted me to come to his location at 5 a.m., which was impractical for me since I needed Taj Bhaiyya's assistance, and he could get to me only after the metro began running. We compromised on a 7 a.m. start. But even then, our training would start later because of his other commitments, such as dropping off his children to school and seeing to his side business. I couldn't help but feel that my training was the side business.

He would leave Taj Bhaiyya and me hanging while he attended to his chores. Often, he would ask Taj Bhaiyya to mow his lawn while I sat twiddling my thumbs.

I began seriously questioning his professionalism when he would get me to warm up only to leave abruptly to take phone calls. By the time he returned, I would have cooled down.

Another red flag that I ignored at the time was his insistence that I buy a full set of Olympic weights. Ostensibly for my training, but soon it became clear that they were actually to build the infrastructure for his own gym.

He convinced me that I was benching 50 kg. When I told Bikram about this, he refused to believe it. Soon, I realized that this was because the coach was actually giving me a hand while claiming that I was doing all the lifting.

He may have been a good coach for able-bodied sportspersons, but for me, he was all wrong. He had me lifting heavy weights for muscle strengthening when he should have been doing the same with Therabands. This inappropriate training regimen resulted in an injury, forcing me to wear a neck collar.

Virendra Vikram was aghast when he saw me. He counselled against overtraining, warning that it could exhaust my neurons and lead to spasms.

Then the real picture began to emerge—the coach's primary interest was leveraging my access to the SAI. He began pressuring me to take him with me to my international events. With the IPC Athletics World Championships in Doha on the horizon, he was particularly insistent. I could not take him—I already had a competition partner and could not have taken a personal coach.

With my coach's incorrect training and the resulting injury, I was barely able to secure fifth place in Doha. I qualified by throwing 3.67 m in my event, just over the minimum requirement of 3.6 m. I made the A mark, but only just.

Based on the overall performance of the women in the Indian contingent—two achieving A, one getting B and Karamjyoti placing in fifth position—we were allotted only one spot for a woman para athlete at the Paralympics.

Upon my return, I severed ties with this coach and redirected all my focus and energy towards qualifying for Rio.

15

Rio

ISHEARTENED BY THE WAY MY COACHES HAD TRIED to use me, I resolved to do it alone. I isolated myself from the para sports community. Everyone was mocking me and my constant fights with my coaches. My Doha performance was sniggered at, and whispers suggested that I was past my prime. The prevailing sentiment was: 'It's Karamjyoti's performance that secured India's quota, so rightfully she should go to Rio.'

I was self-training, away from the SAI, PCI and JLN, blissfully unaware of the narratives being built.

Focusing on my Paralympic dream, I set out to assemble my own support team, starting with finding a new coach.

At Siri Fort, where I did my strength and conditioning training, I came across trainers from Chirag Sethi's Classic Fitness Academy. I often listened to these young trainers telling tennis players about the importance of working their small muscles. I would overhear them talking about working opposite muscle groups. I noticed how attentively they managed athletes through recovery phases.

All this intrigued me—it was so different from how I had been trained so far.

I had begun my para sports journey in 2006 with the FESPIC Games in Kuala Lumpur. Over the course of the next nine years, I had moved from swimming to javelin to shot put, with some discus thrown into the mix. I had won seven gold, three silver and four bronze medals at Asia-level meets while also creating Asian and national records. All this with coaches who had shifted to para sports from able-bodied sports without any specific training in the needs of para athletes.

Now, for the first time, I was hearing trainers talk about the importance of nutrition and the ill effects of overtraining.

I met Chirag Sethi and hired his team using the money I got from TOPS. My commitment to the medal was unwavering, and I meticulously followed Chirag's advice. The first thing we did was overhaul my diet. Sugar was out. Carbs were reduced. Stimulants like tea and coffee were eliminated—Chirag explained that not having caffeine during the training phase would cleanse my system, and reintroducing it during the competition stage would boost my performance.

Creatine was introduced to help quickly build muscle mass, accompanied by a corresponding increase in fluid intake.

I began to do exercises I had never done before. So far, I had focused on strengthening my throw muscles—my push muscles. Now, for the first time, I was introduced to the concept of pull muscles and began to train these too. The rationale was straightforward physics: if your front and back muscle sets are imbalanced, you cannot achieve your optimum throwing strength.

We started using stretch bands to train, targeting opposite muscle sets. We trained the small muscle groups in the fingers, which eventually went a long way in giving me crucial extra centimetres in my throws.

I discovered the importance of muscle releases. After intense exercise, blood rushes to the muscles, forming knots that must be massaged out slowly to ensure optimal blood flow. These massages were extremely painful and left deep bruises. Initially I visited the basement clinic of a specialist for these massages, but eventually my trainer would give them to me right in the gym. This saved money and time, and it spared me the ordeal of being carried down to the basement clinic.

With such rigorous training, my performance had improved from the Doha mark of 3.67 m to 4.00 m. The world record in my category, held by Pamela LeJean of Canada, was 4.48 m. I had to cross that if I wanted gold. But even with my intensive training, I had plateaued. Something was holding me back from improving my distance.

At the 2016 IPC Athletics Asia–Oceania Championships in Dubai, I was determined to break the 4.00 m barrier. On the day of the throw, my small muscle groups came to my aid—the strength I had developed in my fingers provided the extra thrust needed to surpass my previous best. I got to 4.04 m and won a gold for India.

When I was on the podium and the Indian national anthem played, tears streamed down my face and my heart swelled with a sense of achievement.

The challenge on my return from Dubai was how to better my time. Physically, we had maximized our efforts. But something was happening to me during my throws. Just as I gathered all my strength to launch the 3 kg shot put, spasms would seize my body. Originating in my abdomen and lungs, these spasms disrupted the essential jerking motion of my shoulder required for a full throw.

There was no lack of fire, no lack of energy, no lack of training—something else was wrong.

That's when Priti Gupta, a sports psychologist, joined my team. She immediately identified the root of what was holding me back: the barrage of patriarchal doubts clouding my mind, whispering that I was too old, I was past my peak, I was alone, I should be at home looking after my children and husband.

Priti taught me visualization exercises in which I perfected my throw in one fluid motion. I had to throw like this hundreds of times in my mind.

She taught me to disconnect from personal relationships, people's sarcastic comments, gossip, naysayers. While this was good for my form, it came with its downsides. I grew distant and stopped communicating—even with Devika and Ambika. I had to remove myself from their problems because thinking about their issues would leave me restless and increase spasticity.

Although this detachment was a big sacrifice for me as a mother, I was lucky that both my girls were mature and understood. In fact, they were the only two who understood. They sacrificed their time with me for my mental well-being and to support my journey.

And the results spoke for themselves. At the IPC World Para Athletics Grand Prix Desert Challenge Games in Arizona in May 2016, I got both a gold and a silver. Devika, also a part of the contingent, performed equally well, earning a silver and a bronze.

Making the most of our trip, we also visited my sister-in-law in Chicago, a reunion that was long overdue. She had lost a son to cancer several years ago, but circumstances had prevented us from visiting. Now, I could meet her and share her pain in person.

With Rio just a few months away, I was at the peak of my training. I knew that this would be my last attempt at a Paralympic medal. At forty-six, I knew I wasn't going to get a second chance. It was now or never.

For the Rio Paralympics, several significant rules were changed. Often, in para sports, due to a lack of sufficient participants, athletes from different categories of disability are grouped together. These categories are defined by the degree of impairment, which forms the basis for competition pools. When categories are combined, an athlete with a lesser degree of impairment may compete against those with a higher degree of impairment. To evaluate performances in such mixed categories, a complex formula known as the Raza point score system is used to determine winners. This is why in several Asia-level competitions, though I created Asian records, I ended up with silver instead of gold. For spectators, this can be confusing— they may see one para athlete perform better, yet the medal goes to another. This not only discourages viewers and sponsors but also complicates media coverage of para sports.

To increase the popularity of para sports, the organizers decided not to combine any categories for these games. This was good news for me.

The second rule that changed was the removal of Paralympic-assigned volunteers to help athletes transfer from their wheelchairs to their throw frames at the time of the competition. This decision was made to prevent the organizers from being held liable for any injuries the para athletes might sustain during these transfers.

This meant that I needed to find an assistant to take with me. I could not take Devika—given her petite frame and hemiplegia, she struggled with transfers. While I can do most transfers mainly on my own, with only a little help, transferring from the lower height of my wheelchair to the higher 75 cm throw frame is tough. Plus, I didn't want to tire my muscles just before the throw by doing the transfer myself. Bikram should have been the natural choice. Though he had accompanied me to Dubai, he had not stayed on in Delhi. So I wasn't sure whether he would want to go with me or not.

However, it was the third rule change that affected me the most—the one related to the throw frame I used.

The throw frame consists of a metal frame with a seat, a footrest and a backrest, along with a vertical arm on the left side to provide support when the para athlete pulls back the throwing arm to gain momentum.

The new rule stated that the backrest could not exceed 5 cm in width and must be without any cushioning. Further, it required that there be no gap between the back of the athlete's knees and the seat while seated. And at the time of the throw, any lifting of the hips would result in disqualification.

To comply with these new rules, I went to a local welder in Shahpur Jat to have my throw frame modified.

But when I began training, the new design created an unforeseen problem. As I leaned back to build up momentum for my throw, my back would chafe against the now un-cushioned metal backrest. Since the part of my back that was getting hurt is paralysed, I did not feel the worsening blisters.

Since I maintain strict privacy about my body—I even bathe independently—no one detected the injury.

The blisters grew until I had a gaping wound in my back. I could not feel the pain, but as the infection spread to the third layer of my skin, I began to get spasms.

My physiotherapist suggested icing to prevent the spasms but this proved ineffective.

We continued with our usual stretching routine. Typically, I wear tights and a slip under my T-shirt to hide my diaper. But that day I was not wearing a slip, and when my T-shirt rode up during the stretches, he noticed the wound in my back.

We had to stop my training for fifteen days to let the wound heal. But we also needed to find a solution; if I went back to training with the frame that did not have any cushioning, the injury would return. So I made a second throw frame, this one with cushioning, for practice.

I could not waste a crucial fortnight just waiting for the injury to heal. My trainer decided to use this time for weight training. The challenge he threw at me—lift 14,000 kg and I would be ready for Rio!

I was flabbergasted till he explained that this figure did not refer to a single lift but represented the combined weight of all the sets and reps throughout my workout. This included exercises like lifting 10 kg weights—10 reps for 10 sets with each hand, working out to 2,000 kg. I would then bench press 45 kg for 3 reps across 5 sets for a total of 675 kg. At the lateral pulley I would do a total of 2,700 kg. This was followed by 25 throws of an 8 kg medicine ball.

After other such combinations, I would end the session with a super set.

The road to this level of weight training was paved with several trials and errors. Using these machines in the gym was particularly challenging: it took me seven minutes to position myself for a three-minute exercise. I had to be tied into place. One day, I fell backwards while lifting weights—but that didn't stop us; we began using sandbags to stabilize my wheelchair. I needed additional stabilization around my shoulders due to my lack of torso balance from missing seven vertebrae. We innovated with belts, pillows and sandbags, took the help of people and used gravity by altering the angles of my exercises.

As we trained for Rio, I focused on strengthening my co-relative muscles. For the neck we did resistance exercises. For the elbow and wrist muscles—Therabands. Even my rotator muscles were flexed. I used the rowing machine lying on my stomach, tied to the machine for my big muscles. This process was a revelation—I was discovering what a body with chest-below paralysis was capable of.

Once my injury healed, I got back to skill training. I had fifteen shot put balls made, each the same size as the competition ball but varying in weight. Training with lighter balls refined my form, style and muscle memory, while throwing the heavier balls improved my strength. This strategy ensured that when I threw the standard competition ball, I maintained my form and increased my distance.

Three days a week I trained with my cushioned throw frame and two days I used the non-cushioned one to get used to it.

In shot put, the throw frame is placed inside a throw circle. At the beginning of each throw, officials check to ensure that no body part of the para athlete extends beyond the circle. In my case, when I was seated, my feet would rest on the footrest, heels down, with the bulk of my feet projecting forward from the frame. This meant that my throw frame had to be positioned well behind the circle's edge. Now, when I sat with the back of my knees flush with the seat, my toes rested on the footrest.

While this brought my throw frame closer to the edge of the throw circle, potentially increasing the distance of my throw, my legs were now at a new angle, which my paralysed muscles were not used to.

This meant that my legs could spasm, leading to disqualification. To prevent this, we had to do a lot of stretching for my legs as well. We did extension exercises for the flexibility of my ankles and tendons, which hadn't been in use.

That's when I truly appreciated the beauty of sport—each part of the body, whether in use or not, had become so important for my win.

To prevent spasms or any involuntary rise of my hips during throws, we secured my position with belts around my pelvis, knees and calves.

My mind conditioning coach, Saran, had been with me on this journey for about two years at this time. He trained me to harness the energy around me, by practising gratitude and chanting.

Saran helped me realize that if I wanted victory, I had to become one with all the energy that is present in both living and non-living entities. All matter consists of energy: the shot put ball, the throw frame, the leather of my belts, my body. I needed to synchronize these energies and project my intentions into the universe. I was taught to visualize the shot put launching perfectly from my hands and sailing towards the winning distance. I even named my shot put ball and aligned all my energies with single-minded focus towards an affirmation for victory.

Two sports administrators who always had faith in me were Radhika Sriman and Dr P.C. Kashyap. Radhika Ma'am provided immense support throughout my journey, and as I prepared for Rio, she presented me with a framed motivational picture with the words 'You Can Win'. Dr Kashyap, who had been her predecessor at the

SAI, was retiring and gave me a clock as a farewell gift. This clock featured pictures of Olympians at the different hour marks. And it had my picture too—even though I hadn't yet qualified as an Olympian. 'I know what happened before London and I know that you should have been at those Paralympic games,' he told me.

Satyanarayana, who had first placed the torch in my hands at the IPC World Championships in Bangalore, now reaffirmed his faith in me. 'The flame I gave you in Bangalore was the beginning. Just as the Olympic flame goes around the world before finally reaching the Olympics, you will also reach the Paralympics. You cannot retire before that.'

I took these as signs from the Almighty that everything was aligning for my path to Rio.

It was now time to submit names for the long list for accreditation—a preliminary list of probable athletes, not a confirmation of participation. Each probable para athlete is required to include their support team in this submission.

For me, the choice was between Devika and Bikram. I was conserving every muscle of my body and had even stopped doing my daily chores myself for fear of injury. I could slip while bathing, twist something while dressing—it was a risk I was unwilling to take. It made sense to take Bikram. But Devika had been a constant presence by my side, both at Atithi and in Shahpur Jat. Though I was concerned that she would not be able to help with my transfers because of her hemiplegia, I couldn't bear the thought of hurting her feelings by telling her this.

One thing was clear, though: my support person had to be a family member.

But since Bikram had not stayed back in Delhi after Dubai, my ego prevented me from asking him. My mind went back to the Commonwealth Games, when he did not come to see me because he had been too proud to ask. Now I was too proud to ask him to accompany me.

Maybe I should have read *Men Are from Mars, Women Are from Venus*. At that time, I did not understand that, often, men need to have every expectation articulated.

It was a period marked by fear—fear of injury and fear of sabotage.

For fear of fatiguing the small muscles between my fingers, I had even stopped lifting my phone.

For fear of getting into an accident and the ensuing legal complications, I had even stopped driving myself.

For fear of sabotage, I had even stopped buying water from my usual vendor.

I had seen doping scandals impact para athletes close to me—Hitesh Sachdeva and Sharad Kumar. Sharad, a high jumper affected by polio, contended that his protein shake had been drugged to sabotage his career. Despite facing a ban, he made a triumphant return at the 2014 Incheon Games, where he won gold. Hitesh, who had made his debut with me at the FESPIC Games, had been my legs while I had been his eyes. He had qualified for the 2012 Paralympics but was dropped after doping charges. He also claimed that he had been sabotaged.

I was terrified of something like that happening to me. After all, I had no dearth of enemies.

To mitigate this risk, I would buy water from different vendors in totally random places. I stopped having juice from the regular juice stall. I stopped eating any food from outside.

The trials for the Rio Paralympics selection were scheduled for 26 July at the SAI facility in Sonipat. I arrived a day early to be well-rested before the trials.

Along with my sports kit, I carried an induction plate, a cooker and an icebox full of vegetables and fruits. Paranoid about someone tampering with my food or drink, I took every precaution. I also had a lock for my icebox and my room. While everyone else ate at the canteen, I ate in my room.

My only competition was Karamjyoti. Her fifth-place world ranking in Doha had earned us our Paralympic quota. We were both beneficiaries of TOPS and had received Rs 30 lakh for our training. She had gone to Finland to train, while I had chosen to train in India.

Though we competed in different sports—shot put for me and discus for her—the selection would be based on how close each of us could come to the world rankings in our respective events. The one who achieved the distance closest to the world number one ranking would be selected.

That day, all eyes were on us. As we wheeled down opposite sides of the hall, you could have heard a pin drop. People stopped what they were doing to watch us. It had become Deepa vs Karamjyoti.

Sometimes I wonder: did we really need to be competing against each other? We were in different categories and participated in different events. Wouldn't it have been better if we had focused on competing against athletes from other countries instead of wasting our energy in infighting? It all boils down to better professional management of para sports. The first step is accurate medical classification, followed by better training to enable para athletes to perform well and earn more quotas.

During my term as PCI president, I knew what to focus on. To Rio, we sent nineteen para athletes and got four medals. At Tokyo in 2020, when I took the Indian contingent, we won nineteen medals.

Karamjyoti's throw that day mirrored her Doha distance, maintaining her position at world number five.

When it was my turn, all eyes were once again on me. Everyone wanted to see what forty-six-year-old Deepa could do. Of my six throws, two were fouls. But as they measured my distance, I knew I had won the slot. That day, my throw was almost 1 m more than my Doha distance. It matched the world number one distance—I had equalled Pamela's distance of 4.48 m.

The trials were being videographed from multiple angles, both side and hip, not just by the officials but also by Karamjyoti's team. The distance was measured both electronically and physically, with a measuring tape.

I was jubilant and was swamped by the media. After ensuring that the results had been verified, signed and sealed, I returned to Gurgaon.

That night I slept soundly, dreaming of headlines confirming my ticket to Rio. I saw the vision of the clock presented to me by Dr Kashyap being realized—I was going to be an Olympian.

I woke up to headlines, but not the ones I had expected.

Instead of announcements of Deepa Malik becoming the first Indian woman para athlete to be selected for the Paralympic Games, what I read made my world implode.

'Deepa Malik is a cheat,' screamed the news channels. Karamjyoti had filed a complaint against me, the Union of India and the Sports Authority of India. She accused the Union of India and SAI of conducting the trials dishonestly, giving the quota earned by her to me. She accused them of conducting the trials in an unfair and biased manner. She accused me of bribery and undue influence. With just about twenty days left until the deadline to submit the final list of names for the Paralympics, I found myself being dragged to court.

I had faced so much in my journey to get this far that to have my integrity being called into question left me gutted. My first reaction was despair—there was no way that this case could be dismissed in time for the Paralympics deadline.

In this challenging time, my girls, Devika and Ambika, stood like my pillars. They lifted my spirits and told me not to give up. We began to devise an action plan.

The first step was to find out what had happened. I called up the Paralympic Committee of India (PCI) and the SAI office. I learnt that the main complaint was filed against the Union of India and the SAI, and I was one of the parties. I was told that the reply would be filed by the legal department of the SAI, and I could obtain a copy of the complaint if I wished.

Devika and I rushed to the SAI office, where she managed to get the 200-page complaint photocopied. While she did all the running around, all I could do was cry. I had never been so disheartened in my life. In my mind, I saw the clock Dr Kashyap had given me crack. I saw the picture Radhika Shriman Ma'am had given me torn into pieces.

My thoughts spiralled around a painful question: why does one Indian not want another Indian to win? I now understood why it is so difficult for Indians to win medals. When everyone should have been supporting me, here they were, ganged up against me, crushing my medal, India's medal.

All the mocking voices that I had learnt to shut down came flooding back.

I would have to go to court—no one in my family had been taken to court in generations.

My integrity, something I so deeply valued, was being questioned.

While I wept, Devika repeatedly reminded me that the quota is awarded to the country, not to any individual athlete. It is up to the country to select the best sportsperson to use the slot.

It became clear that the case hinged on technicalities, and waiting for the legal department to file its reply might cause us to miss the bus.

The timing and nature of the complaint suggested that its true purpose was not to secure a spot for Karamjyoti but to sabotage my chances.

Gradually, I regained some composure, and my fighting spirit began to come back.

Needing legal advice, I reached out to Rajiv Bhadauria at the Jindals. He told me to come to his office immediately. Once again, I found myself in the Jindal office in Bhikaji Cama Place.

As the reality of the situation began to sink in, I became totally numb. Rajiv Sir and Devika settled me down. I was having a full-on panic attack. Every muscle of my body that I had trained so hard now felt like a dead weight. I could not breathe. It was as though someone were sitting on my chest.

Internally, my mind screamed at the injustice of it all, but I remained silent. I saw all the faces that had mocked me, taunted me, laughed at me. I saw them gloating that they had managed to thwart my Paralympic dream. They had first stopped me from going to London, and now they had stopped me from going to Rio, my last chance at a Paralympic medal.

A storm raged inside me, yet I appeared numb to the outside world.

Devika, on the other hand, had turned into the fiercest form of the Mother Goddess—Chandi. I don't know where she found her strength, but she was a force of nature. From outside the glass-walled conference room, I watched her speak to a team of top lawyers. From her open laptop, she read out the rules to the legal experts, dismantling the allegations in Karamjyoti's complaint.

For four hours the drafting continued. Devika and the team of eight lawyers worked on a detailed brief. We had arrived at 5 p.m. and it was now 9 p.m., not a single person had left their seat. They distilled the brief into a synopsis and printed out copies. By the time we reached home, it was well past midnight.

The next morning, we had to find a lawyer and reach the Delhi High Court, where the matter was listed. Selecting the right lawyer required skill and knowledge. My lawyer had to be one who could match Karamjyoti's lawyer as well as the judge before whom the case was put up. Karamjyoti had hired Nitin Bhardwaj, and on the advice of the Jindal legal team, I hired Sudhir Nandrajog. He came at a cost of Rs 1.75 lakh per hearing—a sum I could ill afford, especially when I was so pessimistic about the outcome.

But Devika was on fire. Like a lioness protecting her cub, she fought for me to bring me out of my catatonic state. 'Mom, you are going to Rio. You are going to Rio,' she told me. 'Keep repeating it. Visualize it.'

We impressed the urgency of the matter on the judge and sought an early date.

At the hearing, we successfully contested Karamjyoti's claim that the quota was assigned to her by name. We presented documentary evidence from the qualifying rules demonstrating that quotas are awarded to the country, not to individual athletes.

The lawyers representing the Union of India and the SAI addressed the legality of trials. Karamjyoti had argued that the trials should not have been conducted at all, and if they were necessary, they should have been overseen by the national federation, in this case the PCI and not the SAI. The SAI lawyers provided letters showing that the PCI had been suspended by the International Paralympic Committee at the time, leaving the SAI as the temporary administrative authority responsible for finalizing the entries for Rio. They added that though the IPC had reinstated the PCI on 31 May, it was only to enable the Indian contingent to participate under the Indian flag at Rio, with the SAI retaining authority over team selection.

The SAI lawyers further proved impartiality in the trials by highlighting the results where I achieved a distance equal to the world number one, while Karamjyoti maintained her position at world number five.

Karamjyoti's lawyer's then questioned the legitimacy of my results, arguing that the rate at which my performance had improved—from 3.67 m in Doha to 4.04 m in Dubai and ultimately 4.48 m at the trials—was unprecedented for any athlete, para or able-bodied. While this was a significant leap, it was the culmination of my intense hard work and scientific training. But they presented charts comparing the performance trajectories of able-bodied sportspersons over time, to call into question both the results of the trials and my degree of impairment. I had to submit medical documents to prove my disability and medical classification, which had been done by the authority in the subject, Rudi van den Abbeele. I had to submit drug test results to prove that I had not taken any performance-enhancing drugs.

They further alleged that my handshake with an official was indicative of bribery. This allegation was dismissed outright by the court.

At the end of the first hearing, worried about the mental toll the trial would take on me, Devika asked me not to attend further sessions. But by now, my fighting spirit had reawakened, and I refused. If Karamjyoti was going to be present in court, sitting in her wheelchair, there was no way that I could stay away.

As Devika and I geared up for battle, my father called Bikram and told him that it was time he came and stood by me. Bikram arrived the next day.

Karamjyoti's lawyers had submitted a misleading video—it had been cleverly edited to play one of my foul throws in a loop to suggest that all my attempts had been fouls. Thankfully, the judge quickly saw through it.

He called for the official video footage. With the SAI project officer dispatched to Bahalgarh in Sonipat to retrieve it, and uncertain of his timely return, I sent Devika with an application asking for a certified copy of a CD of the trials. Our request was denied and, sure enough, the SAI official also got delayed. The hearing was postponed from 11 a.m. to the afternoon session.

As we waited, I called Saran, my mind conditioning coach. Under his guidance, I centred myself and decided to continue with my training, undeterred by being in the court premises. My trainer came with my weights, and I lifted dumbbells right in the courtyard of the Delhi High Court. I did my visualization exercises and created a protective armour for myself with positive spiritual affirmations, to maintain my focus amidst the legal turmoil.

While I was working out, Karamjyoti's brother approached me.

'*Bura mat maan na, ye dharam ki ladai hai*' (Please don't hold it against us, but this is a battle of principles), he said to me.

As his words registered, my mind went back to what Saran used to say to me: my quest for a medal was my dharma. It was my dharma, my duty, to get a medal for my country. I heard the words of Krishna to Arjun before the battle of Kurukshetra, describing it as a dharma yudh—a battle of righteousness. For me, that day, the courtroom transformed into my yudh bhoomi, my battleground, and clearing my name became my dharma.

That night at home, I found solace in reading the Bhagavad Gita.

On 4 August, the CD was presented in court, containing footage of all the trials that had happened on 26 July. Faced with hours of footage, the judge asked whether he was expected to sit and watch the entire day's trials. At this, Devika, unversed in courtroom protocol, jumped up and said, 'Just look at the time stamp. Her event was at 12 o'clock.' The judge took her advice but only after admonishing her.

A junior lawyer hurried to fetch a laptop with a CD drive. He fast-forwarded to the relevant section and showed it to the judge.

When he was convinced of the authenticity of the CD, the judge appointed a committee of experts to assess my fitness. This committee included Coach Satyapal Singh, a Dronacharya awardee; Satyanarayana, an IPC qualified technical official; and Sunny Joshua, president of the Delhi Athletic Association and national technical official for throws at the Athletics Federation of India. They voted by secret ballot, and their verdict reached the court on 11 August at 11 a.m.

Effectively, this was the last full working day before the final date to send entries by name. It was a Thursday before the long Independence Day weekend.

We spent the entire day waiting for the judgement. It finally came at 5 p.m. The envelope with the findings of the expert committee was opened. Sunny Joshua had voted for me. Satyanarayana had voted for me. Satyapal, the coach with whom I had had several run-ins at the Gandhinagar camp before the 2010 Commonwealth Games, had also voted for me.

The next day, 12 August, I was at the SAI office to ensure that my name was sent for Rio.

From the moment I boarded the flight to Rio, all that could go wrong, did go wrong. Bikram was accompanying me as my skill coach, but he clashed with my conditioning coach, who was also with us on the trip, and my mind conditioning coach, who was not.

The root of the conflict pertained to Bikram's approach to training. Bikram's methods were decidedly old school. He had been a sportsman in his youth and had even won gold in pistol shooting while in college. But his approach was stuck in the '80s. He was sceptical of the modern scientific training techniques employed by my conditioning coach and my mind conditioning coach, Saran. The tension between Bikram and my coach was palpable even while on the flight, and it began to overwhelm me. There were heated exchanges between them, which ended with my conditioning coach walking off in a huff.

We had landed in Rio—but my luggage hadn't. Without my throw frames, I would not be able to compete. The airline's offer of cash compensation was of no use. I began to spiral—would my challenges never end?

After a lot of tweeting and getting the Ministry of External Affairs and local embassy involved, my luggage was finally located and delivered just before the opening ceremony.

In the midst of all this chaos, I reached out to my mind conditioning coach. Saran had shown me the power of focus and faith during the court case.

He reminded me to focus and visualize a silver lining to this cloud of chaos and centre myself. My manifestation of this silver lining just before my competition is perhaps why I won silver. Maybe if I had visualized a golden calm or a golden crown, I would have landed gold.

It seemed the soap operatic twists and turns in my life were endless.

In an unexpected international development, the entire Russian Paralympic contingent was banned by the IOC following reports of widespread state-sponsored doping, a scandal infamously dubbed their 'medals over morals' policy.

The beneficiary of this international development was Karamjyoti, as due to the absence of the Russian contingent, their quota was distributed to other countries.

Perhaps her power of manifestation was so strong that it had made her Paralympic dream come true. Despite making it to the Rio Paralympics, she was unable to improve her performance and returned to India without any medals.

Her presence in Rio made me reflect on the futility of our court case. So much precious time—and money—was lost. So much stress was caused.

But even those agonizing hours served a purpose. Expending so much energy grappling with doubt and agony had been almost cathartic for me.

I was now immune to fear.

On the day of my event, I woke up resolute. My goal was within my sight. What began as a quest for a physical medal had evolved into a metaphysical need to defend my integrity. Ever since the court case, I had been branded a 'cheater'. Even the court's judgement in my favour was seen as an example of how much influence I wielded. To truly vindicate myself I needed to achieve a throw of 4.48 m.

This was my moment. This was the opportunity I had been waiting for. This was what I had trained so hard for.

The top three players at the time were Canada's Pamela LeJean, Greece's Dimitra Korokida and Bahrain's Fatema Nedham. At the trials in India, I had already matched Pamela's leading distance of 4.48 m. I was now ready to claim my medal.

Just before my turn, Fatema from Bahrain entered the throw circle. I watched as her first throw was flagged. A wave of concern passed through the crowd. Her second throw followed suit—another red flag. And then, with the audience holding their breath, her third throw too was red flagged. According to the rules, three consecutive fouls meant disqualification.

Without her throws even being measured, Fatema was disqualified.

It was now my turn.

I had done everything that science had told me to during my training.

Guided by Saran, I had become one with the iron of my ball, the metal of my seat, the leather of my belts. The ball was an extension of my body. It was powered by my mind—it was destined to fly.

With no effort spared, I put my faith in the Almighty and chanted the mantra I had learned before I twisted my torso to create the perfect arc for maximum momentum.

With all my might, I let go.

The green shot put ball sailed through the air and landed solidly in the field.

The white flag went up, signalling a valid throw, though I didn't know what my distance was.

I took my second throw.

As the white flag rose again, I saw the distance on the electronic screen: 4.49 m. Just as I was processing that I had surpassed the world number one's distance, I saw right in front of me, sitting in the stands, Karamjyoti, her brother and her coach.

I pointed directly at them with my index finger, making sure they knew I had seen them and for them to acknowledge the distance I had thrown.

This moment was immortalized by photographers. Every time I see that picture, I glow with a sense of righteousness.

I was momentarily transfixed. I had to be nudged to take my next throw. Each athlete is allowed six throws. I continued, with all my remaining energy. My tension had evaporated. For me, Rio was effectively over the minute I threw 4.49 m. The remaining throws were just a way to channel my intensity. I put everything I had into each one.

There is a photograph capturing me in the throes of my sixth throw—I appear almost possessed. Perhaps I was, because that throw surpassed even my wildest expectations. From Doha to Rio, I had improved my distance from 3.67 m to 4.49 m. Yet, in that sixth attempt, I astonishingly reached 4.61 m.

None of the other competitors could match 4.61 m. Pamela was so thrown by my distance, she lost her nerve. The Canadian threw way below me. I had been dreaming of silver, but now gold was within reach.

A cheer erupted from the crowd. I was going to be the first woman para athlete from India to win gold at the Paralympics. I had made history.

But as we were leaving the arena, a stunning development occurred. Fatema returned to compete again. On the technicality that her three foul throws had not been measured, she was granted another chance. With six fresh throws, she exceeded my best, touching 4.72 m.

A wave of protest erupted. The medal ceremony, scheduled for noon, was postponed. The results were withheld.

Within a matter of hours, I had gone from anticipating silver to being certain of gold and then being thrust into uncertainty, unsure of what the final results would hold.

I found myself at the lowest point of this emotional rollercoaster. The suspense was unbearable.

When there were still no results by 4.30 p.m., I approached the technical area where the officials were gathered. I spoke to the Indian chef de mission, who provided some reassurance. He confirmed that my silver was secure and my gold remained a possibility, as other countries had lodged protests against Fatema's second chance.

In that moment I received a profound lesson about human nature and our inherent greed. My desires had gone from *just* wanting to qualify for Rio to *just* matching the world record to *just* vying for silver to greedily eyeing gold.

Finally, the results were announced. Fatema got the gold.

But I made history. I can still hear the announcement: 'Well, here's history. India's first ever female Paralympic medallist in any sport, Deepa Malik.'

All the clouds of my life parted to reveal this silver lining.

Epilogue

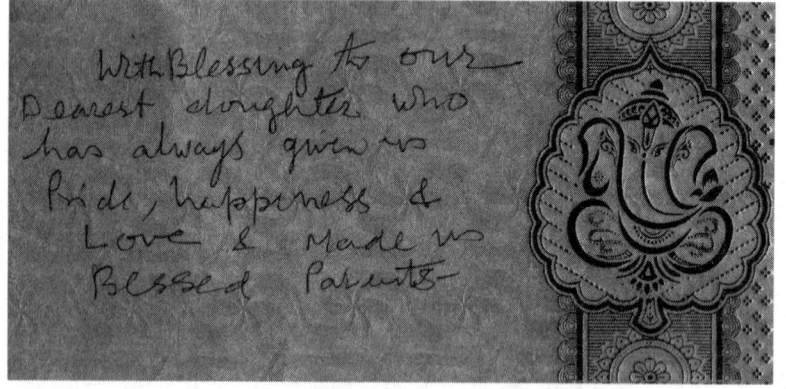

In keeping with the Indian tradition of welcoming home, my parents handed
over this shagun envelope to me after my mother did my aarti and teeka at
the airport arrivals from Rio. My father's handwriting on this note and
the words penned by him remain my greatest award ever, even more
precious than the Paralympic Medal itself.

HAD I RETURNED TO AHMEDNAGAR AFTER
receiving the Arjuna Award in 2012, this epilogue would
have told a very different story.

Winning the silver medal at the Rio Paralympics in 2016 was not
just a personal triumph—it was a historic moment, the magnitude
of which truly hit me when I returned to India.

The reception at the airport was incredible. The air was filled with the sound of drums, and children danced in celebration. My biker friends had roared in on their motorcycles, my army fraternity stood proud and even politicians joined the gathering. Among them, a group stood out to me: the village elders from my husband's home in Bhainswal Kalan, Haryana.

Their arrival to honour a daughter-in-law made me feel like I had struck a blow against patriarchy. They presented me a gada—a mace traditionally given to honour a man's achievement. My achievement transcended gender and shattered generations-old biases. I was told that when the male athletes from Haryana had failed to add to the Olympic medal tally—many had pinned their hopes on a male wrestler from our village—the village elders had told everyone to wait, one more sher (lion) from Haryana was still to perform. That tiger they were referring to was me.

The one thing I had missed in Rio was the honour of hearing the Indian national anthem at the award ceremony. That day at the airport, even that dream was fulfilled when the sounds of 'Jana Gana Mana' reverberated through the air.

I thought I was the happiest person on earth, but there was someone even happier—my father. He was the driving force in my life, constantly teaching me to persevere and push beyond my limits. Two years after Rio, in 2018, he was in a hospital, slipping in and out of consciousness. Even in that condition, during his moments of lucidity, he pushed me towards greatness. The previous year, I had been awarded the Padma Shri and my brother the Sena Medal, and our father had the satisfaction of knowing that both his children had been honoured by the President of India. But he believed I also deserved the Khel Ratna. The deadline to file the nomination for this award was 30 April 2018.

On 26 April, we were in his hospital room, working on the final touches to the file. Ambika had completed her MBA with great success. Meanwhile, Devika had just returned to India from the UK and was showing Papa her speech from the Commonwealth Heads of Government Meeting at Buckingham Palace. His pride in them both was evident, but he remained focused on encouraging me. After Rio, despite my age, I had continued to pursue para sports, setting my third consecutive Asian record in javelin. Although I had won in Rio for shot put, I heeded my father's advice—unlearn to learn. For Rio, I had unlearnt javelin and learnt shot put because javelin was no longer part of the Paralympics in my category. Now, I unlearnt shot put and learnt javelin again, and also strengthened my discus skills. On 26 April 2018, I had my last conversation with Papa before his condition worsened and he had to be put on a ventilator. He wanted to know whether I had submitted my nomination for the Khel Ratna. Despite the stress of his failing health, I had prepared the file with his guidance. I left the hospital that day and went to the Paralympic Committee of India office to submit my file. We lost Papa three days later, on 30 April 2018, but I felt his blessings upon me when I received the Khel Ratna in 2019.

I've continued striving to give my father more reasons to smile. I know he's cheering for me proudly from his seat in heaven—just as he once motivated me while sitting in the balcony of my Gurgaon flat when I trained for the Rio Paralympics. He was there when I appeared on the popular quiz show *Kaun Banega Crorepati* with his favourite star, Amitabh Bachchan. He was blessing me when I spoke at Harvard University in 2024. He was clapping when an India Post postal order was released in my name. And he was smiling when my caricature was featured on the iconic Amul billboard.

The qualities of persistence and consistency are his legacy to me. From my mother, I inherited the genes for adaptability and a capacity to evolve. After Papa's passing, she seamlessly took up his mantle, softening the blow of his absence. One of the highlights of our family trips to Jaipur was having hot jalebis and pyaaz ki kachori for breakfast—a tradition Papa loved and that Mummy has diligently continued. In a society where mothers often get overshadowed in their homes, Mummy has stepped forward and keeps us going with the same fire Papa had. Even at seventy-six she taught me a valuable lesson—she learnt the ropes of social media just to stay connected and to read about my achievements. She learnt not only how to navigate social media but also to type in English. I was so inspired by her that I decided to join the Indian Institute of Corporate Affairs at the age of fifty-three and added a new qualification to my résumé.

When I retired from active sports, I faced the challenge of finding employment. In the absence of viable job opportunities, I learnt a new skill to become an independent director, equipping myself for leadership roles. I became the brand ambassador for TB Mukt Bharat Abhiyan and became a Nikshay Mitra. Beti Bachao Beti Padhao and Swachh Bharat are campaigns I've been closely associated with.

I was one of the 200 Indians selected by Prime Minister Narendra Modi to serve on the committee for Azadi Ka Amrit Mahotsav, commemorating seventy-five years of Independence, and I'm also the brand ambassador for Viksit Bharat 2047. These platforms have given me the privilege of serving my nation. I dream of inspiring new generations of Indians to be more inclusive and sensitive.

My Rio silver had done so much for me, but it did more for people like me. Initially, as a new wheelchair user, I found myself unconsciously restricting my public appearances. But once I returned from Rio, I was inundated with calls from women in wheelchairs, reaching out to ask me how I did it. Inspired by my journey, I found so many people, both able-bodied and with disabilities, who went back to their passions. One friend who played cricket with me in college sold her jewellery and bought a bike at the age of forty-seven; Bikram went back to biking; another wheelchair-using stranger, who later became a friend, learnt to drive and is now a rally driver. I continued with my adventure activities by revisiting my Himalayan rallies, using every platform to advocate for inclusion and accessibility.

The PCI was defunct before I took over as its president. I restarted it and realigned the organization with international regulations. Just as we were getting started, Covid-19 struck. But I used that time to conduct webinars with the help of the Kendriya Vidyalaya Sangathan, my alma mater. Our goal was to educate para athletes on the rules and regulations of their sports. Together with my team, we simplified the complex rules and translated them into Hindi to generate awareness.

When we took our para athletes to the Tokyo Paralympics in 2021, our medal haul was rich. In Rio, 19 Indian para athletes had participated. In Tokyo, we *won* 19 medals, including 3 by women. The following Asian Para Games in Hangzhou, China, in 2023, were even more successful, with our para athletes bringing home an unprecedented 111 medals—29 gold, 31 silver and 51 bronze.

For me Hangzhou felt like I had come full circle. As a child in 1982, I had witnessed the opening ceremony of the Asian Games in Delhi, sitting in the Jawaharlal Nehru Stadium stands with my father. In 2010, Ambika had been in the same stands as I had walked the track with Devika during the opening ceremony of the Commonwealth Games. And in 2023, I found myself in the stands again, this time in Hangzhou, filled with pride as I watched Devika walk with the Indian contingent during the opening ceremony.

As I hung up my boots as president of the Paralympic Committee of India, a bigger opportunity arose: to serve on the Asian Paralympic Committee as the sub-regional representative for South Asia. My mission for inclusion is slowly expanding to encompass regions beyond India, embracing the ethos of vasudhaiva kutumbakam— the world is one family.

The Paris Paralympics were my report card. During my term as president of the PCI, we spotted talent and nurtured it. Half of the 84 member strong contingent was first-timers and we returned with a rich haul of 29 medals—11 of which were won by women para athletes. para sports has come a long way indeed. From 1968 to 2016, we won a total of 12 medals. During my term as PCI president when we sent a contingent to Tokyo, and immediately after my term was over when the team I had nurtured went to Paris, we won a total of 48 medals, 14 of which were won by women.

Much has been written in this book, yet so much remains to be told. From my modest 10x10 room, I've travelled far—my passport now spans three booklets—but my journey is far from over. To borrow from Bollywood: *Picture abhi baaki hai, mere dost.*

About the Author

Deepa Malik is India's foremost para athlete with twenty-three international medals, having created history by becoming India's first-ever female Paralympic medalist with a silver at the Rio Paralympics, and several national and international awards. She has been recognized with the Padma Shri, the Khel Ratna and the Arjuna Award. She is the first Indian paraplegic woman swimmer, biker and car rallyist, holding four Limca World Records.

Deepa has served as the first female president of the Paralympic Committee of India, and has been awarded three honorary doctorates commemorating her dedication to sports and community service. She has also been awarded the Asian Order, the highest sports honour in the para sports ecosystem in Asia.

Dr Deepa Malik is currently serving as the South Asian region representative on the executive board of the Asian Paralympic Committee, the first Indian woman and former para athlete to be appointed to this position.

Her list of achievements is long, and it is being continually updated—because Deepa does not know how to say 'stop'.

To connect with Deepa Malik, please visit her website www.deepamalik.in

About the Co-author

Soni Sangwan is a distinguished journalist and writer, having worked with leading media houses including HT Media, the Times Group, the India Today Group and CNN News18. Soni is married to Maj. Gen. Sandeep Singh, AVSM, and they have a fourteen-year-old daughter, Sonakshi.

 HarperCollins *Publishers* India

At HarperCollins India, we believe in telling the best stories and finding the widest readership for our books in every format possible. We started publishing in 1992; a great deal has changed since then, but what has remained constant is the passion with which our authors write their books, the love with which readers receive them, and the sheer joy and excitement that we as publishers feel in being a part of the publishing process.

Over the years, we've had the pleasure of publishing some of the finest writing from the subcontinent and around the world, including several award-winning titles and some of the biggest bestsellers in India's publishing history. But nothing has meant more to us than the fact that millions of people have read the books we published, and that somewhere, a book of ours might have made a difference.

As we look to the future, we go back to that one word— a word which has been a driving force for us all these years.

Read.

Harper
Collins

HARPER
FICTION

HARPER
NON-FICTION

HARPER
BUSINESS

HCCB
HARPERCOLLINS
CHILDREN'S BOOKS

HARPER
DESIGN

Harper
Sport

HARPER
PERENNIAL

HARPER
VANTAGE

हार्पर
हिन्दी